Contemporary Confucian Political Philosophy

Contemporary Confucian Political Philosophy

Toward Progressive Confucianism

STEPHEN C. ANGLE

polity

First published in 2012 by Polity Press

Polity Press
65 Bridge Street
Cambridge CB2 1UR, UK

Polity Press
350 Main Street
Malden, MA 02148, USA

ISBN-13: 978–0–7456–6129–2 (hardback)
ISBN-13: 978–0–7456–6130–8 (paperback)

A catalogue record for this book is available from the British Library.

Typeset in 11.25 on 13 pt Dante
by Servis Filmsetting Ltd, Stockport, Cheshire
Printed and bound in Great Britain by the MPG Books Group Ltd

For further information on Polity, visit our website: www.politybooks.com

Contents

Preface

Almost twenty-five years ago I fell in love with a young Jewish-American woman, a fellow student of Chinese at the Inter-University Program for Chinese Language Studies in Taipei. This book is certainly not the most important outcome of that event, but in a curious way my coming to write as a Confucian philosopher does stem, at least partly, from the relationship that began in Taipei. The recipient of a brief and forgettable Episcopalian religious education as a child, I became and remain an atheist. The importance of Judaism to Debbie and her family, though, meant that Jewish rituals began to enter my life. First, High Holiday services and Passover, then joining a synagogue, observing and sometimes participating in my daughters' religious educations, and the splendid ceremonies as each of my daughters became a Bat Mitzvah. As all this was going on, my own reading and teaching of Confucian texts led me to reflect on the importance of ritual in our lives – and to see that the Jewish rituals in which I now participated were in fact only one of many types of ritual that inform our lives today. And rituals were not the only facet of my life where I was finding resonance between Confucianism and my own life. It is only as adults that we can become truly aware of the importance of our parents and family in shaping who we are, and also become aware of our own roles in helping to sustain these crucial relationships. Participation in the local community also emerged as something to which I was drawn, and about which I found tremendous insight in Confucian writings. Gradually, I began to wonder: am I a Confucian? What would that even mean, here in Middletown, Connecticut?

I continue to wrestle with these questions. Certainly whatever Confucianism means today – and, as we will see, it has many different dimensions and interpretations – it is more than a vague commitment to ritual, family, and community. It is both broader and more specific. Broader, in that almost any version of Confucianism will also emphasize an on-going commitment to moral growth and a serious involvement with a textual tradition, and many types of Confucianism will add an effort to balance our concern for one another with an apt concern for the environment we inhabit. This is more specifically, both because Confucian ways of valuing family and so on are going to differ, to one degree or another, from other ways of doing so; and also because within the Confucian tradition itself, there are disagreements about the details. So, figuring out what exactly it means to be a Confucian in the contemporary world is complex. In addition, as I will discuss in Chapter 1, in the last hundred years Confucianism has faced greater challenges than ever before, and also has become more global than at any time in its history. It teeters on the verge of possible irrelevance and yet is studied in new ways and in new places. Both within China and without, various interpretations of Confucianism are starting to gain traction as philosophy, as political theory, and as religion – and many of the scholars and practitioners who have been pursuing these Confucianisms are now my friends and interlocutors. If I am a little unsure of whether I am a Confucian, I am confident that I am part of exciting conversations about contemporary Confucian philosophy, and venture in this book both to describe what Confucian theorists have been saying and to prescribe what Confucian theorists should say.

In 2009 I published a book called *Sagehood: The Contemporary Significance of Neo-Confucian Philosophy*. *Sagehood* has two goals: to offer an interpretation of the central philosophical project of Neo-Confucianism – namely, the ethical, metaphysical, psychological, and educational theories surrounding the search for sagehood – and to put these theories into critical dialogue with relevant ideas from contemporary Western philosophy. The hypothesis is that each side can be stimulated by and learn from the other. My main Chinese sources in *Sagehood* are two great Neo-Confucian philosophers, Zhu Xi (1130–1200) and Wang Yangming (1472–1529). I believe their theories in the areas I have mentioned to be fascinating and well worth our attention. In the last two chapters of *Sagehood*, though, I turn to the topic of Neo-Confucian political philosophy, and there I find the approaches of Zhu and Wang to fall significantly short. There are still things we can learn from them but, as I pursued the question of how sages and politics should mix, I found myself drawn to the radical ideas of a twentieth-century Confucian philosopher, Mou Zongsan (1909–95). As I explore briefly in these closing chapters of *Sagehood*, Mou argues that notwithstanding all the insights of the Confucian tradition in many areas, Confucians can only realize their deepest aims if they adopt a different understanding of law and of political authority than had been generally accepted within the tradition. (Mou does note that some of his pre-modern predecessors made moves in this direction, but never in a consolidated way.)

Sagehood, in short, offers a broad view of one version – an attractive and intriguing one, it seems to me – of Confucian ethics, but only some tantalizing hints at what a satisfactory Confucian political philosophy might look like. It left me wanting to think through more thoroughly what such a political philosophy would entail, and wanting to explore what other Confucian philosophers today had to say about these subjects. The opportunity to do this arrived sooner than I ever expected, as I was invited to deliver the inaugural Tang Junyi Lectures at the University of Michigan in the Spring of 2009. Those lectures, collectively titled "Contemporary Confucian Virtue Politics," are the direct ancestors of Chapters 1, 3, 4, and 7 of the present book. I thus owe a considerable debt to Donald Lopez and his colleagues in the Asian Languages and Literatures Department for inviting me, to the appreciative and challenging audiences for the lectures, and to the many old friends and teachers with whom I was able to reconnect (especially Don and Anne Munro). It was then my good fortune to be able to take a year's sabbatical from my teaching and administrative responsibilities at Wesleyan which, coming so close on the heels of the Tang Lectures, provided the perfect setting for building a full book on the foundation already laid in the lectures.

Many friends and colleagues have offered their help over the time I have been writing this book. Daniel Bell did me the great favor of reading over the whole book manuscript and offering many comments, corrections, and suggestions. I am grateful to audiences who responded to portions of the manuscript-in-progress at the 2010 APSA Conference, the Columbia Comparative Philosophy Seminar, Connecticut College, Haverford College, the Institute of Philosophy at the Chinese Academy of Social Sciences, the 2010 Nishan Forum, and Soochow University. My thanks to Routledge for granting permission to use material from my essay in Deborah Mower and Wade Robison, eds, *Civility in Politics and Education* (2012), which overlaps substantially with Chapter 6 of the present book; and also to the editors of《中國哲學與文化》[*Chinese Philosophy and Culture*] for permission to use material from my article in their issue 8 (2010), which is a predecessor of Chapter 3. The following generous people each contributed to my work on one or more chapters: Sebastien Billioud, Fred Dallmayr, Loubna El-Amine, David Elstein, Fan Ruiping, Gu Hongliang, Huang Yushun, Leigh Jenco, Sungmoon Kim, David Little, Kai Marchal, Emily McRae, Deborah Mower, Peng Guoxiang, Marty Powers, Hagop Sarkissian, Sarah Schneewind, Michael Slote, Anna Sun, Sor-hoon Tan, Justin Tiwald, Sean Walsh, Wang Jue, Kathleen Wright, Xiao Yang, and Zhao Tingyang. They all have my sincere thanks. Several anonymous referees gave helpful feedback on my initial book proposal, and two of them read and commented on the entire manuscript. The book has benefitted greatly from their challenging engagement, for which I am extremely grateful. Finally, Emma Hutchinson and her staff at Polity Press have been extremely supportive and responsive; Emma's guidance and good humor have meant a lot to me. With all this help, one hopes that any remaining deficiencies are few and far between, but I suppose they are inevitable, and they are solely my own responsibility.

Introduction: Contextualizing Progressive Confucianism

The title of this book is meant to be at least a little bit provocative. More than 2,500 years after the death of Confucius (551–479 BCE) – not to mention more than six decades after the Chinese communist revolution – is there anything alive and "contemporary" about Confucianism? You might also wonder about both "political" and "philosophy." Confucianism is best known as an ethical teaching advocating benevolence and filial devotion, and its classic texts, which are filled with aphorisms, stories, and dialogues, might seem more like religious tracts or handbooks for spiritual practice than philosophical arguments. As if this weren't enough, the subtitle asserts that the book will articulate something called "progressive" Confucianism. But everyone knows that Confucianism is conservative, looking back to a lost golden age, concerned to revive the rituals and values of an antique era. How can it be progressive?

Let us start with the idea of Confucianism itself. Or perhaps I should say "Confucianisms," because there have been many, even competing, ways in which the legacy of Confucius has been developed over the centuries. As we will see in a few moments, distinct approaches are also proliferating today. As I use the term in this book, Confucianism refers to the broad and dynamic tradition of practice and reflection that includes all of these competing Confucianisms. This means that at any given moment, it may be controversial what the exact parameters of the tradition are. Even seemingly major issues, like the question of whether Confucius is in some sense divine, often divide Confucians. What they agree upon is that the texts and vocabulary of classical Confucianism are a critical source of their own values and practices. In this book I will be diving into some of the current debates about how to best capture and develop the spirit of Confucius and other Confucian masters. To some degree, these arguments are based on historical evidence and textual interpretation, but in a more fundamental sense they are prescriptive rather than descriptive: what are the best, most valuable, most robust insights at the core of the tradition? As I will explain below, I join those who believe that this core should be centered around the ideal of all individuals developing their capacities for virtue – ultimately aiming at sagehood – through their relationships with one another and with their environment.

I am the first to admit that Confucianism spent most of the twentieth century on life-support. And just as China and the world in the twenty-first century are dramatically different from how they were in the nineteenth century, so contemporary Confucianism must successfully remake itself if it is to again be significant. The goal of this introductory chapter is to sketch the context within which the refashioning of contemporary Confucianism is already underway. We will see that while Confucianism today is certainly not only a philosophy, philosophy is an important element of contemporary Confucianism: among other things, it is the most international aspect of Confucianism. The philosophers I will introduce in this chapter are from China, Taiwan, Hong Kong, and Singapore; and also from the United States and Canada. Some are ethnically Chinese and some are not; some write primarily in Chinese and some in English.[1] Most of these Confucian philosophers are sure that political philosophy is an important part of Confucianism, though they also acknowledge that this is an area in which contemporary Confucianism faces significant challenges.

What, finally, of "progressive"? I mean this word to function in two different ways. On the one hand, it helps to describe the core Confucian commitment to individual and collective moral progress, and many of the other Confucian philosophers to whom I will refer would agree that this kind of progress is critical to Confucianism. On the other hand, it is meant as a label for the particular approach to Confucian political philosophy that I will be advocating throughout this book. "Progressive Confucianism" bears certain similarities to other contemporary "progressive" social and political movements, and I will argue that some contemporary Confucians are mistaken in not adopting these progressive values and institutions. A key part of my argument will aim at convincing readers that Progressive Confucianism is indeed "Confucianism." As we will see, I build on the foundation begun by Confucian philosophers in the twentieth century, and especially on the work of Mou Zongsan (1909–95). My ultimate goal is showing that Progressive Confucianism has much to both teach and challenge us today.

A Difficult Century

The twentieth century was difficult for Confucianism. In 1905, a last-ditch effort to reform a floundering empire led to the abandonment of the ubiquitous civil-service exam system, around which higher education in China had been based for centuries. Since the exams were based in large part on mastery of Confucian classics, the end of the exams marked a major challenge to the significance of Confucian learning. This was followed, in 1911, with the collapse of the last dynasty itself. In 1915 Chinese intellectuals inaugurated a "New Culture Movement" that sought fundamental changes to Chinese values, practices, and even the Chinese language. In many ways this movement was a more pervasive "cultural revolution" than the later Maoist movement of that name. The values of "modern civilization" were on the rise and older traditions like Confucianism were roundly criticized. Confucianism did not die, but after the first decades of the twentieth century, it would need to find new ways to be relevant in Chinese society.

After this unpromising start, the twentieth century continued to pose obstacles to any rebirth of Confucianism. Some political leaders tried to manipulate it as a shallow ideology of loyalty to power. Chinese intellectuals increasingly were drawn to either liberalism or Marxism as they endeavored to work out what a "New China" should look like. The rhetoric and values associated with science were hugely popular and widely seen as incompatible with traditional Confucianism. As Mao pushed Communist ideology in increasingly radical directions, the space for Confucianism shrank even further, reaching its nadir during the 1973–4 "Criticize Lin Biao and Confucius" campaign. Mao's goal was to wipe Confucianism completely from the hearts of China's citizens.[2]

Admittedly, there were some important exceptions to this bleak picture. In 1921, a young scholar named Liang Shuming (1893–1988) generated considerable discussion with the publication of his *Eastern and Western Cultures and Their Philosophies*, which argued for the continued value of a reformed Confucianism and pointed toward problems with Western materialism. The early 1920s also witnessed a spirited intellectual debate sparked by Zhang Junmai (1886–1969)'s criticism of his contemporaries' unthinking endorsement of science as a solution to all problems; Zhang drew on Confucian ideas to argue for the importance of humanistic values.[3] Another important figure in this era is Xiong Shili (1885–1968). Like Liang Shuming, Xiong was intrigued by Buddhist metaphysical theories, but gradually developed an influential critique of Buddhism, on the basis of which he articulated his own understanding of Confucian metaphysics. Although when in his twenties Xiong had been involved in the republican movement to overthrow the Qing empire, most of Xiong's career was spent as a college professor. Liang and Zhang, by contrast, balanced their philosophical writings with political and social activism – under very challenging circumstances – throughout much of their lives.

The Confucian philosopher whose work is the most important for the present book, Mou Zongsan (1909–95), is sometimes referred to as among the "second generation" of twentieth-century Confucians. Other members of the second generation include Tang Junyi (1909–78) and Xu Fuguan (1902–82) who, like Mou himself, studied with Xiong Shili, began academic careers in mainland China, and then left China after 1949 to live and teach in Taiwan and Hong Kong. All three were active scholars, with Mou and Tang being particularly prolific. Their combination of historical re-interpretation, openness to and engagement with Western philosophers like Kant and Hegel, and commitment to democracy and the rule of law, has come to be called "contemporary New Confucianism" and has made a major impact on the Sinophone academic world.[4,5] Outside of the academic community, though, the felt presence of New Confucianism was very slight throughout the 1950s, 1960s, 1970s, and into the 1980s. One often gets the sense, especially in their more popularly oriented writings from this period, that Mou and his colleagues feel isolated and frustrated. Despite their somewhat lonely voices, that is, the twentieth century remained a difficult time for Confucianism.[6]

Starting in the 1980s and 1990s, and picking up steam in the early years of the 2000s, signs of renewed interest in Confucianism began to appear in China. The earliest indications of changing attitudes could be seen in academia, as research and writing on Confucius, Confucianism, and even New Confucianism (despite the fact that many of the New Confucians were fierce anti-Communists) emerged and grew. We will look at some of the key figures in these discussions below. A second important arena is governmental, in which Confucian symbols come to play some significant roles. Jiang Zemin, China's leader from 1989 to 2002, was fond of emphasizing the importance of "rule by virtue," which – though he did not emphasize it – is a deeply Confucian theme. Jiang's successor, Hu Jintao, soon announced his own major initiative to cultivate a "harmonious society"; harmony is another key Confucian value, though once again the connection to Confucianism was not made explicit. A large-scale program to promote the study of Chinese language and culture overseas began in 2004 under the title of "Confucius Institutes." These institutes, of which there are now more than three hundred around the world, rarely engage in activities that are explicitly connected to Confucianism, but they certainly emphasize the role of Confucius as an important symbol of Chinese culture. Many observers were struck, finally, by the central role that Confucianism played in the Opening Ceremonies of the 2008 Beijing Olympic Games. The spectacle began with 2008 drummers clad in ancient-style costumes chanting the opening lines of the *Analects* of Confucius, and "harmony" was a repeated motif throughout. There is of course a difference between Confucian symbols and Confucian values, and the gap between the two is often very wide. Still, official use of Confucian-sounding rhetoric can help to legitimize the discussion of Confucian themes throughout the society.[7]

Another important dimension of the revival of Confucianism in contemporary China is taking place in popular culture and civil society. A variety of educational experiments – some private, and some supported by local governments – are taking place. The most common model is after-school or weekend classes in memorizing and chanting Confucian classics (often, depending on the school, mixed with Shakespeare). More elaborate options also exist, including private schools that are developing curricula based on traditional culture. Books and television series expounding the lessons of Confucianism have been very popular, the poster child for which is Beijing-based professor Yu Dan. Her 2006 book, *Yu Dan's Insights Gleaned from the Analects*, has sold more than ten million copies. It is a charming book, drawing widely on contemporary examples and world folklore to elucidate the lessons from the *Analects* that Professor Yu finds relevant to present-day China. Chinese scholars have frequently been dismissive of the book, but this is somewhat unfair, as it makes no pretensions of presenting a scholarly interpretation of the *Analects*. The observation of Daniel Bell, a Canadian political theorist currently living and teaching in Beijing, is perhaps more pertinent: he notes that Yu's version of the *Analects* has been thoroughly "depoliticized," since she confines her lessons to matters of personal growth and interpersonal relations.[8] At any rate, all agree that the enormous sales of Yu's book speak to a desire in contemporary China for a more robust ethical culture to combat what many see as rampant materialism and even nihilism.

The last three decades have witnessed extraordinary growth in China of religious organizations and practices (both officially sanctioned and not), and of secular civil-society organizations (like environmental NGOs). Both types of groups have at least sometimes worked to get around government limitations via the internet. These trends have been intertwined with complex responses from the government, which has variously encouraged, suppressed, and tried to coopt these organizations. Confucians and Confucianism have been playing their part in these developments.[9] Confucian civil society organizations, both formal and more informal (like the community of like-minded people who contribute to a particular internet site), have also begun to serve more than merely academic functions. A mix of scholars and what can only be called Confucian activists have started to take and publicize positions on matters of public interest, sometimes in direct opposition to governmental entities. In December of 2010, for example, criticism began circulating on Confucian websites of the local government in Qufu City, Shandong province – the city most closely associated with the birth of Confucius and the hometown of his family – because it had approved construction within the city limits of a large Christian church.[10] In April of 2011, a similar event took place. Apparently bowing to pressure from other factions within the government, authorities removed a large statue of Confucius that only a few months earlier had been unveiled on the edge of Tiananmen Square, the symbolic center of modern China. Confucians again howled in protest; one open letter posted anonymously on an internet site cited the *Analects* on the importance of "trust (*xin*)," suggesting that a government that lost the trust of its people could not stand.[11] Compared with the carefully apolitical stance of Yu Dan, these recent developments suggest a more confident attitude that is reminiscent of the traditional Confucian responsibility of intellectuals to remonstrate with superiors (be they parents or rulers) who deviate from the Way.

A final dimension of the on-going growth of Confucianism is its international aspect. Most basically, from 1949 to the 1980s, New Confucianism lived in Taiwan and Hong Kong, not in mainland China. Relations among these three polities have changed dramatically in the years since, and the study and development of Confucianism is now shared – and even the subject of some healthy competition.[12] There have of course been scholars outside of East Asia studying Confucianism for many decades; what is new in recent years is Americans and others taking up the Confucian philosophical project as their own. Robert Neville's 2000 book *Boston Confucianism: Portable Tradition in the Late Modern World* is a fine symbol of this trend; we will look at more examples below. Explicitly Confucian practices have not taken off in the United States, unlike American Buddhism, which according to some measures is the fastest-growing religion in America. The lack of Confucian practices is perhaps unsurprising, given that even in today's China, it is somewhat murky exactly which practices make sense. Finally, Confucian philosophizing is a small but growing part of the international philosophical scene, and some of these philosophers' work is making its way back into Sinophone philosophical discourse. The present book seeks to build upon these trends.

Confucianism as Philosophy

The Chinese word for philosophy, *zhexue*, is of recent vintage. Like a number of other words in modern Chinese (including *zongjiao* for "religion"), it is a neologism coined in Japan in the latter part of the nineteenth century (the same two-character compound is used in both languages; it is pronounced *tetsugaku* in Japanese), specifically as a translation of "philosophy" and its cognates in other European languages.[13] It was only in the twentieth century that scholars began to talk about "Chinese philosophy (*zhongguo zhexue*)."[14] Two works in particular introduced the idea that Confucianism and other Chinese traditions could be thought of as "philosophy": Hu Shi's 1918 *Outline of a History of Chinese Philosophy* and Feng Youlan's 1934 *History of Chinese Philosophy*. These works set out to analyze the texts, thinkers, and ideas of China's intellectual tradition in terms of the categories of Western philosophy: epistemology, metaphysics, ethics, and so on. Chinese "philosophers" were identified as idealists or materialists, as realists or nominalists. It was also in the late 1910s that philosophy departments in Chinese universities – themselves quite new – began to hire faculty to teach "Chinese philosophy." This arrangement has continued down to the present day (notwithstanding certain disruptions during the Mao era): Chinese philosophy departments contain significant numbers of scholars whose research focuses on Chinese traditions and especially on Confucianism.

Despite this seeming success of "Chinese philosophy," the aptness of thinking of Confucianism as "philosophy" has recently come in for significant criticism. I refer not to Western philosophers questioning whether Confucianism counts as real philosophy – these doubts, thankfully, seem to be receding[15] – but rather to worries within China that categorizing Confucianism as philosophy does violence to key aspects of the tradition.[16] The concerns tend to cluster into two areas, and if we are to have solid footing for our exploration of contemporary Chinese political philosophy, both of these issues need to be addressed. First, it is charged that by shoehorning the writings of the ancient Chinese masters into Western philosophical language (no matter whether one is writing in Chinese or another language), one inevitably misunderstands one's sources. Examples of such problems are easy to find, and so we should readily agree that things can go wrong when new terms, derived from foreign traditions, are used to interpret an existing discourse.[17] However, the fact that things *can* go wrong does not mean that problems are unavoidable. After all, the Confucian tradition itself contains many instances in which Confucians draw on concepts from outside the then-existing tradition in order to find better answers to age-old challenges or to respond to newly arisen problems. As a dynamic tradition of reflection, Confucianism has grown and changed, enriched by encounters with Mohism, Daoism, Buddhism, and various strands of Western thought (in the twentieth century). At a number of points in this book, I will directly face the challenge of justifying why the positions I advocate should count as good Confucianism, as well as raising questions about the Confucian legitimacy of others' positions. My general strategy will be to ask whether a given innovation (or resistance to innovation) is true to the core concerns of the evolving tradition.

The second charge leveled against those of us who take Confucianism to be philosophy is that we sunder the connection that existed throughout the pre-twentieth-century tradition between reflection and a full-fledged way of life. Confucianism, it is said, is not a mere profession: its practices are intimately related to improving oneself and one's world. It cannot flourish if confined to the libraries and lecture halls of universities. To these critics, philosophy professors like Mou Zongsan are not true Confucians.[18] I have a two-part answer to these criticisms. First of all, I am quite sympathetic to the idea that a genuine, contemporary flourishing of Confucianism will require that it find a way to be relevant once more to people's full lives. It is not just a set of rules or an abstruse understanding of the ontology of the universe – things that one could read in a book and then count as "knowing." As Wang Yangming (1472–1529) famously put it, true knowledge and action are unified. A Confucian education orients one to the ethical dimensions of the situations one encounters throughout one's life, and thus changes the way one perceives and acts in the world.

The second part of my answer, though, is that these truths about the broad aims of Confucian education do not show that philosophical reflection, dialogue, and argument[19] are not a critical part of Confucianism. Rather, they show that if one rests content with the professional aspects of Confucianism-as-philosophy and ignores its deeper lessons, one is not a very good Confucian. In defense of Mou Zongsan and Confucian philosophy professors everywhere (myself included), it may not be as easy to know how to practice Confucianism today as it once was. At least, pre-twentieth-century Chinese society had various well-trodden paths to follow, based in part in a deeply ingrained ritualization of life. It might be a mistake, though, to conclude that Confucianism was easy to practice under those circumstances. Looking superficially Confucian was certainly easier then. But was it easier to be a good son? Was it easier to cultivate one's "humaneness *(ren)*" and show apt concern for all aspects of one's world ("to form one body with all things")? I am not so sure. In fact, some of the arguments of the present book aim to show that critical modern innovations like broad political participation, the rule of law, and the active rooting out of social oppression, actually better enable one to be a good Confucian.

Trying to demonstrate these conclusions right now would get me too far ahead of myself, so let us return to the issue of philosophy. The reflection, dialogue, and argument that lie at the core of philosophical practice are important parts of Confucian practice as well. Confucian philosophers insist that this aspect of their practice is not an end in itself, but rather contributes to their life-long commitment to learning – and through this learning, to coming as close as they can to the ideal of sagehood. The striking thing is that for all their differences, many great Western philosophers believed essentially the same thing. For Greeks and Romans, philosophy was a "way of life" that aimed at personal transformation.[20] So, too, was philosophy intimately related to personal growth for Dewey, Wittgenstein, Foucault, and many others.[21] Of course, Confucians might not be very happy with the models of personal growth offered by these ancient, modern, or post-modern Westerners, and it is an unfortunate fact that many professional philosophers – East and West – do not take the broader implications of their philosophical work very seriously.[22] But, once again, it has never been easy to become a better person.

The final point I would like to make in this section is to further clarify the relation between the existing Confucian tradition and various non-Confucian sources of inspiration in the generation of contemporary Confucian philosophy. In previous work I have employed a method called "rooted global philosophy" which is again very apt in the present context. Rooted global philosophy means to work within a particular living philosophical tradition – thus its rootedness – but to do so in a way that is open to stimulus and insights from other philosophical traditions – thus its global nature.[23] New Confucians like Mou Zongsan were rooted global philosophers, seeking to develop their tradition in constructive ways by drawing on stimulating ideas from various parts of the globe.[24] It is important to emphasize that rooted global philosophy is not premised on our ultimate convergence on some single set of philosophical truths. Perhaps this will take place, but the plurality of human concerns and historically contingent differences in traditions provide us with no guarantees. In the realm of political philosophy, this book argues for a certain degree of convergence between Confucianism and the liberal tradition, but also for continuing differences from existing liberal values and institutions.

Contemporary Confucians

Mou Zongsan plays a special role in this book. One of the central themes of his New Confucianism was the need for Confucianism to develop a new political philosophy and political practice – what he called a *"xin wai wang,"* literally "new outer kingship," which can more loosely be rendered as "new politics" – that would better enable the realization of "inner sage-hood *(nei sheng)."* I am persuaded that in this respect, Mou's approach is the right one for Confucianism to pursue, and in particular that his idea of "self-restriction *(ziwo kanxian),"* which I will explain in depth in Chapter 2, is crucial. The idea of self-restriction allows for a reorientation of the relation between individual ethical insight and publicly agreed-upon norms like laws and human rights; the resulting partial independence of laws and rights is a key part of my argument in Chapters 3, 4, and 5, though in each case I move considerably beyond anything that Mou himself actually said. In two other ways, as well, there is significant distance between the project of this book and Mou's own philosophizing. First, I believe it is possible to separate Mou's insights into political philosophy from the rest of his philosophical system, and then to develop a version of these insights that can stand independently from Mou's other ideas. Indeed, I find some of the other aspects of Mou's system to be philosophically problematic. His controversial ideas of moral metaphysics, intellectual intuition, perfect teaching, and so on will therefore play no role in this book – though *some* version of Confucian ethics will be necessary in order to motivate many of the book's arguments, about which I will say more below. My approach is bound to be controversial, because Mou understood his various ideas to be intimately related, all parts of a unified philosophical system. Without denying that different aspects of Mou's vision are mutually reinforcing, I will show in Chapter 2 that "self-restriction" is indeed both separable from, and meaningful without, the rest of Mou's system. Second, Mou had little or nothing to say about some of my topics, especially the issues raised in Chapters 6 and 7. Still, in an important sense my project here is to further develop Mou's New Confucian approach to political philosophy, including defending it from some contemporary critics who have quite badly misunderstood its motivations and arguments.

Mou Zongsan serves as an important source of the Progressive Confucianism I will be developing in later chapters, but now we should turn to the rapidly expanding world of contemporary Confucian theorizing, since these are the voices with whom I am most directly in dialogue. Many of the individuals whom I discuss in this section come up repeatedly in later chapters, both positively and negatively. In order to make sense of the complex contemporary scene, I tentatively offer some categories into which various thinkers and approaches might be put, but please understand that these groups are overlapping and sometimes shifting: contemporary Confucianism is a live and increasingly vibrant tradition. In formulating these categories, I have generally emphasized the method by which people approach contemporary Confucianism, rather than the specific normative views they hold.

Begin with a group that is both the largest and yet the least involved in the issues that will concern us in the balance of this book: the *philosophical historians*. Representative figures include Chen Lai (Tsinghua University), Guo Qiyong (Wuhan University), and younger scholars like Peng Guoxiang (Peking University) and Wu Genyou (Wuhan University). The main activity of scholars like these is the production of interpretive studies of thinkers, texts, periods, or concepts from the long history of Confucianism (including the twentieth century). Unlike intellectual/cultural historians who foreground the political and cultural contexts in which Confucians lived and wrote, these philosophical historians emphasize the charitable understanding of Confucian philosophy and, to some degree, spiritual practice. They are not primarily interested in the creative, contemporary development of Confucianism, however.[25] This is not to say they are uninterested in the contemporary fate of Confucianism; sometimes they reflect on the possible contemporary relevance of the doctrines they explicate, and some of them are quite active as essayists or public intellectuals. Some self-identify as Confucians. Their primary work, though, is historical scholarship.

Another group to which I will make little subsequent reference is the *Confucian revivalists* (although there is considerable overlap between this category and the following one). I mentioned this loose category above as the source of public complaint about the planned church in Qufu and about the removal of the statue of Confucius from Tiananmen Square. Revivalist organizations include both scholars and non-scholars and tend to be supportive of both research on, and efforts to revive the practice of, "Confucian [Religious] Teachings (*rujiao*)."[26] The journal and website *Yuandao*, founded in 1994 by Chen Ming, is one of the chief organs of the revivalists, although relevant websites are proliferating.[27] Revivalism is often motivated by a sense of cultural pride and sometimes also by a concern about a moral or spiritual crisis in today's China. Revivalists may be interested in one or more of the theoretical approaches to contemporary Confucian political thinking, but contemporary theorizing often plays a minimal part in the projects or aspirations of revivalists.

The category of political philosophizing most closely associated with revivalism can be called *institutional Confucianism*, the leading thinker of which is Jiang Qing (1953–).[28] In 2003, Jiang published *Political Confucianism: The Changing Direction, Particularities, and Development of Contemporary Confucianism.*[29] This book represents an importantly different approach to contemporary Confucianism from the work of the New Confucians. In works like the 1958 Manifesto referred to above, Mou Zongsan and other New Confucians had advocated Confucianism in terms of "Learning of the Heartmind-and-Nature (*xinxing zhi xue*)," by which they meant that the core of Confucianism involved realizing the "inner sagely" potential each of us has. According to Jiang Qing, this is to emphasize the wrong aspect of the Confucian tradition. Rather than its metaphysics and ethics, Confucianism's political and other institutions are what Confucians today need to rediscover, reinvent, and advocate – if Confucianism is to be able to play a constructive role in Chinese society. Based on a complex notion of legitimacy that Jiang believes can be found in earlier Confucian justifications of political institutions, he proposes some dramatically new kinds of institutions that he believes are apt for contemporary China.[30] When coupled with his efforts to revive traditional Confucian educational practices by leaving his university post and founding a private academy, Jiang's writings have garnered him considerable attention as a public intellectual. Like some figures from the early twentieth century, Jiang believes that Confucianism must be institutionalized as a formally organized religion, building these institutions on models found in China's past. Jiang sees Confucianism as intimately tied to Chinese history, culture, and popular practice; for him, any talk of global values is problematically utopian. Still, Jiang's faith in the truth of Confucian teachings and, strikingly, in the reality of *Tian* (or "Heaven") as a kind of deity seem to be deeply held, and he views Confucian institutions as eventually able to have a positive impact on the rest of the world.[31] His confidence that Confucianism must be the source of Chinese values has led him to outline a dramatically different set of political institutions from those currently in place in China.[32] This new political structure would have a place for the democratic expression of people's views, but the upper two houses of its tricameral legislature would be designed to give voice to learned Confucians with special insight into moral reality, on the one hand, and to experienced representatives of Chinese cultural and social institutions, on the other.[33]

Jiang is not alone in thinking that properly modified institutions should form the core of our thinking about Confucianism's future. Born in 1963 and initially trained in physics, Kang Xiaoguang is a social scientist and public intellectual who has become persuaded that China must replace its communist ideology with a soft authoritarianism based on Confucianism.[34] Kang is deeply unhappy with failings of the current regime in the area of social justice and is concerned that China's present political system lacks legitimacy. He writes of an alliance of political, intellectual, and economic elites that is leading to increased corruption, inequality, a rise in the power of organized crime, and other social maladies; he sums it up by saying that these elites are robbing the masses.[35] He (quite rightly) sees that such a system cannot possibly be legitimate in any type of Marxist framework. At the same time, Kang argues that liberal democracy is no panacea. Instead, he accepts and seeks to justify authoritarian, one-party rule. His goal is to show how a version of authoritarianism can both deal effectively with the social justice problems he has identified, and simultaneously be legitimate in its own terms. His basic idea is to show that a certain type of authoritarian, "cooperativist," welfare state can be justified largely by a rebuilding of Confucian-style institutions. Fan Ruiping's *Reconstructionist Confucianism: Rethinking Morality after the West* shares with Jiang Qing and to some degree with Kang Xiaoguang an enthusiasm for Confucian ritual and other fairly specific forms of life, especially the traditional family structure. Like Jiang, Fan sets his version of Confucianism up against the "New Confucianism" of Mou Zongsan. Fan identifies his "reconstructionist Confucianism" with the "project of reclaiming and articulating moral resources from the Confucian tradition so as to meet contemporary moral and public policy challenges."[36] According to Fan, philosophers like Mou advocate greater changes than Fan himself; in fact, they strive to "recast the Confucian heritage in light of modern Western values." As a result, Fan alleges that the "Confucian heritage is in great measure colonized by modern Western notions" as the New Confucians engage in "naive presentism" in order to "read social democratic concepts into Confucianism."[37] Starting in the next chapter, I will take issue with this characterization of New Confucian political philosophy, and will engage with other arguments from Jiang, Kang, and Fan throughout this book.

Mou Zongsan has many followers today, many of whom are primarily engaged in reiterating and defending various of Mou's theses.[38] There is a creative trend among philosophers who are generally supportive of Mou's vision, though, which we can label *Kantian New Confucianism*, the leading exponent of which is Lee Ming-huei of Taiwan's Academia Sinica. There is a debate among interpreters of Mou concerning how deep Mou's engagement with Kant really runs: is Mou fundamentally a Confucian who comes to express many of his ideas using Kantian language, or are Mou's ideas genuinely Kantian (perhaps because even earlier Confucianism itself is deontological)?[39] Lee is an influential voice among those who think that the connections are very deep. For our purposes, what is most significant about Lee's approach is the way he draws on Kant and on more recent Kantian philosophizing, much of it from Germany, to develop themes in political philosophy about which Mou said comparatively little. For example, in one discussion of democracy, Lee argues as follows.[40] First, Confucianism has two key theses concerning democracy: that democracy is connected to humans' innate good nature, and that political freedom must be based on moral freedom. Second, Lee says that this approach to democracy is different from mainstream Anglo-American theories, but resonates strongly with Kant's democratic theory, which he proceeds to explicate and defend. Third, Lee uses the parallel with Kant to suggest ways in which Confucian democratic theory may be developed, filling in many of the gaps left by Mou and other New Confucians. Another example of Lee's approach relates to Jiang Qing's emphasis on the institutional dimension of Confucianism. Lee agrees with Jiang on the importance of Confucian institutional theories, but he wants to show that this is still compatible with the centrality that Mou (and Lee himself) places on the pure moral heartmind. Lee's strategy is to show that in Kant, the fundamental commitment to moral autonomy can undergird an "ethic of responsibility" that is concerned with practical political outcomes, and that Confucianism, in parallel fashion, can build its institutional values on the foundation of its theories of moral heartmind.[41]

Max Weber argued that a key aspect of modernity was that it has become "disenchanted": we had lost the deep-seated religious and meta-physical commitment to values that was characteristic of earlier ages. One of the defining features of what I will call *Critical New Confucianism* is an agreement with Weber on this point.[42] The Taiwanese philosopher Lin Anwu, from whom I borrow the term "Critical New Confucianism," criticizes what he calls the "magical" dimension of Mou Zongsan's thought. He advocates a post-modern, practically and socially embedded Confucianism that stresses social justice and political responsibility and would critique autocracy, patriarchy, and male chauvinism; he now sometimes refers to this as "civic Confucianism (*gongmin ruxue*)."[43] As one analyst has noted, the details of how this might come about are far from clear, and Lin's work remains "hamstrung by its piecemeal formation and overly self-referential character."[44] Still, the broad outline of Lin's objectives resonates reasonably well with the arguments and goals I will be making in subsequent chapters. Another "critical" view that is generally compatible with Lin's can be found in the work of the young mainland scholar Tang Zhonggang, though as yet his scholarship has been more focused on the interpretation and criticism of Mou's political philosophy, as opposed to the constructive development of a "Critical New Confucian" perspective. Tang sees a future for a liberal, post-modern Confucianism that abandons Mou's moral monism and metaphysics and enters into the actual lifeworld (here he cites Habermas).[45] Tang is less explicit than Lin about the role or type of democracy that he envisions, but as is the case with Lin, many of the positive statements that Tang makes about the nature of the polity he envisions head in the same directions that I will endeavor to move – albeit more concretely – in the rest of this book.

Another approach to Confucian political philosophy that is finding increasing favor can be called *Neo-Classical Confucianism*. What these scholars have in common is a certain kind of ahistoricism: rather than looking at how the Confucian tradition has evolved (up through the twentieth century), they ask: If Confucius or Mencius or Xunzi were alive today, then based on what we know of their ideas from their writings, what might they have to say about contemporary social and political challenges? Would they endorse democracy, and if so, of what type? What would they say about human rights? Distributive justice? Capitalism? And so on. Theorists like Joseph Chan of Hong Kong University, Bai Tongdong of Fudan University, and perhaps Fan Ruiping (already mentioned above under Institutional Confucianism) can all fit under this heading.[46] A shared neo-classical approach does not guarantee shared conclusions: Chan, Bai, and Fan differ quite dramatically. Some of the writings of Canadian theorist Daniel Bell also fall into this category, though his recent reflections on "Left Confucianism" are more synthetic or comparative and thus belong in the next group I will mention.[47] A general goal of the Neo-Classicists tends to be showing that the recovery and creative development of classical Confucianism leads to the articulation of new and valuable positions within political philosophy: positions that may pose significant challenges to the existing Marxist or liberal wisdom. It is also often claimed that political philosophy built on the ideas of classical Confucianism has more chance of taking root and flourishing in Chinese soil, as opposed to theories of Western origin. Given the ahistorical nature of these positions and given the success of Western ideologies like Marxism, I have serious doubts about the persuasiveness of this latter argument, but as creative interpretations and developments of the founding texts of the Confucian tradition, Neo-Classical analyses are often very valuable.

My last category is the most diverse. By *Synthetic Confucians*, I designate Confucian philosophers who draw centrally on non-Confucian philosophical traditions. These individuals may identify with multiple traditions, seeing value and significance from multiple perspectives, and seek to integrate these in one synthetic form of Confucianism. The synthetic approach goes beyond the "rooted global" approach that I mentioned earlier, since it is explicitly rooted in more than one tradition. One prominent strand of this group – including Roger Ames of the University of Hawaii, Robert Neville of Boston University (who is also a Christian), and Sor-hoon Tan of the National University of Singapore – emphasizes the resonances they see between American Pragmatism and Confucianism, and seeks to develop Confucianism in concert with Deweyan and Peircean insights.[48] Huang Yushun of Shandong University offers a different kind of synthesis, taking inspiration from Heidegger in order to develop what he calls "life Confucianism."[49] Daniel Bell has recently been exploring the idea of "Left Confucianism," which pushes Confucianism and socialism to learn from one another.[50] Yet another example is the historian and political theorist Thomas Metzger who, especially in his magisterial *A Cloud Across the Pacific: Essays on the Clash between Chinese and Western Political Theories Today*, has sought to bring Confucianism and Mill's liberalism into a constructive and synthetic dialogue.[51] As can be seen from this extremely diverse list, synthetic approaches to Confucian political philosophy are emerging within many philosophical cultures and traditions, and are taking place in multiple languages. Roughly, we might be able to discern two different motivations within this synthetic philosophizing. In some cases, one is motivated to accept the synthetic version of Confucianism only insofar as one has an antecedent, independent commitment to the other doctrines with which Confucianism is being synthesized. A clear example of this is Bell's Left Confucianism: insofar as one is gripped by socialist values, then a Confucian will be attracted to a version of Confucianism that has developed in ways that accommodates and enhances socialist insights.[52] A different pattern of motivations occurs when the synthesis aims to solve a problem that, according to the theorist, can be perceived from within the perspective of Confucianism. Metzger's work is perhaps the best example of this approach, since he argues that both Confucian and Millian philosophies face complementary problems (he calls this the "Seesaw Effect") that can only be solved by some kind of creative synthesis.[53] The only other generalization we can make about synthetic approaches is that they are obviously premised on the existence of enough commonality between the respective traditions to make synthesis a possibility.

To conclude this section, let me add two caveats. First, contemporary Confucian political philosophy is complex enough, and its development is proceeding and proliferating at such a pace, that no set of categories is going to be completely satisfactory. The taxonomy I offer here is simply meant to help us to grasp the salient dimensions of the current discourse, in part so that the positions I take (and the positions I reject) in the coming chapters will make more sense. Second, we must note that current conversations often include non-Confucians who nonetheless interact in significant ways with, and thus contribute to, contemporary Confucian philosophizing. The early twentieth century political theorist Zhang Shizhao (1885–1973) is one such example; as we will see in Chapter 4, despite his clear commitment to liberal values and institutions, his arguments can contribute to a proper Confucian stance on the rule of law. Another example is the contemporary philosopher Zhao Tingyang, whose discussions of human rights and of "all-under Heaven (*tianxia*)" will figure prominently in Chapter 5. Zhao is an eclectic thinker, drawing both on a range of traditional Chinese ideas and on more recent Western perspectives, but Confucians can learn a great deal by taking his arguments seriously.

Progressive Confucianism

In light of all this, where does "Progressive Confucianism" fit in? I said at the outset that I mean "progressive" to function in two different ways: to describe the core Confucian commitment to individual and collective moral progress, and to label the particular approach to Confucian political philosophy that I will be advocating, which bears certain similarities to other contemporary "progressive" social and political movements. In terms of the categories I have just outlined, Progressive Confucianism probably fits in between the Kantian and Critical New Confucianisms. It is like the former in endorsing the importance of Mou Zongsan's "self-restriction" argument, though it is agnostic about the exact form that an account of Confucian ethics must take.[54] It is like the latter in being much more social-critical than Mou ever was, though it parts company with at least some of Lin's and Tang's criticisms of Mou. In addition, throughout the following chapters I will draw on what I see as the most persuasive parts of the Institutional, Neo-Classical, and Synthetic varieties of Confucianism.

"Progressive" is often opposed to "conservative," and yet there are senses in which the Confucian tradition – including my reading of it – is progressive and conservative at the same time. As Mou's fellow New Confucian Tang Junyi (1909–78) put it, "conserving is based on one's self-conscious affirmation of the value of the existence of one's life," and this understanding of value ultimately leads to a realization of the values of all things, and this latter understanding is the ground for progress.[55] Mou puts it this way: "If one is without a firm commitment to life, penetrating wisdom, and pervasive ethics, then one cannot speak of 'conserving.' True conserving is concretely embedded in the practice of creativity: the two are not opposed."[56] According to the New Confucians, in other words, insofar as we "conserve" the virtuous characteristics and affirmation of life that the tradition (as they interpret it) has shown us to be vital, we are thereby progressing – both growing ethically and making things better in our world. Mou acknowledges that if "conserving" is understood as a fixed set of habits or attitudes, and creativity is glossed as unrestrained, radical novelty, then they are obviously opposed, but asserts that these descriptions fit with neither conservation nor creativity in their true and valuable forms.

The idea that ethical insight leads to progressive political change, which in turn leads to greater realization of our potential for virtue, lies at the heart of Progressive Confucianism. The institutions advocated by Progressive Confucians are valued not because of their ancient pedigree but because of their capacity to assist in the realization of the fundamental human virtues that Confucians have valued since ancient times. Social structures that set barriers to the realization of virtue, therefore, need to be critiqued and changed. Progressive Confucian criticism of social, economic, or political oppression – a central topic of Chapter 7 – will often resemble the criticisms raised by other sorts of progressivism, but as I will show throughout the book, Progressive Confucianism remains true to its founding insights in many ways. Versions of hierarchy, deference, ritual, and state-sponsored ethical education, among other things, are all endorsed in the coming pages. Progressive Confucian political philosophy argues that our narrowly political institutions and values must be understood to exist in a balanced, mutually dependent relationship with two other distinct sources of value and practice, the ethical and the ritual.

I said a moment ago that Progressive Confucianism is based in part on the aim of realizing "fundamental human virtues that Confucians have valued since ancient times." There are two ways to read this. On the one hand, one might emphasize the fact that Confucians value these virtues as a reason for taking them seriously. If you are a Confucian, I might argue, then you must value these virtues (humaneness, righteousness, propriety, wisdom, and faithfulness): accepting these virtues as central is part of what it is to be a Confucian. On the other hand, one might emphasize the fact that these are "fundamental human virtues": early Confucians recognized that they deserved to be valued, but the reason to value them is because they are valuable, not because Confucians have traditionally valued them. By framing this book as a work in political philosophy, I take myself to have adopted the latter of these two approaches. Political philosophy aims to tell us what is true about human lives and values insofar as they relate to our lives together in political society. This is distinct from simply explicating what one or another tradition has said. I thus agree with Bai Tongdong's insightful discussion of the difference between the universal openness of political philosophy, which Bai sees as his own enterprise, and the particularist focus encouraged by Jiang Qing's viewing Confucianism (that is, *rujiao*) through the lens of religion.[57]

So the audience of this book is not confined to those who identify themselves as Confucians. Still, there are limits to what I can hope to establish here. In particular, I will not be arguing for the truth of either the general framework of Confucian ethics, nor of any particular way in which historical Confucians have tried to flesh out their general ethical commitments.[58] I will rely on a rough and general understanding of Confucian ethics as involving, among other things, the following key ideas: humans are capable of developing our attunement to and care for all aspects of our social and natural environment, which most centrally involves those people with whom we have particular relationships; our care for distinct dimensions of value in our environments (e.g., family responsibilities, the well-being of strangers for whom we are responsible, and concern for our friends) must be harmonized; well-lived human lives and the flourishing of our communities both depend on people successfully developing the afore-mentioned capacities to significant degrees; these capacities can be usefully explained through reference to individual virtues like humaneness and propriety, though these virtues are at least somewhat inter-related (and perhaps, depending on the specific account, ultimately just different aspects of a single capacity); and the ultimate goal of Confucian ethics is the full development of these virtues on the part of all people.[59]

Stated this generally, Confucian ethics obviously has both similarities with and differences from various Western ethical views. The same can be said for Progressive Confucianism itself: as I begin to lay out its key ideas in the chapters to come, both similarities and differences from liberal, republican, and Aristotelian political theories will emerge. The differences are sometimes subtle rather than dramatic, especially when comparing

Progressive Confucianism to its closest Western correlates (for example, those versions of liberalism that find substantial room for state moral education and stress civic virtues). Progressive Confucianism is committed to a kind of constitutional democracy, though this is neither imposed from outside Confucianism – through a desire to emulate the West, say – nor does it mean that Progressive Confucianism is "simply" constitutional democracy. The roles played by the constitution, laws, and representative institutions are distinctive and always to be understood within the broader framework of balance with Confucian ethics and ritual. Further convergence is always possible, of course: indeed, I would hope that those working within congenial strands of Western traditions will learn from this account of Progressive Confucianism, so that future liberalisms (for example) might share even more with future Confucianisms.

This Book

The balance of this book contains six chapters and a conclusion, the goal of which is to defend a Progressive Confucian perspective on political philosophy through critical engagement with alternative Confucian and non-Confucian approaches. I proceed topically; the main issues I address are authority, law, human rights, ritual, oppression, and deference. This list will look quite idiosyncratic from the perspective of Western political philosophy, but I have chosen the topics to reflect what is distinctive and controversial about contemporary Confucian political philosophy in general, and my Progressive Confucianism in particular. Human rights and the critique of oppression are not traditional Confucian topics, but they must be important to contemporary Confucianism. Law and authority are discussed to some degree within the tradition, though my approach to each is in important ways a departure from the tradition. Ritual and deference are traditional topics that rarely, if ever, are mentioned within Western political thought; one of the keys to my overall argument here is to show how they are critical to a comprehensive Confucian political philosophy in ways that political philosophers working within other traditions should find stimulating.

The argument in each of the chapters builds upon points established earlier in the book. Since a version of Mou Zongsan's "self-restriction" argument is central to several subsequent chapters and yet is virtually unknown in Anglophone philosophy, I make it the topic of Chapter 2. I believe that Mou had considerable insight into the idea of self-restriction; I agree with him that it is a creative development within the Confucian tradition that, while not already implicit in early Confucian writings, can nonetheless count as a distinctively Confucian theory. However, much of my argument in Chapter 2 departs from the specific context and commitments of Mou's philosophical system. I will show that self-restriction makes sense and retains its importance even independently from Mou's other theories: it can be grounded in any version of Confucian ethics that meets the criteria I spelled out in the previous section.

The question of legitimate political authority is critical to any political philosophy, and has been at the center of debates within Confucian political philosophy for the last century. Early Confucianism saw *"Tian"* or Heaven as the source of authority, as kings ruled in accord with its "mandate." The clearest communication of *Tian's* intentions comes through the actions of the "people" (*min*), whose well-being thus forms the bedrock of Confucian politics. Chapter 3 begins by rehearsing both the strengths and the limitations of such a framework, as well as pointing to a tension concerning the status of the "people" that runs throughout traditional Confucianism. Next, I analyze Institutional Confucian Kang Xiaoguang's contemporary effort to justify an authoritarian state by means of an only modestly revised version of the early Confucian view. Finding fault with this approach, I then articulate an alternative approach to Confucian authority, drawing in significant ways on Mou's "self-restriction" argument. Very roughly, on this model something like *Tian* remains the source of authority, but a re-conceptualized "people" themselves are the holders of authority. This authority is delegated through democratic processes to a government, and its exercise is constrained and influenced in two ways: by a constitution and by a particular kind of state moral education.

The role played in Chapter 3 by a constitution and laws pushes me to address more directly the potential tension between virtue and law, which is the main topic of Chapter 4. The relations between "rule of law (*fazhi*)" and "virtue politics (*dezhi*)" have been repeatedly debated in China over the last century. After a brief introduction to pre-twentieth-century Chinese discussions of these themes, the chapter turns to two such debates, from the mid-1910s and from the late 1950s and early 1960s. Within these contexts, I pay special attention to the arguments of Zhang Shizhao (1885–1973) and Mou Zongsan, respectively. The latter parts of the chapter survey more recent Chinese discussions of the inter-relations between law and virtue, and then suggest various ways in which the arguments of Zhang and Mou point toward a Progressive Confucian stance on these issues that can contribute to current dialogue, both within and without China, on issues like the limits on moral authority and on the role of virtue in politics, the relations between public and private, and the need for political and legal value to be rooted in morality.

Chapter 4 concerns domestic law; in Chapter 5 I turn to international law and, in particular, human rights. Much of the debate in the last two decades concerning the relationship between Confucianism and human rights has foundered on whether "human" and "rights" – in the specific senses in which these are used in Western human rights discourse – can find homes within Confucianism. My point of departure in this chapter is the idea of contemporary Chinese philosopher Zhao Tingyang that organizing our global political thinking around the Chinese idea of "all-under-heaven (*tianxia*)" can serve us better than alternative frameworks. I add to this Mou Zongsan's "self-restriction" argument as a way to understand how rights come into the picture. Still, Mou said little about rights with the scope of "human rights," so much of this chapter moves beyond both Zhao and Mou to show how we could arrive at the "rights of all-under-heaven," and furthermore how they might be institutionalized.

The next chapter turns in a quite different direction, exploring how the Confucian concern with ritual (*li*) can serve as a robust model of civility, which in turn is critical to a flourishing state-and-society. (The ineliminable interconnections among self, state, and society, and their consequences for Confucian "political" philosophy, are major themes of the book's Conclusion.) My interpretation of ritual has four main characteristics. First, it is minimal, in the sense of placing only modest demands on people and being accessible to those without advanced levels of ethical cultivation. Unlike maximal views of ritual, the view developed here is comfortable with the idea that ethical value goes beyond and can potentially critique any given set of rituals. Second, ritual has a partial independence from context-sensitive ethical judgments. Because it plays a central role in the constitution of our communities, partly through the way it expresses a commitment to shared values, ritual has a viscous nature and is not easily changed. Third, ritual as we practice it meshes with the ethical virtue of propriety. Propriety is an important dimension of an ideal ethical response to a given situation. It disposes us to focus on the apt manner in which one should act, rather than simply on the intention, type of act, or outcome. In many cases, the apt manner of action is socially understood (as ritual), though the virtue of propriety should be seen as outrunning existing rituals. Finally, ritual is distinct from, but compatible with, the rule of law.

Chapter 7 is concerned with social criticism: in particular, with the necessity for contemporary Confucians to recognize and root out oppression. I show that Confucianism long ago anticipated an important finding of contemporary psychology: namely, our social and physical environments have significant effects on the ways and degrees to which we can be virtuous. Confucian insights in this regard have been limited by their ethical particularism, however, so Confucianism has sometimes been blind to the systematic effects of large-scale social and economic arrangements. A particularly worrisome type of social arrangement is oppression – when a group is systematically immobilized or diminished – and so Progressive Confucians must stand against oppression, notwithstanding historical Confucian complacency concerning many types of oppression. Still, non-oppressive forms of hierarchy and deference are both possible and important, as any Confucian political philosophy must recognize. Like Chapter 6, Chapter 7 pushes the boundaries of the "political" well beyond a narrow concern with the state.

The book's Conclusion revisits themes from the preceding chapters in order to make explicit the ways in which Confucian political philosophy depends on a dynamic harmony – one could almost say productive tensions – among ethical, narrowly political, and ritual dimensions of value. In this context, I dwell for some time on the relations between the state and both education and ritual, and finish with some reflections on the challenging question of the institutional home for Confucianism in our contemporary world.

2

Self-Restriction: The Indirect Link Between Ethics and Politics

Traditional Confucianism conceived of the ethical and political realms as continuous and unified. Either the most virtuous should rule or, in a concession to hereditary monarchy, rulers should strive to be as virtuous as possible and be guided by their still-more-virtuous ministers. In theory, the possession of virtue enabled the ruler to care for all in the realm; the exemplary nature of the ruler's character, especially as manifest in his concern for members of his family, was supposed to lead all in the realm toward virtue as well. To be sure, a variety of intermediary institutions evolved to enhance and spread the effects of the ruler's virtue, including ministers, bureaucrats, and the system of examinations that produced them; a broad system of rituals; and a penal code designed to preserve order when all else failed. "Order" was a central goal, but it was conceived in ethical terms and virtuous rule was understood to be both necessary and sufficient for its attainment.

At the core of Mou Zongsan's New Confucian political project is an effort to pry apart ethical and political values. Mou was worried about any political system that relies on leadership by individuals who claim to have highly developed moral insight. He had in mind the periodic, terrible excesses of both the traditional Confucian state and the modern Communist one: in both cases, leaders who believed in their own virtue sometimes sought to impose their vision of morality on the realm, with bloody consequences. Mou characterized this as politics being "swallowed" by morality.[1] To be sure, Mou was deeply committed to the importance of striving for sagehood. Among other things, he saw laws and rights themselves as rooted in and emerging from moral struggles, as we will see. Without morality, there would be no politics. Nonetheless, he recognized that "achieving sagehood is an endless process."[2] Politics (including law) must, therefore, be independent from morality, or else it, too, would be endlessly unfinished and inadequately protective. Mou thus found himself advocating a position that fell between liberal right-based theories and traditional Confucian (or Communist) good-based theories. Unlike the liberals, Mou held that moral and political value must retain a continuity, lest politics be unmoored from the underlying source of all value, in which case we would have no reason for confidence that the outcomes of our political processes were ultimately aimed at making our lives better. Unlike the Communists and earlier Confucians, though, politics and law must nonetheless stand on their own, independent of morality. In other words, Mou rejected both a direct connection between morality and politics, and a lack of connection. His alternative is an indirect connection. Political value, he says, emerges out of morality, but achieves an independent status because the further development of moral value requires what he terms "self-restriction (*ziwo kanxian*)."[3]

I am persuaded by Mou that self-restriction is critical to a fruitful contemporary Confucian development of political philosophy. However, let me make clear from the outset that my explication and development of this idea differs in some crucial ways from Mou's. Self-restriction plays key roles in at least three different areas of Mou's philosophy. It explains how cognition of the empirical world is possible for creatures whose moral heartminds also respond to the lifeworld in a non-empirical way; it explains how and to what degree scientific norms can govern our activities, at least partly independently from morality; and it explains how laws and rights can structure our political lives without being over-ridden by individual claims to better moral insight. In each case, Mou argues that what is being "restricted" is the direct, intuitive grasping of moral reality by the moral heartmind. Understanding this latter idea, which he frequently terms "intellectual intuition," would be critical to a full account of Mou's theory of self-restriction. I believe, though, that with some re-interpretation, we can detach the idea of self-restriction from the rest of Mou's "moral metaphysics" without losing its significance for political philosophy. Self-restriction must certainly be grounded in an account of ethical value but, as already suggested in Chapter 1, there is a range of views that all meet the general criteria I have laid out for Confucian ethics. I will use some of Mou's specific discussions of self-restriction as my point of departure, and in fact I believe that Mou would accept virtually everything I say here about self-restriction. (The contemporary Kantian New Confucians, in addition, should be able to follow and accept my argument here.) But we do not need to take on board all of Mou's system in order to see the value of self-restriction, and this approach opens it up to a much wider audience.

Mou himself glosses "self-restriction" as meaning "self-negation (*ziwo fouding*)" in a Hegelian sense: that is, the limitation of one thing by something else of a fundamentally distinct kind.[4] This is a good start on its meaning, but before pursuing that further, it will be worthwhile to attend a bit to the term *ziwo kanxian* itself, which is unusual and was invented by Mou. "Self-restriction" is formed by combining the common noun "self (*ziwo*)" and the decidedly uncommon verb "*kanxian*," which Mou constructs from two related terms from the *Book of Changes*. "*Kan*" is one of the eight trigrams out of which the sixty-four hexagrams of the *Changes* are composed. Its bottom and top lines are broken or *yin* lines; the middle line is a solid, *yang* line. The contemporary scholar Richard Lynn gives "sink hole" as its basic meaning, and it is clear from a number of early commentaries that it has the connotation of water flowing through it. One such commentary also associates *kan* with the "rain, by which things are moistened (*run*)." Flowing water and moistening are both positive-sounding, despite the negative connotations of sink hole. In addition, two of the earliest commentaries define *kan* as "*xian*," or "pit."[5] With all this in mind, we should think of *kanxian* primarily as a lowering and limitation, like sinking into a pit. This justifies translating it as "restriction." However, its associations with water and especially with moistening are also crucial, because Mou sees self-restriction ultimately to be a vital, positive stage in broader processes of cognition and moral growth.

Self-Restriction in Politics

I mentioned already that Mou uses self-restriction in three distinct contexts: cognition, science, and politics. His earliest introduction of the term occurs in an effort to argue that Wang Yangming (1472–1529)'s theory of moral cognition implicitly includes the idea of self-restriction.[6] Given the strategy I have outlined above, though, I will focus instead on Mou's most approachable account of self-restriction's function in politics, and demonstrate that we can draw from it an idea of self-restriction that is compelling even when freed from Mou's other theoretical commitments. Key to Mou's discussion is a distinction between the functional presentations of ethical reasoning and the structural presentations of analytical reasoning. By the first of these ideas, he means an individual's particularist, situation-specific ethical judgments, which he sees as the core modality of Confucian ethics.[7] He understands these judgments to come from the properly cultivated moral heartmind, and in this sense to be subjective; he also puts this in terms of the individual's virtuous character.[8] The structural presentation of analytic reasoning, on the other hand, refers to general, objective rules or frameworks. With this in mind, here is Mou:

A democratic political structure is something that emerges from the conscious decisions people make in their political lives; based on this clue, we can connect it to ethical reasoning. But such political structures are objective frameworks belonging to objective practice, and thus cannot be completed by the functional presentation of ethical reason. The inner logic of the political structure itself is a manifestation of the structural presentation of reasoning; this reasoning temporarily cannot be thought of in terms of individual virtue or practical reasoning, but has shifted into analytic reasoning without ethical meaning .... But this overall political structure itself is something desired by ethical reasoning. In other words, the realization of this political structure is also the realization of a highest ethical value. This shows that in order to realize this ethical value, ethical reasoning must from within the midst of its functional presentation restrict itself (*ziwo kanxian*), step back a pace, and shift into the structural presentation of analytical reasoning. Observed from within this structural presentation of reason, politics has its independent significance, forms its own, independent realm of value, and has temporarily left ethics behind; it seemingly has no connection with ethics. From within the structural presentation, the various aspects of this political structure – like the organization of power and the definition of rights and duties – are all on par with one another, and thus can be the subjects of an independent political science. People can discuss these aspects using pure political discussion, striving to clearly establish a reasonable, impartial framework (*heli gongdao*).[9]

As we can see, for Mou that which restricts itself is a certain kind of reasoning, in favor of a different modality of reasoning. From elsewhere in Mou's writings, though, it is clear that the difference between ethical and analytic reasoning is more dramatic than I have been making it sound. He really has in mind two fundamentally different kinds of consciousness: an innate moral consciousness that has the ability to directly intuit the basic moral nature of the cosmos, and a cognitive, analytical consciousness that works by distinguishing subject from object.[10] One key to my appropriation of Mou is to realize that self-restriction still makes sense if we give a much less metaphysically charged interpretation of the two forms of reasoning. As I noted above, Mou takes "the virtue of one's moral character (*renge zhong de dexing*)" to be roughly equivalent to the deliverances of one's moral heartmind; I propose simply to see ethical reasoning in terms of the perceptions and reactions of virtuous character to particular situations. This is consistent with Mou's more elaborate story, but does not require that we follow Mou in all the specifics. Furthermore, my version still provides a solid (and solidly Confucian) normative grounding for ethics, based in the general framework of Confucian ethics I outlined in Chapter 1.[11]

What about the reasoning that takes place within the political realm? How is this different from ethical reasoning? I accept much of what Mou says: it is reasoning in terms of different values and in keeping with general, objective rules. Rather than basing one's judgment and behavior on one's own perception of the situation, one is bound by laws and works within political processes. Among other things, this means accepting the messiness and imperfections of the political process (as I will discuss further in Chapter 4). As he puts it succinctly in one of his lectures: if a sage wants to be a president, he must "observe the political rules."[12] There are some key questions about the nature of reasoning and judgment from within the political perspective that I will put off for now – questions concerning the ways in which ethical reasoning might still make its presence felt within the political realm. Instead, let us take note of the first sentence from Mou's long quote: it is important that politics emerges out of the ethical activity of individuals as they merge together in political life, because Mou's basic picture is that a certain kind of political structure is ultimately needed as the indirect means to more complete ethical practice. Ethical reasoning "restricts itself" in order to more fully realize itself, and thereby allows for an independent realm of political value to exist. It is independent in the sense that it cannot, at least under normal circumstances, be overridden by an individual's claim to superior ethical insight. As Mou puts it later in the same book,

> No matter how great or spiritual the attainments of one's [virtuous] character, when manifested in politics, one cannot override the relevant limits (that is, the highest principles of the political world), and in fact must devote one's august character to the realization of these limits. When one is able to successfully realize these limits, in ancient times one would be called a "sage-king"; in modern times, a "great statesperson." If one cannot, in ancient times one would be called a "hegemon," "tyrant," or "autocrat"; in modern times, a "totalitarian ruler" or "dictator."[13]

Mou ignores here the differences between ancient and modern politics; on his more considered account, even the best of ancient politics suffers from its lack of independence.

Let us take a step back. There are two key things that we need to understand about self-restriction: what it is, and why it is necessary. So far in this section we have made some progress toward understanding what it is, at least with respect to the relation between ethics and politics.

I will have more to say about the details below. Here, let us focus on the justification of self-restriction (as it applies to ethics/politics). In summary outline, the argument is as follows. Our subjectively felt, internalized morality implicitly points toward an ideal of full, sagely virtue. Full virtue must be realized in the public, political world. Without objective structures (like laws), the public goals of full virtue are inaccessible. Since these objective structures restrict the ways in which our subjective moral feelings can be manifested, Mou concludes that the achievement of virtue requires self-restriction. Objective, public standards are thus related to inner virtue, but they are also distinct from one another. Before I unpack this argument, let me emphasize why it is important. Mou's idea, which I endorse, is not that a constitution, laws, and rights are merely *compatible* with Confucianism, but rather than these objective political structures are *required* by Confucianism if it is to realize its own goals. Mou's argument does not depend on an independent commitment to constitutional democracy, but is a critique internal to the Confucian tradition. The fact that he draws on Hegelian language does not change this fact, just as the ways in which earlier Confucians drew on Buddhist ideas does not render their critiques external to the tradition.

In any event, turn now to the argument itself. It has three premises: (1) We (Confucians) are committed to seeking full virtue; (2) full virtue must be realized in the public world; and (3) the public realization of full virtue requires objective structures that are independent from claims of virtue. The first premise should be uncontroversial: The pursuit of ethical self-improvement and the criticism of those who rest content with moral mediocrity are perennial themes in Confucian writings. Some writers over the last century have sought to resist the second premise, arguing that Confucianism can only have a continued role in the modern world if it confines its aspirations to the development of an inner virtue that has no necessary expression or influence in the outer world. We can see something of this attitude in Yu Dan's extraordinarily popular recent book on the *Analects*, and the eminent scholar Yu Ying-shih has repeatedly made arguments to this effect.[14] However, it is absolutely central to the Confucian conception of virtue that inner states and dispositions have an outer manifestation and influence. Indeed, this is one of the real insights of the tradition that we are now beginning to see confirmed by modern psychology.[15] More certainly can be said about this premise, including its dependence on the lack of a firm distinction between "private" (like family) and "public" (like political); on this score, Confucians and feminists find themselves both supporting the latter's slogan that "the personal is political."[16] Still, it should be clear that the core of Mou's argument comes in the third premise.

The premise that the public realization of full virtue requires objective structures can itself be spelled out in three steps. First, publically realized full virtue means that everyone is also and simultaneously realizing virtue; as we read in *Analects* 12:1, "If one day he can overcome himself and turn to humaneness, the world will turn to humaneness along with him."[17] Similarly, *Analects* 12:16 says that the good person "completes the good in others"; *Analects* 4:25 tells us that "virtue is not solitary; it must have neighbors." It is possible to read these latter two statements in a narrow way, perhaps only including the elite stratum of society, but as I argue in Chapter 3, this tendency within early Confucianism is something that a contemporary Progressive Confucianism has good grounds for rejecting. The fundamental inter-relationship of people on which these sayings from the *Analects* are based should include all people.

Second, the attainment of virtue by others must be their individual and active achievement. As Mou explains at one point (partly using Hegelian language), actual freedom requires self-awareness, which in turn requires struggle; each person must feel that he or she is an independent individual. This is connected to the pervasive Confucian commitment to "getting it for oneself (*zi de*)"; slightly later in *Analects* 12:1, the text continues: "To be humane comes from oneself; how could it come from others?"[18] Third, only when rights to exercise agency with respect to matters both large and small are guaranteed, via external political structures, can the possibility of individual, active engagement with one's own self-cultivation be assured. People need to have opportunities to take responsibility for various aspects of their world, even up to the possibility that they are most qualified to serve as the head of government.[19] Virtuous insight must therefore be restrained – restrict itself – by adherence to the objective structures that protect the rights of all. Only then is full virtue a possibility.

Is this Confucianism?

One of the persistent criticisms of Mou's theory of self-restriction is that it, and therefore the constitutional and democratic structures it purports to require, are not really Confucian. At its most extreme, this line of criticism alleges that self-restriction is a purposeful obfuscation designed to conceal the wholesale borrowing of Western political values. Although I am not adopting Mou's full theory, some of these same challenges are still relevant to my more minimal understanding of self-restriction, so we should consider them here. Mou believes that his self-restriction idea is necessary in order to preserve the value and relevance of Confucianism – as a whole – in the contemporary world. Even though Confucianism is not a single, systematic philosophical theory, but rather a more than two-millennia-long tradition of philosophical theorizing and practice, it still has recurrent and mutually reinforcing key parts that we can think of on the model of a single theory. If Mou is right that self-restriction is necessary to save the body of theory and practice that is Confucianism, then if adopting self-restriction is to abandon Confucianism, all hope for Confucianism would seem to be lost. This would have consequences both for people's identity and also for the other ideas and values of Confucianism, since if the theory as a whole is no longer tenable, each part of it is thereby called into question. Perhaps its several aspects might be combined with other ideas into a new whole; or perhaps their resonance will linger on in somewhat distinctive versions of liberalism, socialism, and so on. But if Confucianism cannot be combined with self-restriction and if self-restriction is necessary, dramatic consequences surely follow.

Advocates of Confucianism thus have three strategies: (1) reject the idea that there are distinctive challenges to Confucianism today and hold that there is no problem for self-restriction to solve; (2) accept that there are challenges, but argue for a different solution to them; or (3) adopt something like Mou's approach. For example, the contemporary Institutional Confucian thinker Jiang Qing shares Mou's concern about the contemporary challenges to Confucianism, but both thinks that a different solution is available, and that self-restriction is deeply non-Confucian. I will deal with the latter charge below. Jiang's own solution can be quickly sketched: he argues that the Confucian tradition has ample resources on which it can draw to develop a robust and successful contemporary politics. According to Jiang, Mou ignores these institutions because Mou is convinced that "outer kingship" must somehow emerge from "inner sagehood." That is, ethics (which Mou connects strongly with the inner moral heartmind) has priority in any theorizing. Jiang disagrees, and says that inner and outer are two parallel aspects of the tradition; their relation is structural rather than causal. He therefore urges that political philosophers set aside an obsession with the heartmind and focus on creatively adapting Confucian institutions to China's current situation.[20] Jiang also argues that Confucians not take democracy to be an indispensable guide to their institutional innovation, since this is to unjustifiably privilege a type of institution that happens to have been successful in the West, but has no universal validity. Both here in this chapter and in the subsequent course of this book, we will see the following response to Jiang unfold. Jiang's idea that inner morality and outer politics are independent, parallel tracks is only tenable if moral development does not depend on a particular political form. We will see that Mou lays the groundwork for me to argue to the contrary: political (and social) institutional forms do matter to moral development, and often matter enormously. This is why Confucians must advocate participatory politics and must critique oppression. This is not unjustifiably privileging "Western" democracy because to whatever degree Progressive Confucianism converges with Western models – and it is likely to be distinctive in several respects, as we will see – this follows from the internal logic of Progressive Confucianism, not from a desire to copy the West.

Mou himself sometimes argues that self-restriction is a plausible interpretation of what earlier Confucians, and especially Wang Yangming (1472–1529), had in mind.[21] In other places, particularly when addressing politics and science, Mou does not read the idea of self-restriction back into the tradition. Instead, his argument – one instance of which we have already seen above – is that core Confucian commitments demand a certain kind of approach to political legitimacy and to scientific independence, even though this was never fully realized by historical Confucian philosophers.[22] The needed approach relies essentially on self-restriction. Mou does on occasion cite brief bits from Confucian classics when spelling out this kind of argument, but his point in these contexts does not seem to be claiming that the need for self-restriction was already understood. Rather, we can see Mou as employing a variety of more subtle strategies. One of his goals is to show a resonance, or at least lack of contradiction, between self-restriction and the earlier Confucians' explicit statements.[23] Another tactic is to maintain that Confucians did largely grasp the inner spirit of legitimate (democratic) politics, even though they missed the crucial role of self-restriction in actually making a polity legitimate.[24] Finally, Mou argues rather plausibly that certain Confucians – he stresses Gu Yanwu (1613–82) and Huang Zongxi (1610–1695) in particular – at least partly saw the need for a development of Confucianism in the direction that Mou now insists upon, although they were not radical enough.[25]

What should we make of these various claims? First of all, it is hard not to agree with Jiang Qing when he says that a careful reading of Wang Yangming makes clear that (on Wang's account) innate good knowing "can only manifest (*chengxian*) itself, and cannot restrict itself (*kanxian*)."[26] Jiang shows that Wang repeatedly uses language calling for the direct manifestation of innate good knowing, and never hints at the much more involved and indirect process that Mou has in mind.[27,28] I propose that we accept the idea that self-restriction is implausible as an interpretation of pre-existing Confucian texts. However, the question of whether self-restriction is a creative development of Confucianism remains. Jiang argues that it is not, but instead amounts to abandoning Confucianism. He reasons as follows. First, as we have seen already, self-restriction cannot reasonably be seen as an interpretation of pre-existing elements of the tradition. Second, Jiang canvasses the multiple foreign sources of Mou's idea of self-restriction: Hegel, Kant, Buddhism, and even Aristotle. From this he concludes that Mou has transformed his Confucian discourse into a fundamentally Western framework; Mou's so-called "Third Era" of Confucianism is actually "Western Learning (*xixue*)."[29]

Jiang is mistaken in two key ways, both with respect to Mou's own version of self-restriction (which is of course Jiang's target) and with respect to my more generalized understanding of self-restriction. First of all, I agree with a number of other commentators who maintain that while it is true that Mou has digested a wide range of inspirations, East and West, his fundamental goals and conclusions are Confucian, rather than Kantian, Hegelian, or Buddhist.[30] The entire structure of his philosophy, including the "New Politics (*xin waiwang*)," is designed to enable the realization of a Confucian socio-ethical vision. The issue is slightly different for my own account of self-restriction, which does not rely on a particular Buddhist- and Kantian-influenced version of Confucianism, but the same conclusion still applies. Second, Mou has argued that self-restriction is in fact *necessary* in order to realize the Confucian ideal of full virtue, and I have already begun to develop my own version of these arguments (which will be further supplemented in chapters to come). This is a vital part of Mou's justification that Jiang neglects; it means that not only is Mou's (or my) approach to creatively developing Confucianism acceptable, it is actually required.

Ethical and Political Values

The core idea behind self-restriction, I have said, is to provide an "indirect" connection between ethical and political values. Political values must be rooted in ethics, and yet independent from it; ethical values must be restricted within the political realm, yet ultimately served by this relationship. In this final section of the chapter, I propose to clarify three aspects of this complex relationship. First, I will review what has been said so far, and summarize some of the arguments to come in subsequent chapters, on the topic of politics emerging out of ethics. Second (and relatedly), it is important to emphasize that while political values are, strictly speaking, "non-moral," the political realm is nonetheless governed by important and valuable norms: it is not a bare realm in which only power matters. Finally, I will close with some thoughts on the temporal relationship between ethical and political values: do they alternate, coexist, or what?

I noted above that politics emerges out of the ethical activity of individuals as they merge together in political life, and that a certain kind of political structure is ultimately needed as the indirect means to more complete ethical practice. Underlying this relationship are two key thoughts: that the emergence of political norms depends on the actual interaction of ethical agents seeking to better realize their ends, and that any actual set of political norms can be assessed in light of its contribution to furthering ethical development. I will flesh out these two ideas in considerable detail in the rest of the book. In Chapter 4 and especially Chapter 5, I explain and expand upon Mou's argument that rights emerge as a result of interactions among groups in society seeking ways to protect and balance their interests. Chapter 7 then argues for what might be called a legitimacy constraint on this process – that is, a perspective from which the actual results of political construction can be criticized. To what degree does the resulting framework enables individuals in all groups to develop ethically? Insofar as barriers are placed in front of any group's capacity for moral growth, the legal, political, or social framework is subject to Confucian criticism.

In the long quote from Mou that I used to introduce his approach to political self-restriction, we saw him say that "observed from within this structural presentation of reason, politics has its independent significance, forms its own, independent realm of value, and has temporarily left ethics behind; it seemingly has no connection with ethics." Similarly, he says that within the political realm, we rely on "analytic reasoning without ethical meaning." According to some of Mou's critics, this means that when one has engaged in self-restriction, one is operating in a realm free of moral values: the pure search for scientific truth or the pure "political science" of manipulating power.[31,32] But in light of what was said in the previous paragraph, it should now be clear that when Mou says that politics has "temporarily left ethics behind," he does not mean that politics is simply about power. Politics is a "realm of value" structured by rules, and throughout his political theory, Mou takes impartial laws to be paradigm instances of "political" rules. He criticized traditional China for lacking a genuine rule of law. Without its own, independent justification and meaning, law is no more than a dispensable, manipulable tool of control; it has no genuine authority over us, nor do we have any genuine rights.[33]

The "highest principles of the political world" are embodied in a state's constitution; only these sorts of principles have the "objectivity" that is needed for genuine political authority. Subjecting oneself to such objective rules is precisely the nature of self-restriction.[34]

Finally, let us consider in more detail the idea that the relationship just described between ethics and politics is "temporary." In fact I think that self-restriction is a persistent feature of our lives, rather than something to which we temporarily or periodically resort. This is an area in which Mou's own language can be somewhat misleading. For example, he often uses the word "temporary (*zan* or *zanshi*)" to characterize self-restriction. At one point, he characterizes the perspective or realm within which politics is independent as "temporarily leaving behind (*tuoli*) ethics; seemingly (*si*) unrelated to ethics."[35] Mou's contemporary, Tang Junyi, seems to have understood the idea of self-restriction as involving a series of temporally distinct stages.[36] Many current commentators on Mou's theory of self-restriction take it as obvious that it involves temporal stages.[37] But I think that metaphors of temporal stages are seriously misleading. For one thing, once we have acknowledged that ethical and political values (for example) interlock in the way I have described above, then we see that ethics always is present in politics, albeit not in a direct or crude way. It is not a matter of leaping in and out of an ethical perspective, but rather an embracing of properly designed political values and institutions as a central part of being ethical. The sage does not begrudgingly follow the law, but reveals his or her virtue through willing self-restriction by political norms. At the same time, when the contemporary scholar Wang Dade says that according to Mou, ethical insight waits in the background, ready to manifest itself when politics goes awry,[38] we might conclude that he is at least partly right, for does this not offer an interesting way of understanding civil disobedience? Legitimate self-restriction does not mean that one's full-fledged and independent ethical judgment disappears, so one should be capable of judging when the violation of the law might be ethically justified without abandoning the general commitment to law that self-restriction demands. If one's ethical values lead one routinely to break the law, though, then this is not civil disobedience but rather the denial that any legitimate law is actually in play.

3

Rethinking Authority and Rejecting Authoritarianism: Giving the People their Voice

In his treatise on political philosophy, Mou Zongsan argued that the Chinese traditions were very strong in theories of governance ("zhidao") but unfortunately weak in the more fundamental area of justifying political authority ("zhengdao").[1] I believe that there is significant insight in Mou's thesis. As in the prior chapter, my goal here is not to defend Mou's specific position. Rather, I will develop my own argument concerning the proper way for Confucians to think about political authority, in dialogue with other contemporary Confucian thinkers. I draw on Mou's self-restriction argument at a key point in the chapter, and the overall conclusion is one that Mou might have endorsed. The structure of my argument is quite different from Mou's, though, in part because I believe it is rather clear that early Confucians had a powerful account of political authority – even if it turns out to be subject to an important tension, as I will show below. In particular, early Confucianism saw "*Tian*" or Heaven as the source of authority, and kings ruled in accord with its "mandate (*ming*)."[2]

Contemporary analysts make distinctions among sheer power, *de facto* authority, and legitimate authority. The difference between the latter two turns on whether legitimacy is genuinely merited: unlike sheer power, all forms of authority depend on claims to legitimacy. In the case of *de facto* authority, enough people accept these claims for the government to maintain public order, even though the actual legitimacy of the regime may be questionable. Different systems of thought articulate what is needed to earn genuine legitimacy in strikingly different ways. In some cases, it makes sense to call legitimate political authority "sovereignty," but I will follow the historical and contemporary uses of this latter term and restrict it to the supreme political authority within a bounded territory. That is, the word "sovereignty" and its cognates emerged in early modern Europe within a system of states, and it has continued to be used in this limited way.[3] The Confucian concern with authority is not limited to authority within a specific state: in classical and imperial times, the authority of the Son of Heaven was understood to be universal,[4] and I will argue for a

Confucian conception of authority in contemporary times that retains at least part of this structure.[5]

I take the early Confucian conception of authority as my starting point.[6] As we will see, it is crucial that the clearest communication of *Tian's* intentions comes through the actions of the "people (*min*)," whose well-being thus forms the bedrock of Confucian politics. I begin by rehearsing both the strengths and the limitations of such a framework, as well as pointing to a tension concerning the status of "the people" that runs throughout traditional Confucianism. My second step is to analyze a representative contemporary "Institutional Confucian" effort to justify an authoritarian state by means of an only modestly revised version of the early Confucian view. Having found fault with this approach, I then articulate an alternative approach to Confucian authority, and here I draw on the idea of self-restriction. The Progressive Confucian picture that I defend here is "Confucian" in several ways: it is motivated by concerns that have lain at the heart of the Confucian tradition throughout its long history; it builds from and comments on critical Confucian texts; some of the key terms in which the essay's ideas are developed are distinctive of the Confucian tradition; and it is addressed in part to those in the contemporary world who consider themselves to be (or are sympathetic to) Confucians. Like the rest of the book, it is also addressed more generally to anyone interested in the issues of legitimate political authority and the potential justification of authoritarianism. Understanding the way that Confucians today should understand political authority, and the reasons why Confucians should reject authoritarianism, has the potential to stimulate creative, critical philosophical thinking no matter what one's antecedent philosophical convictions.

A Tension in the *Mencius*

The famous "Mandate of Heaven" theory has its roots in the way the Zhou people legitimized their conquest of the Shang.[7] Passages in the *Book of History* tell us that *Tian*[8] has transferred its "mandate (*ming*)" to the Zhou, as a result of the Shang people's misrule. How did the Zhou leaders know that they had received the mandate? Through oracle bone divination. The Zhou adopted the Shang method of divination, but put it to the new use of justifying the shift in Heaven's favor.[9] Part of what was new was the transformation of *Tian* into a moral figure, a god who made judgments based on the conduct of the ruler. By the time of the Warring States era and the foundational texts of Confucian philosophy, though, there has been another shift: *Tian* is no longer a "figure" at all, but closer to an abstract sense of the normative order of the universe. For Confucian writers at least, its intentions are no longer accessible via divination. Sacrificial rites are understood to play different roles, and the relationship between humans and *Tian* has become more indirect. In what follows I will focus on the views found in the *Mencius*.

For our purposes, the key passage in the *Mencius* is 5A:5, which explains that "the people (*min*)" are the intermediary through which the *Tian's* intentions are communicated. It is worth quoting at length:

> Wan Zhang said, "Is it the case that Yao gave the world to Shun?"
> Mencius said, "It is not. The Son of Heaven cannot give the world to another person."
> Wan Zhang asked, "In the case, when Shun had the world, who gave it to him?"
> Mencius said, "Heaven (*Tian*) gave it to him."
> Wan Zhang said, "When Heaven gave it to him, did it openly decree (*ming*) it?"
> Mencius said, "It did not. Heaven does not speak, but simply reveals the Mandate through actions and affairs."
> Wan Zhang asked, "How does it reveal it through actions and affairs?"
> Mencius replied, "The Son of Heaven can present a person to Heaven, but he cannot make Heaven give him the world. The various lords can present a person to the Son of Heaven, but they cannot make him give that person a state . . . Formerly, Emperor Yao presented Shun to Heaven, and Heaven accepted him. He made him known to the people (*min*), and the people accepted him. Hence, I say that Heaven does not speak but simply reveals the Mandate through actions and affairs."
> Wan Zhang continued, "May I ask how he recommended him to Heaven and Heaven accepted him, how he presented him to the people and the people accepted him?"
> Mencius replied, "Yao put Shun in charge of the ritual sacrifices, and the various spirits were pleased with him. This was Heaven accepting him. He put Shun in charge of affairs, and the affairs were well-ordered, and the people were at ease with him. This was the people accepting him. Heaven gave it to him, and the people gave it to him . . . The *Great Announcement* says, 'Heaven sees as my people see; Heaven hears as my people hear.' This expresses what I mean.[10]

In other words, the people play a critical role in manifesting *Tian's* acceptance of the proposed ruler. It is not the case that one can know independently of the people's actions – say, via divination – what *Tian* decrees. Treating the people well is not just a responsibility of the ruler, but a necessary condition for legitimating authority in the first place.[11] Conversely, a ruler who treats the people extremely badly has – on at least one reading of the text – thereby lost his legitimacy and authority. No direct divination of *Tian*'s intentions is available or needed. In the famous words of 1B:8:

> King Xuan of Qi asked, "Is it the case that, when they were their subjects, Tang banished Jie and Wu struck down the Tyrant Zhou?"
>
> Mencius replied, "That is what has been passed down in ancient texts."
>
> The king said, "Is it acceptable for subjects to assassinate their rulers?"
>
> Mencius said, "One who mutilates benevolence should be called a 'mutilator.' One who mutilates righteousness should be called a 'crippler.' A crippler and a mutilator is a mere 'fellow.' I have indeed heard of the execution of this one fellow Zhou, but I have not heard of it as the assassination of one's ruler."[12]

By virtue of his tyrannical treatment of the people, Zhou lost his legitimacy, no longer merited the designation "ruler," and could be overthrown and executed.[13]

By building such a critical role for the people into what we might call his authority system, Mencius helped to see that the people's interests, as seen from their own vantage point, would be taken seriously by Chinese leaders ever after. The people's contentedness with their well-being was not just a good policy goal, but the actual conduit of the state's legitimacy. (To be sure, in actual practice this commitment to the people's interests was all too often honored in the breach. Still, the ideal was clear.) It is important, however, not to exaggerate the status of the people. They are not the source of authority, but only its sign. Mencius is not offering a theory of popular sovereignty. Neither – contrary to frequent readings of 1B:8 – is he offering a theory of popular rights. The people do not have the "right" to rebel against a tyrant. Mencius says that it is predictable that people will resist bad rule, and in a sense people cannot be blamed for striving violently after the necessities of life. He says that only the cultivated gentlemen have "constant hearts" such that their moral commitment does not flag even in straightened circumstances, but he goes on to say, "As for the people, if they lack a constant livelihood, it follows that they will lack a constant heart. No one who lacks a constant heart will avoid dissipation and evil. When they thereupon sink into crime, to go and punish the people is to trap them."[14] Trapping the people is not something of which any good ruler would be proud; Mencius adds, "When there are benevolent persons in positions of authority, how is it possible for them to trap the people?" Nonetheless, what the people are doing is still a crime, rather than a just rebellion. This is even clearer in 1B:4. In response to a question about whether worthy people delight in beautiful surroundings, Mencius says, "They do. But if others do not also enjoy it, they will certainly condemn their superiors. Those who condemn their superiors because they do not share in such delights are wrong. But those who are the people's superiors and do not share the same delights with the people are also wrong."[15] There is no hint here of a "right" to such delights. Denied their share, the people will predictably complain. There is a kind of justice in their complaint, since as Mencius also says, those who hoard delights are themselves wrong. We can summarize all this by saying that the people are reliable indicators of good or bad rule, but they are not themselves in a position to exercise choice or agency. *Tian* remains the source of authority. The people are like thermometers, measuring the quality of rule and thereby indicating the presence or absence of legitimate authority.

Admittedly, in the *Mencius* and in other early Confucian texts, there is a theme that stands in considerable tension with the account I have just given. Mencius famously argues that "all people (*renren*)" have the rudimentary, spontaneous moral reactions that justify his claim that people's natures are good.[16] He also says in one place that the great sages Yao and Shun "were the same as other people (*yu ren tong er*)," which affirms that "everyone can become a Yao or a Shun."[17] As Donald Munro long ago emphasized, Mencius asserts that all people have equal moral potential. In addition, as Irene Bloom in particular has argued, we can find passages in the text that articulate something like a common human dignity. It is put in terms like the "nobility of Heaven," as opposed to the more prosaic nobility of man; and the "honorable" quality that all people have within themselves, which is different from "the honor that derives from men."[18] The problem with all of this, in light of my foregoing account of authority and "the people," is that this latter set of passages foreground the shared moral nature and equal potential for moral and political agency of all. We should also keep in mind that Mencius repeatedly speaks of the ability of "gentlemen" to make independent moral and political judgments, to remonstrate with rulers (or parents), and in certain extreme circumstances, to remove rulers. In other words, some people are clearly capable of agency. While perhaps not an outright contradiction, there is at least something awkward about speaking in some moments about the fundamental similarities among all people, and in others moments treating "the people" as a mere reactive mass, incapable of agency.[19,20]

An ingenious solution to this difficulty emerges from a distinction made some time ago by Roger Ames and David Hall. My translations have been obscuring an important difference in Mencius's Chinese: when he is speaking of "the people," his term is *min*; when he says things about the commonalities of "all people," his term is *ren*. We could clarify the difference by rendering *min* as "the masses" and *ren* as "persons." Ames and Hall note that *min* tend to act collectively and that early uses of the term *min* have strong connotations of blindness, ignorance, and sleep. In contrast, *ren* is typically used in the sense of "a particular person *qua* human being" and carries a positive connotation; Ames and Hall also argue that one "becomes *ren* as a consequence of that personal cultivation and socialization that renders him particular." In other words, "Edification permits one to move from the indeterminate masses (*min*) to the expression of one's particularity (*ren*) and, ultimately, to the expression of one's authoritative humanity (*ren*)."[21] While some aspects of this account have proven controversial, we can prescind from those and still accept the basic *min–ren* distinction as helping to explain the tension observed above. Insofar as people are conceptualized as individuals distinct from the mass, they are of the same type as Yao and Shun.[22]

Even if this distinction helps us to understand how Mencius could say all the things he does, though, it does not entirely dissolve the tension. Few mechanisms seem to be considered for systematically moving people from the category of *min* to *ren*. Furthermore, contemporary thinkers might well find the characterization of the "ignorant masses" as hopelessly condescending and deeply out of touch with these people's lives. One does not have to be a radical individualist to think that there is something missing, in terms of the ability of Mencius to conceptualize life from the perspective of a given peasant farmer.[23] His universalist talk about *ren* calls for such an "extension" of perspectives and of caring, but his political ideals seem far too restricted to allow for taking the people's distinct perspectives seriously.[24] He sometimes analogizes the ruler to a parent, but should not a parent treat children as distinct – as making unique demands on the parent-child relationship – rather than as a mass with set needs? Problems like these ultimately drive recent Confucians to rethink the authority system that we have seen in *Mencius*.[25]

Kang Xiaoguang

I turn now to contemporary China, and a notable effort to revive Mencius's understanding of authority. I introduced Kang Xiaoguang in Chapter 1 as an Institutional Confucian. Kang's main Confucian sources include the classical canon (especially *Mencius*), some Han dynasty developments, and the turn-of-the-twentieth-century Confucian reformer Kang Youwei, who argued that Confucianism had to be installed as a state religion if China was to rise again.[26] In addition, he draws on the contemporary Confucian thinker Jiang Qing – especially as regards the key idea of legitimacy. On this basis, Kang explains his idea of a contemporary Confucian authoritarianism, which unfortunately preserves (and even exacerbates) precisely the tension we have already seen in *Mencius*. As already mentioned, Kang is not a scholar of Confucianism, and many scholars are quite dismissive of him. I focus on him because his arguments are particularly clear and, I believe, also representative of an important (and, in some ways, troubling) strand in contemporary Confucian thinking.

Before getting into the details of Kang's argument, we should reflect for a moment on the relation between legitimate political authority and authoritarianism. We can start from Hannah Arendt's three-fold distinction among coercion, authority, and persuasion. As she sees it, authority is a demand for obedience based on hierarchical superiority, which is different both from the "external" threat of violence that supports coercion and from the egalitarian order within which persuasion finds its home.[27] This typology fits very nicely with what Kang has to say; as I will elaborate below, he claims that for Confucianism, the "most basic distinction is between 'ruler' and 'ruled'," and that Confucianism rejects the false modesty of liberal democracy: rather than pretending that everyone is equal, Confucianism gives authority to the elite. The responsibility of the "ruled" is simply to obey.[28] On this understanding, "authoritarian" states are fundamentally anti-egalitarian; authority accrues to an elite group. A significant worry to which we will return is whether such a group is self-identifying and self-perpetuating, or in other words, whether there is any standard of legitimacy outside of the rulers' self-assertion.

For our purposes this can stand as the meaning of "authoritarian," but some further discussion of its implications for the more basic idea of (legitimate) authority is needed. As I will use this term, the government (including the judicial system) of a properly constituted egalitarian democracy also has authority and so citizens have obligations to obey its laws.[29] Such a government does not have to *persuade* its citizens to follow the laws. Rather, persuasion plays a key role in how the government's authority comes to be legitimized. For example, each individual citizen is treated as capable of forming judgments about matters of public import, and therefore engages in political participation (such as voting) subject to the persuasion, but not coercion or authority, of others. As we will see, a key difference between Kang's vision and the alternative I propose turns on the degree to which something like persuasion is able to play a role in legitimating the authority of a Confucian government.

A good place to begin our examination of Kang's substantive claims about authority comes when Kang considers how a modern authoritarian state in China should deal with the question of leadership succession. After a brief contrast between ancient Chinese practice (heredity, palace coup, and violent revolt) and the methods advocated in Confucian classics, Kang endorses the latter as appropriate to today's China. Specifically, he writes:

> Today, when we think about the principles of succession for the highest leaders, pride of place ought to go to recommendation by the community of Confucians (*rushi*), after which comes abdication, after which comes revolution. In actuality, recommendation by the community of Confucians is a form of elite democracy. Abdication in fact comes down to recommending the worthy. Revolution is the worst option, but we cannot deny its legitimacy, which is just to say that we must acknowledge the right of the masses to overthrow a tyrannical government.[30]

Strikingly, Kang then goes on to argue that this Confucian practice of succession is already being practiced in contemporary China. He suggests that the transitions from one CCP leader to another have been "abdications," and furthermore that – just as we read in *Mencius* – only abdications that are accepted by the masses are truly legitimate. Mao Zedong's abdication in favor of Hua Guofeng failed because the masses did not support him. Deng Xiaoping's abdication eventually succeeded (with Jiang Zemin), despite the masses' rejection of Hu Yaobang and Zhao Ziyang.[31]

The difficulties with Kang's position are numerous. At the surface-level, it seems a grotesque distortion of recent history to say that the "masses" were an obstacle to Hu Yaobang's or Zhao Ziyang's rising to the position of central leader. These were matters of policy disagreements, jealousies, and simple power disputes among a small group of elite Party leaders. A deeper problem has to do with whether, on either Kang's own view or on the classical Confucian view he is invoking, the masses (*min*) can accurately be seen as judging, choosing, accepting, or in some other way exercising agency. I have already argued that the correct reading of *Mencius* shows the *min* to be passive and reactive; their acquiescence or resistance to a leader is a reliable index of whether the leader rules well, but does not represent any kind of judgment or considered endorsement of the ruler. Furthermore, and *pace* Kang's reading, the masses have no "right" to rebel, even though they will do so if ruled badly. Finally, there is the question of *Tian*: Does Kang believe that *Tian*, as viewed through the insights of the gentlemen and the reactions of the masses, is still the ultimate source of legitimacy?

Kang's answers to these challenges build on an idea that has been put forward by his fellow Institutional Confucian Jiang Qing, namely, that the legitimacy of Confucian political authority is evaluated along three distinct dimensions, all of which are necessary for a government or ruler to count as having authority.[32] The three dimensions of legitimacy are sacred, cultural, and popular, which Jiang sees as corresponding to the Confucian triad of *Tian*, earth, and humanity. Let us look at and critique Kang's view of each in turn.

Given what I have said above about Kang's goal of an elite-based authoritarianism, it will come as no surprise that when it comes to the sacred dimension of legitimacy, Kang stresses the role of an elite group of authoritative interpreters of *Tian*'s intentions. Without saying anything about what he takes *Tian* to be or mean, he proposes manufacturing a Confucian state religion with distinctive emphasis on Confucian "believers." He criticizes those who treat Confucianism merely as an academic theory, characterizes traditional bureaucrats as "priests (*jiaoshi*)," and views the premodern masses as "believers (*xintu*)."[33] The "community of Confucians" whom he imagines offering recommendations in the course of leadership succession are presumably the modern instantiations of the traditional bureaucrats; at one point he imagines them associated with various Confucian churches, and even speaks of a "new-style theocracy."[34] The curious thing about all of this is that while Kang can see and argue for the usefulness of a Confucian religion with priests and believers, he is fairly explicit that all of the talk of religion is motivated by its usefulness toward achieving the ends of a stable Confucian authoritarianism.[35] It is hard to see what he himself takes "believing in *Tian*" to amount to, other than ceding authority to his so-called priests.

It is much easier to understand how Kang's second dimension of legitimacy, culture, is supposed to legitimize authority. In fact, Kang argues that cultural legitimacy is important for three reasons, though he is not always careful to distinguish them. The first approach is most common: Kang argues that cultural continuity is vital to the continued existence of the Chinese. He says that the Chinese people can survive the loss of their state, but even if their state were to persist, they could not survive the loss of their culture.[36] In another essay, he invokes the persistence over many centuries of Jewish cultural nationalism to support his point that a state is less important to a people than a culture.[37] If this is right, and if one is committed to the continuity of the Chinese people, and if Chinese culture can be substantially identified with Confucianism, then Chinese people have a distinctive reason to endorse the authority of a Confucian government.

Let us call this the Continuity Argument. Unfortunately for Kang, his Continuity Argument is based on several mistaken premises. Let us grant that culture is one of the key marks of a people. But neither culture nor people are ever static configurations. Perhaps it is true that in the absence of a homeland, greater weight may fall on textual and interpretive continuity, though the many differences among the various American Jewish movements would seem to call even that into question. Another problem for Kang is the virtual identification of Chinese culture and Confucianism. This is problematic both because of the many other philosophical and religious movements that have contributed so greatly to Chinese culture, and because there is an enormous difference between the elite textual tradition that he calls Confucianism, and the plethora of ways in which loosely "Confucian" values came to be realized and practiced throughout Chinese society. So we cannot conclude that Chinese people today have any strong reason to endorse the authority of Kang's version of Confucian government.

An adjunct to the Continuity Argument could be labeled the Competitive Argument: This is the view that we live in a world of global competition among civilizations, and Chinese should embrace cultural nationalism just as other peoples have. Successful cultural competition makes a nation, and its people, stronger. Individuals can shift from one culture to another, says Kang, and emigrants can be seen as cultural colonizers.[38] Kang puts a political and competitive spin on the idea of "cultural China" that Tu Weiming has sought to popularize for quite different reasons:[39] Kang sees it as part of a nationalist competition that transcends borders. The Competitive Argument clearly rests on two major premises. First, we should (or have no choice but to – although in this case the argument may collapse into the Continuity Argument) engage in inter-civilizational competition. Second, promoting Chinese culture means promoting Confucianism. This second premise has many of the same problems as the "Chinese culture equals Confucianism" premise in the Continuity Argument. Because we are now talking about forward-looking competition, though, I suppose that if Confucian values were particularly convincing to foreign and domestic audiences, that would provide reason to embrace them to even greater extents than had traditionally been the case.

Kang's final approach is the Unity Argument: it is culture, rather than economics, military force, politics, or ideology, that will hold China together despite the many centrifugal forces at work.[40] Perhaps the biggest problem with this argument is that Kang's approach to promoting Confucianism in China – which involves mandatory study throughout the educational system and its installation as China's "national religion" – looks much more like the imposition of an ideological system than like the natural flowering of existing elements of Chinese culture. As such, one wonders what success it would have in promoting unity, especially in outlying regions of the Chinese state.[41]

In sum, Kang's various appeals to culture as legitimator for Confucian authority-claims are each quite problematic. Let us turn, then, to the third dimension, popular legitimacy. From the passage concerning leadership succession with which we began, it is clear that Kang wants to follow something like the view found in *Mencius*. He says there that, "We must acknowledge the right of the masses to overthrow a tyrannical government." Elsewhere he notes the importance of attending to the "people's intentions (*minyi*)"[42] and cites many of the same passages that I discussed above.[43] At the same time, however, Kang recognizes that there are real problems with the way in which *Mencius* treats popular opinion. He writes: "How do politics express the people's intentions? This is a challenge that contemporary Confucianism faces, and an area in which Confucianism's reserves of knowledge are not substantial. We must seek to learn from contemporary political theory and political practice."[44] He suggests that free mass media, institutions of political consultation, and corporatism offer adequate answers to guaranteeing the "masses' right to political participation."[45] Kang then offers an astute analysis of the potential weaknesses of these solutions, but contends that the right to free association and full-fledged democracy *within* each "functional constituency" will be adequate to fend off abuses of the system by government and capitalist interests.

Kang's ideas here are quite interesting, as are his related and extensive arguments that liberal democracy is neither theoretically unproblematic, nor the practical panacea that some have claimed. The problem is that he is trying to have his cake and eat it too. He wants the *min* to be agents, capable of forming judgments, the holders of rights, and appropriately requiring free access to information and extensive (if still limited) forms of democratic participation.[46] At the same time, though, he is still committed to his "authoritarian" premise and its clear distinction between the elite rulers and the "mass" who are ruled. This latter commitment fits with the idea of *min* as thermometer, but if the *min* is made up of agents capable of individual judgment, it is not so clear what justifies a rigid distinction between rulers and ruled. In other words, Kang is running into almost exactly the same tension we saw in *Mencius*. In fact, since Kang is explicit about the people's status as rights-holders, he faces not just a tension but a full-fledged dilemma. If the *min* is merely a reactive mass, which would be needed to see them as requiring elite rule and thus as legitimizing a Confucian authoritarianism, then they are not suited to be rights-holders nor to participate in democratic processes (even within functional constituencies). In contrast, if the *min* is made up of individual rights-holders who can make judgments and participate in democratic governance, then they fail to justify the strong form of elite rule that Kang desires. This does not mean that as soon as one has acknowledged the need for certain basic rights and for some democratic participation, one is obligated to adopt liberal democracy. In the balance of this chapter, I discuss one form of legitimate participatory politics that is not authoritarian, but also not egalitarian, liberal democracy. I will return to this theme in the book's Conclusion, where we will have an opportunity to reflect on how other contemporary Confucian proposals that seek to make room for participation measure up to the criteria of Progressive Confucianism.

Progressive Confucian Authority: Reconceptualizing the People

By attending to the question of mass political participation, Kang Xiaoguang recognized a limitation of Confucianism and sought to provide an answer, but I have argued that his solution is not radical enough. It is now time to offer a different way that Confucians can think about legitimate authority – a model that will allow for more robust realization of core Confucian commitments, as well as resolve the tension inherent in the *Mencius* that I discussed above. On this model, something like *Tian* remains the source of authority, but a re-conceptualized "people" themselves are the holders of authority. This authority is delegated through democratic processes to a government, and its exercise is constrained and influenced in two ways: by a constitution and by a particular kind of state moral education. Several aspects of this model will be familiar from other kinds of democratic frameworks, but even these aspects are justified by distinctively Confucian arguments. In the rest of this chapter, I will sketch what I have in mind in three steps: the new version of *Tian*, the new version of the people, and some thoughts on the specific political processes that one would find in a Progressive Confucian polity.

I mentioned earlier that understandings of *Tian* underwent an evolution in early China, from a personal deity toward a more abstract conception of normative order.[47] Another important stage in this process is taken by the Neo-Confucians in the eleventh century CE. (Neo-Confucianism is a major philosophical and spiritual movement that lasts from the eleventh through eighteenth centuries.) Neo-Confucian philosophers identify *Tian* with their central normative concept of *li*, which I will translate as "Coherence."[48] *Li* is the valuable and intelligible structuring of the cosmos such that all things can fit together into a single, dynamic harmony. It is not just any "coherent" arrangement of a set of things, because local Coherence (e.g., of the relations between you and your parents) is determined by the way in which the local fits into ever-larger patterns of more global Coherence (e.g., all human relationships, or the relations among humans and our environment). *Li* or Coherence is based on the insight that the identity and role of anything depends on its relations to many other things and purposes – ultimately, in fact, on its relation to all things, intentions, and desires. For example, why is this an "oar"? Because of the ways that it fits with boats and rowers, lakes and water molecules, spruce trees and the manufacturing of carbon fiber, and so on. Figuring out the best way to interact with other people and with our environment demands that we understand and honor these inter-connections. Neo-Confucians are committed to a more expansive vision of harmony than are their classical forbearers; they strive to realize (that is, both perceive and actualize) a balanced community with each other and with the universe that honors the fundamental connections we feel for one another.

Let that stand as an account of Neo-Confucian Coherence. Many – though by no means all – contemporary Confucians continue to speak of Coherence, and I will join them. This means continuing to take seriously the idea that all things are fundamentally interrelated and that, especially as guided by our emotionally tinged perception of these interconnections, we can at least begin to see Coherence in our world. Seeing Coherence is not, at least in everyday cases, any kind of mystical awareness. When we respond positively to a harmonious configuration of people, or to a harmony between people and their environment, this is a perception of Coherence. When we see a way to nudge a relationship in a constructive direction, this, too, is a perception of Coherence. Or at least the approximation of Coherence: perhaps there are larger dimensions of which one is ignorant, and which need to be worked into the overall balance in order to get even closer to full harmony. According to this model of what it is to be a Confucian, one must be committed to the ideal of Universal Coherence (*tian li*): there is a best, most valuable, most life-affirming way for things to be at a given point in time, and seeking this is following the Way.

It would be natural to ask at this point whether Coherence is actually the type of ideal that anyone, or at least very many people, can take seriously in the modern world. One of the reasons that some thinkers today with considerable sympathy for Confucianism adopt Neo-Classical or Synthetic approaches to developing contemporary Confucianism, rather than an approach like mine that follows the tradition's own development more closely, lies in their skepticism about Coherence. I have no arguments to offer that can show either that we all – no matter what our backgrounds – must embrace Coherence, or even that all Confucians must follow this path. By its very nature Coherence is an ideal that outruns the specific evidence we might have for its reality. Still, to say that it "outruns" our evidence is not the same as saying that our evidence and experiences are irrelevant. The kinds of interrelationships to which Neo-Confucians point are easy enough to understand, and the more we are conscious of them, the more they can motivate us. In addition, many powerful contemporary voices have spoken of the importance of unifying ideals of goodness. If Coherence is one such, and furthermore an ideal that can ground an attractive ethical and political vision, then perhaps it is worth taking seriously after all.[49]

How does Coherence relate to political authority? For all Confucians, even early Confucians who had no notion of "Coherence," one has authority when one values what is truly valuable and thus others defer to you. (The *Analects* contains some beautiful metaphors for this, such as the many stars bowing to the central North Star or the grass bending before the wind of the gentleman's presence.) Supposing that we take seriously an ideal like Coherence, we can then ask: to whom can we look to see how to properly value it? One answer might be "a sage," and certainly contemporary Confucians share with their predecessors the belief that some people have more developed perceptive sensitivities to Coherence than others. Nonetheless, there are two key problems with designing an authority system around a sage-ruler. First – and this is only slightly controversial within the tradition – despite the fact that sagehood is accessible in principle, there are few if any actual sages, and certainly none that can be confidently identified at any particular point in time. As Mou Zongsan puts it, achieving sagehood is an "endless process."[50] Second, limiting authority to sages leaves out all the rest of us, yet it is a central Neo-Confucian teaching that everyone has at least some sensitivity to Coherence. In terms of the argument from earlier in the chapter, limiting authority to sages would be to leave unresolved the tension in *Mencius* between its claims about the "masses" and its claims about all persons. Instead of vesting authority in a sage, therefore, I suggest that contemporary Confucians should vest it in the people.

If the people are to have authority, the idea of "the people" must be conceptualized differently than in ancient Confucianism. "The people" will be the collection of all individuals. Each of us is part of the authoritative entity because each of us has a unique and valuable perspective on Coherence. As Confucians as different as Mencius and Zhu Xi (1130–1200) both emphasized, each of us has the capacity to recognize and respond to ethically salient aspects of our world. Of course, we are each going to be more sensitive to some areas of potential value and harmony, and less sensitive to others. Furthermore, some of us will be better at attaining the broad and balanced vision that is necessary to integrate diverse perspectives and approach closer to Coherence. I will say more about this below, since it should factor into the design of our political system. Nonetheless, even if our perceptual capacities are not all equal, "the people" in a contemporary Confucian polity should not be functioning as a passive indicator of the will of *Tian*, but as our best and indeed only access to what is genuinely valuable.

Perhaps this sounds too individualist, given the widely recognized Confucian emphasis on groups and relationality that is often put in terms of a "social conception of the self." My reply is that relationality does in fact figure deeply into how a contemporary Confucian should conceive of "the people," but it should not lead to the conclusion that distinct individual perspectives are of no consequence. Rather, each individual perspective is itself shot through with relationality. My own perspectives on matters before me are articulated by the facts that I am son, father, spouse, and teacher, as well as member of a variety of partly overlapping communities. To various degrees, the perspectives of others (for example, my daughter's and my wife's experiences in middle school, as I understand them) shape how I view things. Capacious relationality will tend to correspond to a broad inclusiveness of perspectives, though seeing the way to harmonize many different perspectives is not always easy, and it is important that the perspectives of distant others not drown out one's concern for those close to one.[51] At the idealized extreme, a sage is able to appropriately honor all relevant perspectives. In light of actual human limitations, though, we cannot and should not wait for a sage to appear, but must collectively do our best to realize Coherence.[52]

It should be clear that the conceptualization of the "the people" being advocated here is quite different from the notion of "the masses" that seemed to have a home in much early Confucian discourse. It might be objected that in so revising the meaning of *min*, and thereby losing track of the difference between reactive mass and individual (albeit relationally ramified) agent, I have lost the ability to capture the key Confucian idea that people need to develop. After all, though they understand our innate moral state somewhat differently, both Mencius and Zhu Xi are clear that individuals vary greatly when it comes to actualizing our moral potentials. On this basis, some scholars have argued that according to any version of Confucianism, rights (like the rights to vote or to be heard) should be due to people only on account of their "actualized humanity" – their possession of virtue – rather than on account of mere potential for agency.[53] If there is a high threshold that must be met before someone counts as a member of "the people," then even if we say that this narrow "people" has authority, we have still ended up with a highly restrictive authority system that puts no weight on the first-person perspectives of most individuals.

The strongest response to this objection will invoke the idea of "self-restriction" and its concomitant requirement of objective, institutional protections for the rights of all. I will return to this idea in a few moments. First, though, we should agree that personal and social progress is indeed a core objective of Confucians. People's perspectives are valuable because they are partial windows onto Coherence, and we can get better at seeing it. Children only gradually get better at integrating others' perspectives with their own; both informal and formal educational processes are aimed at helping them along. Many adults, it must be admitted, still see the world through relatively privatistic lenses. In some cases this can lead to behavior that is officially or scientifically designated as "anti-social"; in other cases it might be manifested by a retreat into a gated community. As I will mention briefly below (and discuss further in the book's Conclusion), one of the distinctive features of a contemporary Confucian polity is its continuing concern for the education of both these categories of adults. What all this means to the scope of authority, though, is by no means set in stone. Once we have acknowledged that authority will not be confined to perfect humans with all-encompassing vision – that is, to sages – then anyone with Confucian sympathies must acknowledge that the specific design of an authority system will be a matter of balancing different priorities. If there are strong reasons for making our notion of "the people" very inclusive, as I will continue to argue, then so long as we also do our best to further our educational objectives, there is no obstacle to a comparatively low threshold for membership in "the people."[54] To be sure, we will exclude children from full membership. Nothing in what I have said so far, in fact, requires that each adult get an equal say in the political process. Perhaps we conclude that somewhat older people often enough have broader perspectives, such that we wish to reflect that in our system.[55] We would do well to keep in mind, though, that many structures are easily moralized and normalized by the powerful, who may have no particular insight into Coherence. I will return to these themes repeatedly in subsequent chapters, showing different ways in which Progressive Confucianism balances the genuine values of hierarchy and deference with the need to design political space in such a way that the maximum number of people have access to playing non-trivial roles in public deliberation and choice.

Political Structures and Participation

Grant, for now at least, that a contemporary Confucian political philosophy should hold that the people have political authority. What is the process by which this is exercised? If a government is to be formed and rule as the delegates of the people, how is this to take place? Suppose some individual has, or claims to have, deep insight into Coherence; could he or she justifiably rule as a dictator? Philosophers will be familiar with the distinction between value systems that give priority to the good, as versus those that give priority to the right. In both European and Chinese history, philosophies that take the realization of the good to be fundamental have been prone to authoritarian excesses at the hands of leaders who claimed to see what was good for everyone. Philosophies that stress the right have their own failings, but they have often been able to justify procedural limitations on the exercise of power that has protected the weak. While I will not here be spelling out exactly what procedures Confucians should adopt, I will draw on the self-restriction argument from Chapter 2 in order to demonstrate that the Progressive Confucian commitment to the good (in the form of Coherence) in fact requires that individuals constrain their pursuit of this good in accordance with the objective processes and limitations encoded in a constitution. Progressive Confucians must hold that a constitution, laws, and rights have a status that is in important ways independent from claims about moral insight. As I concluded in Chapter 2: "People need to have opportunities to take responsibility for various aspects of their world, even up to the possibility that they are most qualified to serve as the head of government. Virtuous insight must therefore be restrained – restrict itself – by adherence to the objective structures that protect the rights of all. Only then is full virtue a possibility." One result of this argument is that a Confucian polity should not be authoritarian.[56] There is no way within the framework I have offered to motivate a strict separation between the rulers with authority and the ruled who, if they are even allowed to express opinions, still have no authority of their own.

Which rights are to be protected and what sorts of electoral and representative mechanisms are to be enshrined in the constitution is a further matter. Contemporary Confucian scholar Tu Wei-ming, who was a student of Mou Zongsan, has said that "Confucian personality ideals – the authentic person, the worthy, or the sage – can be realized more fully in the liberal-democratic society than either in the traditional imperial dictatorship or a modern authoritarian regime."[57] Tu may be correct as far as he goes, but we should not limit ourselves to existing liberal democracies as the best and only fit with the various criteria that I have begun to outline. A number of years ago, Daniel Bell proposed that a future, Confucian-influenced Chinese state might have a bicameral legislature composed of a democratically elected lower house and a meritocratic upper house.[58] Bell's idea fits into the category of Synthetic Confucianism: he is seeking a way to combine democratic and Confucian values, and assumes an independent commitment to each. Bell focuses on explaining and justifying the upper house, and on exploring pros and cons of different relationships between the two houses: is the upper house stronger, which Bell terms a "Confucian" solution? Or should the "democratic" option be chosen, giving more power to the lower house?[59] Throughout his various discussions he largely takes the need for a lower house for granted – which makes sense, given his synthetic approach – offering only brief arguments to the effect that there is a "profound need to institutionalize the democratic virtues of accountability, transparency, and equal political participation."[60]

Institutional Confucian Jiang Qing takes a different approach, seeking to justify a proposal for a tricameral legislature on existing Confucian grounds. Starting from the early Confucian triad of "Heaven, Earth, and Humanity," Jiang develops the idea of "three-fold legitimacy," which consists of sacred, cultural, and popular dimensions.[61] On this basis, Jiang argues that for a legislative system to be legitimate in China, it would have to have three houses: the "House of Confucian Tradition (*tongru yuan*)," the "House of National Essence (*guoti yuan*)," and the "House of the People (*shumin yuan*)." One obvious question about all of this is whether the connections among the Confucian triad, the three dimensions of legitimacy, and the three houses are plausible. We might wonder, for example, why Jiang does not take the "Earth" dimension of legitimacy to correspond to ecological values. More fundamentally, as David Elstein has pointed out, the institutions that Jiang proposes have virtually no precedents in Chinese history and Jiang acknowledges borrowing from Western democratic thought.[62] The democratically elected House of the People, in particular, seems extremely novel, especially in light of my arguments above that it is a mistake to see classical Confucians as according agency or will to the "people."[63] This is a problem for a position that claims to root itself in continuity with past Confucian institutional practice, as opposed to the New Confucian emphasis on continuity with ethical norms like universalizing virtue.

A third approach to designing a Confucian legislative system has been offered recently by Bai Tongdong. As mentioned in Chapter 1, Bai's approach is Neo-Classical: he combines a reading of select classical Confucian texts with various facts or theoretical insights that have come to light since the period of Confucius to produce a contemporary Confucian political philosophy. The *Analects* and especially *Mencius* are the textual sources of Bai's theorizing about democracy; as he reads them, these sources ground notions of popular will and a demand for accountability, and we can infer from the state's responsibility to educate its citizens that it must protect their basic civil and political rights.[64] Bai is quite sympathetic to a number of John Rawls's views, and even argues that his own version of Confucianism should count as a version of Rawls's "thin" or "political" conception of liberal democracy. Bai believes that fuller versions of democracy stumble, however, in part because they ignore what he calls the "sixth fact of modern democracy," which is that because of the limited intelligence, education, and interest of most citizens, combined with the ability of the powerful to distort information and general selfishness, a liberal and deliberative democracy in which every citizen participates equally is impossibly utopian.[65] As a result, he believes there is excellent reason to prefer a limited, Confucian version of democracy. Bai suggests that Daniel Bell's bicameral proposal fits the bill quite nicely, especially the version in which the upper house is more powerful, thus limiting the role of the popular will to "consultation."[66] Note that while Bell's own version of this proposal is Synthetic, combining independent democratic and Confucian values, Bai argues for a thoroughly Neo-Classical foundation: he makes no separate appeal to the value of democracy.

Readers will not be surprised to learn that I find Bai's rather breezy claims about Mencian support for popular will and accountability to be unconvincing, and I view his derivation of implicit Confucian support for civil rights as equally suspect. Furthermore, I find it rather unclear exactly what the "sixth fact" is supposed to be, and believe that the empirical evidence Bai has offered to support it is quite scanty. I will not pursue these matters here, though, because what I want to emphasize is the different approach that Progressive Confucianism recommends to the question of political participation and institutional arrangements. By no means do I want to reject out of hand everything that Bell, Bai, and even Jiang have offered, but our starting point needs to be different and our goal much broader than simply the design of a legislature. More specifically, Progressive Confucianism urges that Confucians adopt the following four-point framework. First, the Confucian conception of political authority needs to be based in the people, where "people" is understood as the collection of all individuals, each with a distinctive perspective and each with some degree of agency and judgment. Each voice has something to offer concerning what is truly valuable. In addition, participation is important for its broadly educational effects as well: learning to more broadly contextualize one's own viewpoint, and learning some of the "supportive values" (like dialogue and fallibility) that I will go on to discuss below, in Chapter 7. This provides a Confucian foundation for participatory politics that is lacking in any of the three proposals I have just canvassed. Bell imports the need for democracy from outside Confucianism (which is legitimate, but not a *Confucian* foundation), while Jiang and Bai, in different ways and based on somewhat different sources, mistakenly read a demand for popular participation back into early Confucianism. Admittedly, they qualify and restrict the power of popular will, but the very insertion of an active popular will into the political process is inadequately grounded.

Second, nothing in the Confucian justification for political participation requires that participation or power be equal. Indeed, equality has not emerged from this account as a central Confucian value. Limits on inequality are important to the ideas of balance and harmony – as we will see in the discussion of distributive justice at the end of Chapter 7 – and some forms of equality may well turn out to be required in order to protect other, deeper Confucian values. But equality-for-equality's-sake is not a goal of Progressive Confucianism, which is part of the reason that I have said we should remain open to certain aspects of Bell's, Jiang's, and Bai's proposals. Despite all the genuine difficulties that the idea of meritocracy faces, and the even deeper practical challenges to systematically identifying virtuous people, there is no question that putting virtuous and talented people into positions of power is a Confucian goal; insofar as it is achievable and consistent with the other criteria mentioned here and elsewhere in the book, it should be a Progressive Confucian goal as well.[67]

My third point is to recall that on all Confucian views, there are no hard-and-fast lines separating personal, social, and public/political domains. Because of this, participation can take many forms. Some of it will take place via legally defined political processes, such as voting or standing for election, but activity in civil society or even in quite personal domains can also count. The key reasons Progressive Confucianism emphasizes participation, remember, are its roles in helping to discover and articulate what is truly valuable, and in helping to improve oneself and those with whom one interacts. Personal activities like caring for an ailing parent or nurturing a vegetable garden can count as participation insofar as they bring one into contact with significant aspects of our shared reality, and one does them in ways that share what one is learning with others. Simply growing vegetables and eating them is not participating, but joining a garden club or encouraging family and friends to share in the joys and frustrations of the garden both carry some degree of participation. Blogging about your experiences, writing an Op-Ed piece for the local newspaper, taking on a leadership role at the garden club, or speaking at a City Council meeting each represent an increased level of participation. All else being equal, more participation and higher-level participation are better, but since participation is not an end in itself, all else may not be equal. There are many ways to shape a good and virtuous life, and how much participation is called for will depend in part on the nature of one's state and society. Given the many challenges that face our societies and our world today – oppression, rigid hierarchies, dramatic and thus problematic inequalities, cultures of self-centeredness, gaps in the rule of law, and violations of human rights – considerable participation seems to be demanded.

Fourth, Progressive Confucianism must insist on strong mechanisms aimed at ensuring all are heard and none are oppressed. Institutional design is not the only arrow in a Confucian quiver: as I will discuss in Chapter 7, individual virtue, especially when aided by explicit attention to the history and dimensions of oppression, can be an important tool in the struggle against oppression. But, at the very least, individuals must have means of informing and mobilizing others through participation, and ultimately of changing the problematic attitudes, patterns of behavior, and institutions. So – again, at the very least – civil and political rights must be protected, since the abilities to speak up and to organize are vital to such participation. Laws against discrimination and a legal system designed to be accessible and fair to people of all means are also essential; here, note that equality before the law is an essential part of the very idea of rule by law, so Progressive Confucians will endorse this kind of equality. Bai's book contains a thoughtful discussion of the "one person, one vote" principle, arguing that Confucians should reject it. Granting that political equality is not a foundational principle for Confucians, Progressive Confucians should see arriving at the best possible voting scheme as an empirical question: what voting system, when combined with all the other social-political institutions we have been discussing, best achieves the key values that we have identified? Given how many variables we are talking about, it in fact seems unlikely that a single institutional arrangement will uniquely satisfy the equation, especially when background variations in culture and history are taken into account. However, no matter whether they are the large majority in a Confucian society, or a small minority in a pluralistic polity, Progressive Confucians will seek to justify their political proposals in the same general terms.

4

Debating the Rule of Law and Virtue Politics: Zhang Shizhao, Mou Zongsan, and Today

This chapter's title can be parsed in two different ways, leading to the question: are we concerned with the relations among three things, or two? On the one hand, we might ask what the proper role virtue has – if any – in politics, and then ask how the rule of law relates to virtue and to politics. On the other hand, we might take "virtue politics" as a single idea, just as we tend to think of the "rule of law" as a unit. In fact it is this latter approach that I will adopt, in part because lying behind my English title are the two Chinese terms *fazhi* and *dezhi*. The former is typically translated as "rule of law" or "rule by law"; the latter is often rendered "rule by virtue." As we will see, talk of "ruling" can, in both cases, be too narrow; thus my preference for "virtue politics." In this spirit, *fazhi* might even be translated instead as "law-governed politics." In any event, my primary concern here is with *fazhi* and *dezhi*. I begin with a brief look at the development of these ideas in the Confucian tradition, wherein we will see that although law and institutions have a role to play, Confucians throughout the tradition have put much more weight on virtue politics. I then turn to two moments in the twentieth-century Chinese debates about the relations between *fazhi* and *dezhi*. Despite the fact that little attention is being paid to the protagonists of these debates – one a Confucian, and the other not – today, we will see that their themes resonate well with one another, that current discussions both in China and abroad will be constructively enriched by taking seriously the conclusions suggested in these earlier debates, and in particular that my two protagonists point the way toward a Progressive Confucian stance on the balance between rule of law and virtue politics.

Pre-Modern Confucianism on *"Fa"*

Before turning to the twentieth century, let us begin with earlier Confucian ideas.[1] The Chinese term *fa* 法 is usually translated "law," but for Confucians, *fa* has broad and narrow meanings. Narrowly understood, *fa* refers to legal codes; when used more broadly, it is often better translated as "institution" or "system," and there are also contexts in which it is best understood as "model," which is its earliest sense.² Legal codes are one type of institution, but when *fa* is used in its broad sense, a much wider range of institutions is envisioned: one famous discussion of *fa* lists property arrangements, schools, marriage ceremonies, and expectations for military service.³ As for what role *fa* (in either sense) plays, we should start with a famous saying from the classical Confucian Xunzi: "There is only governance by men, not governance by *fa*."⁴ This belief, that it is the interpreters and implementers of *fa* (in both senses) who are decisive rather than the *fa* themselves being crucial, would also dominate Neo-Confucian thinking on these topics. The great twelfth-century philosopher Zhu Xi (1130–1200) said that legal codes (*lü*) "are, after all, of some help in teaching and transforming people. But fundamentally they are deficient to some extent."⁵ Speaking of *fa* in the broad sense, he wrote:

> Generally speaking, any institution (*fa*) must have its drawbacks. No institution is perfect. The important thing lies in having the right men. If there are the right men, even though the institutions are no good, there are still many benefits. But if there are the wrong men, there may be excellent institutions, but of what benefit would they be?⁶

Similar sentiments can be found in many Neo-Confucian writings. Although the important Ming dynasty thinker Luo Qinshun (1465–1547) recognized the importance of institutions, writing "only after institutions (*zhidu*) have been established is it possible to improve customs and increase material prosperity," he still maintained that "if one wishes to change the *fa*, the essential consideration is to get hold of the right men."⁷

At the same time, we should keep in mind that Luo Qinshun is not idiosyncratic in his assertion that institutions are necessary (even if they, in turn, depend on good men). Admittedly, many Neo-Confucians were harsh critics of the radical institutional reforms instituted by Wang Anshi (1021–86) in the early Song dynasty. Rather than top-down institutional reforms, thinkers like Cheng Yi (1033–1107) wanted stress put on personal moral cultivation; interpreters have labeled this an "inward turn." It is a mistake, though, to see Neo-Confucians as relying solely on individuals' solitary efforts at moral cultivation. Several scholars have emphasized the "middle level" institutions that Neo-Confucians came to rely on as critical supports for individual improvement and, ultimately, as a basis for reforming the state apparatus itself. Zhu Xi was worried about what one scholar has called "the politics of selfishness" at both central and local levels, and therefore argued for a focus on re-establishing the link that had once existed between "inner (moral) reform and outer (institutional) reform." Zhu believed that "the key to China's moral regeneration [was] to establish a set of middle-level institutions that [would] enable the concern for one's household to extend to the village, and so on."[8] Zhu therefore both worked to promote and wrote extensively about institutions like academies and village compacts, thereby "redefining the terms of political involvement through his commitment to institutional reform on [this] middle level."[9]

My second qualification is to note that some thinkers from the Song dynasty and later wanted to push the role of institutions even more into the foreground. The clearest cases of the trend come from the late Ming and early Qing dynasties, and in particular from the trenchant political manifesto *Waiting for the Dawn*, completed in 1663 by Huang Zongxi (1610–95).[10] For our purposes the key is the emphasis Huang puts on *fa*, which he uses in the broad sense discussed above. A healthy polity is based on well-designed institutions like schools, property regimes, and ceremonies that train people to be social citizens, rather than selfish egoists. Huang contrasts these institutions with those promoted by recent rulers, which he characterizes as "anti-institutional institutions" (or, if you prefer, "unlawful laws"; *fei fa zhi fa*): in this case, the educational system, property regime, and ceremonies are designed solely to glorify the one family who happens to occupy the throne – whether they deserve it or not. Huang then famously asserts: "Should it be said that 'There is only governance by men, not governance by institutions (*fa*),' my reply is that only if there is governance by institutions can there by governance by men." He goes on to explain: "If the institutions of the early kings were still in effect, there would be a spirit among men that went beyond the institutions. If men were of the right kind, all of their intentions could be realized; and even if they were not of this kind, they could not slash deep or do widespread damage."[11]

Let us take stock. The proper role and content of *fa* are matters of debate throughout the Confucian tradition. Law and legal codes were not seen by Confucians as having any special place within the larger universe of institutions. Confucius's discomfort with litigation is well-known, and legal specialists were anathema to the later imperial state.[12] Still, the practice of both civil and criminal law was extremely widespread and a key responsibility of state officials. Properly managed, law was a tool that not only could help keep order, but actually encourage harmony and moral growth.[13] Nor is law the sole institution that could be constructive as well as pernicious. Schools could train students to be good people, or they could encourage a selfish focus on passing the civil service exams at all costs; rituals could enable and encourage the expression of apt emotions, or they could be wooden and oppressive impositions. At their ideal best, each of these institutions embodied the Way, a universal morality of virtuous people and flourishing, harmonious society. Each had its role to play in nurturing such people and such a society. Because of the fusion between the moral order and institutions, there were no independent, "procedural" criteria by which justice was regularly assessed.[14] What ultimately mattered was putting in place virtuous people who would see that the institutions of the state and society functioned so as to bring about the Way, based on the ability rooted in their own virtue to perceive the demands of the Way in any given situation.[15]

Zhang Shizhao and the First Debate

Now fast-forward to the mid-1910s. The Qing empire collapsed in 1911 and the Republic of China was founded the next year. Yuan Shikai (1859–1916), the military strongman who has become President, harbors monarchical ambitions. Many of those who had, in the final years of the empire, called for a transition to constitutional monarchy now come to distance themselves from Yuan. He makes efforts to cloak himself in the language and trappings of the sage-king, even declaring that "virtue is the substance; laws are merely instrumental."[16] One of the reasons that Yuan and his supporters offer for re-instituting the monarchy is that only an individual, an emperor, can command enough respect and loyalty to unify the nation.[17] Indeed, the republic and its political institutions – assembly, provisional constitution, laws – seem to many to be impotent or even irrelevant. This is the context for the first of the twentieth-century debates we will examine.

A rough characterization of the debate pits the famous early reformer Liang Qichao (1873–1929), as champion of "rule by man (*renzhi*)," against Zhang Shizhao (1885–1973), the student of British liberal institutions who favors "rule by law (*fazhi*)." Drawing on important new research by the contemporary scholar Leigh Jenco, though, we will soon see that this way of understanding the debate is seriously misleading. Some in Liang's camp were indeed focused on the need for *genuinely* virtuous individuals to lead the polity; their main objection to Yuan Shikai was that he was not virtuous, and so they advocated various means for producing more virtuous elites. Liang's own position, in partial contrast, was that only if there were a wholesale change in Chinese culture and society would Chinese people be able to play effectively the political roles of leader, citizen, loyal critic, and so on – no matter what the exact political system. Social and cultural changes, rather than changes to political institutions, were therefore what mattered most to China's future, because it is the people, in the end, who make the difference.[18] A related dimension that we see in the writings of some of Liang's lesser-known associates more explicitly than in his own work is that engagement in politics is not only less vital than engagement with social change, but is actually inimical to the sort of moral improvement that Chinese people require. Dirtying one's hands with political dealings undermines one's virtue. Participation of an apolitical sort – in literary reforms and other social movements – is to be preferred because it is consistent with moral purity.[19]

The general framework of Liang's position, in short, resonates strongly with traditional Confucian arguments, even if the radical social and cultural changes he advocated departed from Confucianism in many ways.[20] It is with Zhang Shizhao that the "rule by man" versus "rule by law" dichotomy truly breaks down. His contemporaries (and some more recent scholars) took him to be naively arguing that British parliamentary institutions and laws were a panacea for China's problems. To the contrary, Jenco has shown that Zhang's nuanced arguments contain two main strands: worries about a simple-minded approach to rule by virtue, and arguments that individual development and institutional development mutually interact with one another. Taken together, Zhang's position is far from a thorough rejection of core "rule by man" contentions, even while he insists that political institutions and personal engagement in politics are much more consequential than Liang and the rest believe. While Zhang is no Confucian, we will see that his arguments both resonate well with those of someone who is (namely, Mou Zongsan), and contribute very constructively to what a Progressive Confucian ought to believe today.

There are two sides to Zhang's worries about "virtue." First, he observes that talk of virtue typically operates in a socially normative, rigid fashion. Society's elites get to define what is "virtuous" and typically do so in ways that exclude the less educated. Even setting aside Yuan Shikai's tendentious (or perhaps just cynical) claim to virtue, Zhang is concerned that the more distant people are from the supremely literate elite culture, the more tenuous is their claim to "virtue." Politics, in contrast, he sees as more open and inclusive.[21] He says, "Politics uses institutions to regulate an entire state, from the leader to the ordinary people, from the extremely worthy to the extremely dissolute. In the eyes of the law, there is no distinction between them. All have a fixed space that circumscribes them."[22] As Jenco puts it, the institutions that Zhang promotes "subject the activity of non-elites to both regulation and recognition, which has the effect of registering such activity both legitimate in, and efficacious for, a republican government."[23] Zhang's second point about virtue is that no one ever actually attains the level of virtue that would justify unrestrained political authority: "The absolute authority of virtue, no one but sages can attain . . . [But] there never has been this kind of sage."[24] Zhang's point is not that virtue is irrelevant or non-existent. In fact, he believes that when a country has good institutions in which all are able to participate, "the virtuous and able will come to increasingly display their abilities" [Ibid., 439]. But sagely virtue is neither necessary nor sufficient for political authority.

The last quote from Zhang points in the direction of his other main theme: namely, what Jenco calls the "interactive potency of institutions and virtues."[25] Zhang's main point is that *pace* Liang Qichao, society and politics are not independent of one another. The nature of government institutions has an effect on the development of talent and virtue among people of all classes. He writes: "A good government is nothing other than creating an organization and encouraging all the courageous, intelligent, clever, and strong people in the country to contribute to it, directly or indirectly, as the quality of their talent dictates."[26] In many ways, this position has "rule by man" overtones: "In general, the course of politics is directed by the most talented people in a society."[27] Still, as noted above, virtue is not the criterion for political authority. Virtue and laws are complementary but distinct. "The foundation of a 'republic' is virtue, when considered from the perspective of ethics; when considered from the perspective of politics, it is institutions."[28] Developing people's talent and virtue is critical, but it cannot be done in a way that is blind to the inclusiveness and ubiquity of politics. As one of Zhang's colleagues put it, "If you seek to correct the deficiencies in rule by man by relying only on law, you risk inviting the problems of [pure] rule by law [regimes]; but simply waiting on a hero will also produce imbalance."[29]

Zhang insisted on distinguishing ethics and politics, yet also saw that they are related. I will return to this point in the final section, below. For now, let us note that Zhang's position – influenced by his early education in Confucianism as well as by his time in Britain – did not rest exclusively on what we would now call the "rule of law." He is interested in the broader role played by all manner of political and legal institutions, and in this his use of "*fa*" follows from earlier meanings. He is obviously no pure proceduralist, though neither does he have a very specific vision of substantive justice toward which he believes society should be moving. He does talk occasionally of a "flourishing" society, but the exact parameters of flourishing remain to be worked out as the polity seeks to mobilize the talents and perspectives of everyone. As we each seek to put our talents to use, while at the same time consciously "accommodating" the differences we find from others (on which more in the final section, below), we will work out together the way forward to a better world.

Mou Zongsan and the Second Debate

Zhang Shizhao and his interlocutors were writing in the early years of the Republic of China. In 1949, Communist forces are victorious and establish the People's Republic of China (PRC). Chiang Kai-shek and his supporters retreat to Taiwan, where they re-establish the government of the Republic of China. The British colony of Hong Kong also remains outside the control of the PRC. In the following years, one can discern another debate about rule of law versus virtue politics, this one carried on in Taiwan and Hong Kong between self-identified liberals and self-identified Confucians; in the background was their understanding of the Communism that was being advocated on the mainland. My focus here will be on the Confucians, but first let us look briefly at the liberals. Yin Haiguang (1919–69) argues against "taking morality as the foundation for democracy," which he takes to be the Confucians' position, because it will inevitably lead to totalitarianism. He writes: "Morality itself actually does not have the function of preventing immoral behavior from appearing. Therefore, morality is not even remotely able to serve as the foundation for democratic order. Taking a step back, even if we say there are no such harms, morality after all belongs to the ethical realm. It is external to institutions, and because of this morality and political institutions are still two different entities."[30] Yin's distinction between morality and politics sounds very much like Zhang Shizhao. As we turn to the Confucians, though, we will find that at least some among them had nuanced views that seek to combine elements of rule of law with the importance of virtue politics – and perhaps are the more genuine developers of Zhang Shizhao's ideas.

My chief representative of the Confucians will be the "New Confucian" Mou Zongsan, who has already featured prominently in Chapters 2 and 3. In 1961, Mou published *Authority and Governance* in which he spelled out his understanding of contemporary Confucian political philosophy. At the core of this work is the distinction between "politics," which Mou characterizes as the justification of political authority, and "governance," which encompasses institutions of social control.[31] As I mentioned above, Mou argues that while its institutions of governance were highly developed, traditional China lacked institutions that implemented political authority. Mou often uses law as an instance of the kind of political institution he is talking about. For instance, without its own, independent justification and meaning, law is no more than a dispensable, manipulable tool of control; it has no genuine authority over us, nor do we have any genuine rights.[32] Legal authority is thus a species of political authority, and we can conclude that the more general category covers one's rights and duties to legitimate, general, or public institutions (in Chinese, the category is *gong*). These publically specifiable rights and duties are at least analytically distinct from our moral responsibilities, which Mou takes to be particularistic and rooted in our subjective conscience.

Confucianism has traditionally stressed the development of an individual's moral consciousness with the ultimate goal of attaining sagehood – a state in which one perceives and responds to all opportunities to fulfill the nascent, life-affirming harmony of the universe (or Coherence, as discussed in Chapter 3).[33] Mou both endorses and develops these ideas in distinctive ways, but for our purposes, his most novel and important arguments concern the relation between this moral striving, on the one hand, and law and politics, on the other. Partly echoing themes we saw in Zhang Shizhao, Mou worries about any political system that relies on leadership by individuals who claim to have highly developed moral insight. As already mentioned, he characterizes this as politics being "swallowed" by morality [Mou 1991, 140]. Mou is deeply committed to the importance of striving for sagehood. Among other things, he sees laws and rights themselves as rooted in and emerging from moral struggles. Without morality, there would be no politics. Nonetheless, he recognizes that "achieving sagehood is an endless process" [Ibid., 127]. Politics (including law) must, therefore, be independent from morality.

Unlike the liberals with whom he was debating, Mou held that moral and political value must retain a continuity, lest politics be unmoored from the underlying source of all value – in which case we would have no reason for confidence that the outcomes of our political processes were ultimately aimed at making our lives better. Unlike the Communists and earlier Confucians, politics and law must nonetheless stand on their own, independent of morality. In other words, Mou rejects both a direct connection between morality and politics, and a lack of connection. His alternative is an indirect connection, based on the idea of "self-restriction (*ziwo kanxian*)" that I discussed at length in Chapter 2. One way of summarizing "self-restriction," as it applies in the political realm, is that even sages cannot violate the constitution.

I will say more about Mou's vision of virtue politics – which retains a significant role, notwithstanding the limits placed on it by morality's self-restriction – later in this chapter. For now, we might reflect on the relation between "partly independent political and legal value," on the one hand, and other contemporary notions of "rule of law," on the other.[34] Scholarly discussion of "rule of law" is complex and often founders on terminological ambiguities, in both English and Chinese. Let us begin with the two extreme possibilities. At one end of the spectrum, there is the use of law – or at least, of pronouncements that look like laws – at the ruler's discretion to achieve the ruler's own desires. If a ruler fails to achieve his or her will by the use of such "law," he or she will turn to other means of governance: law has no pride of place. I will call this "rule by law."[35] Turning now to the other end of the spectrum, there is general agreement that for the most full-blooded versions of "rule of law" – which many call "thick" versions of the rule of law – broader issues of moral and political value must enter into the definition, such that good laws can be distinguished from bad ones by the failure of the latter to support an appropriate concept of justice, among other things.[36] In between these extremes lies "principled rule by law" or "thin rule of law," according to which for something to count as law, it must satisfy a list of procedural requirements. Scholars generally agree on the requirements that need to be satisfied; two examples are that laws must treat people in similar situations alike, and laws must be made public.[37]

Mou rarely spends much time distinguishing among "political value," law, rights, and human rights: the key for him is simply that all of these are instances of the sorts of things that have to have partial independence from morality. My next chapter is devoted to building an account of human rights on the foundation Mou gives us, so we can set that issue aside for now. As for the rest, it is clear that Mou understands law and rights in at least the "thin rule of law" sense. Procedural requirements like publicity and treating similarly situated people the same are a way of specifying wherein lies the "independence" of law. In fact, Mou's view is probably stronger than this: based on the idea that law emerges from morality, he insists that a system of law include protection for various rights, and so we should conclude that he endorses a thick version of the rule of law. Still, he nowhere suggests that individual laws must be held sacrosanct. As far as I can tell, Mou's position is compatible with civil disobedience, so long as these acts are not aimed at undermining a fundamentally legitimate constitution.[38]

Contemporary Debates

Discussion of rule of law and virtue politics is flourishing in contemporary China. In order to understand why and to draw some conclusions about the relevance of the two earlier debates we have just examined, let us start with the context for the current, post-Cultural Revolution conversations about law and virtue. The idea that law had a status independent of revolutionary goals or the imperatives of Party policy had been criticized during the Anti-Rightist Movement of the late 1950s and it was ridiculed during the Cultural Revolution itself. Red Guards claimed that Mao had taught, "depend on the rule by man, not the rule of law," and talk of "equality before law" or the "presumption of innocence" were construed as insidious policies of benevolence to protect class enemies.[39] China's existing legal institutions were dismantled during the Cultural Revolution era. In 1978, the beginning of the post-Mao reform era, China had virtually no functioning legal system. Few laws existed, the Ministry of Justice had been disbanded in 1959, and there were only a handful of lawyers in the entire country.[40] With Deng Xiaoping's ascendancy in 1978, "rule of law" began to be emphasized in statements from the leadership, in academic research, and in institutional changes. "Rule of man" was typically associated with the chaos of the Cultural Revolution; the exact meaning of "rule of law" was extensively debated, with many scholars starting to draw on arguments and distinctions from Western legal philosophy, among other sources. With comparatively few exceptions, the 1980s and 1990s featured little positive discussion of virtue politics, although mass campaigns aimed at combating corruption via the promotion of virtue did continue.[41]

The relation between law and virtue became a vibrant topic again in the 2000s, though, spurred on by statements by Jiang Zemin in 2000 and 2001. In a January 10, 2001 speech, he invoked a pair of terms that have subsequently been much discussed:

> We should persistently strengthen the construction of a socialist legal system and govern the country according to law (*yifa zhiguo*). At the same time, we should persistently strengthen the construction of socialist morality and use virtue to govern the country (*yide zhiguo*). In the administration of a country, rule of law (*fazhi*) and virtue politics (*dezhi*) complement and promote each other. Neither should be overemphasized to the neglect of the other.[42]

Jiang's statements led to an explosion of academic and commentarial writing on virtue politics and its relation to the rule of law.[43] Writers draw on four main sources: the writings of Marx, Lenin, and various Chinese communist leaders; figures from the history of Western legal and philo-sophical thinking; contemporary Western legal and moral philosophers; and ancient (almost exclusively classical-era) Chinese thinkers. In addition, they draw on or engage with other contemporary Chinese contributors to the burgeoning literature.

Several themes can be discerned in these current debates. First, authors repeatedly stress the rich discourse concerning the development of virtue and its role in governance that is found in Confucianism, and rely on these resources to suggest the possibility of a distinctively Chinese approach to balancing law and virtue. Distinctions (sometimes very broad and vague) between Chinese and Western theories of law, virtue, and governance are quite common. Second, many explain that one importance of virtue or morality is in providing a source or foundation for law. Third, virtue is important not just for leaders, but much more broadly. Many authors emphasize the need for virtue education to reach all members of the Communist party; their leading role in the society demands greater inner-party "quality" and discipline.[44] Some authors take "virtue politics (*dezhi*)" to apply even more broadly still, reaching out into the entire society and serving as a premise for the development of both a "good government" and a "good society."[45]

Finally, many of the authors argue that recognizing the importance of virtue politics is not the same as a return to "rule by man." The distinctive values and procedures stressed in the "rule of law" are critical to China's continuing progress toward a modern, harmonious society. Li Lanfen argues, for instance, that basing the distribution of goods on judgments about virtue or political enlightenment – even though intended to moti-vate the further cultivation of virtue – has the contrary effect of blocking and suppressing the development of moral values. Democracy and liberty, rather than dictatorship, are therefore the proper basis for bringing rule of law and virtue politics into a dialectical unity.[46] Wang Keping cautions that even though rule of law and virtue politics are both important – his meta-phor is that they are like the two wheels on a cart – yet given China's long history of rule by man and only very recent efforts toward rule of law, it is critical not to over-emphasize the role of virtue right now. He writes:

> Under [current] circumstances, if the socio-political function of rule by virtue is utilized merely as an expedient measure and deliberately exaggerated or enlarged out of its right proportion, it will threaten to hinder or cancel out the progression and enforcement of the rule by law. Moreover, it might lead to a half-way turning or branching-off in the name of adjusting governing policies. That is to say, with moralized

rhetoric or the external form of rule by virtue, the underlying tactics of rule by man would be employed to condition or deconstruct the frame structure of rule by law.[47]

As a result, for the foreseeable future, rule of law must be treated as primary, and rule by virtue as secondary.

It is important for us to keep in mind that very few of these scholars – including those who draw on classical Confucianism – think of themselves or their arguments as "Confucian."[48] Many would assert that they are offering a version of "socialism with Chinese characteristics," but this rubric has been used in so many different ways as to be empty of virtually all significance. Most of the authors who draw on Confucian terms or texts find isolated ideas to be stimulating, without making any larger commitment to Confucian values (like the realization of virtue for all, or an understanding of virtue in specifically Confucian terms). In general, therefore, we can conclude that a robust contemporary Confucian discourse about the relation between the rule of law and virtue politics has yet to emerge. There is at least one interesting exception, though: the "institutional Confucian" Fan Ruiping has argued that any contemporary discussion of "civil society," no matter from what perspective, must accept that it is a social order grounded in the rule of law. If there is to be a Confucian civil society, therefore, there must be a Confucian rule of law.[49] On this basis, Fan sets out to show that the rule of law does, after all, have a basis in Confucianism. His main argument turns on an interpretation of the famous "conflict" cases from *Analects* and *Mencius*, in which there appear to be conflicts between government authority and filial responsibilities. The conflict cases (*Analects* 13:18 and *Mencius* 5A:3 and 7A:35) are well-known, but Fan argues that they are often misunderstood as calling for virtuous people to "bend the law for the benefit of one's own family." To the contrary, he says they are really about "what kinds of laws a society should make."[50] For instance, with regard to *Mencius* 7A:35 in which Mencius is speculating about what the sage-king Shun should do if his father were to kill someone, Fan says that Mencius "was making a legislative proposal: a law should be made to require the emperor to resign the position and be exiled with his parents . . . in order to save his parent's life." After all, Fan says, "as a Confucian moralist, Mencius could not encourage people to break a law if the law's requirements are well-constructed."[51]

I find this fascinating, and agree with part of Fan's underlying motivation, but believe that Fan's specific idea is highly implausible, both textually and philosophically. The underlying idea that I endorse is that Confucians must be able to specify distinct senses for "rule of law" and "rule of virtue." Fan rightly criticizes the conflation of these notions, though he believes this is mainly a matter of the last one hundred years and the partial result of Western influence. It is indeed important that public laws have authority independently of anyone's claim to virtue, even though (as Fan goes on to suggest) it might well be the case that the laws in a Confucian society will take familial relations into account in a way, or to a degree, that other societies will not. However, this does not solve the matter of *Mencius* 7A:35. First, there is no hint in the text (or anywhere else in *Mencius*) that either Shun or Mencius had in mind a legislative proposal. What is illustrated is the perception-and-reaction of a sage to a challenging and complex situation, only one dimension of which had to do with the legal code. As such it fits with the extensive discussion throughout *Mencius* of particularistic, situational responsiveness, which is several times put in terms of "discretion (*quan*)." Second, there are enormous barriers to solving conflict cases in the way that Fan recommends. For one thing, Fan's approach implies that Shun did not act ideally, since there was no suitably qualified law in place. This runs against the tenor of the text and against explicit later interpretations. More fundamentally, Fan's solution would mean that we would somehow need laws to anticipate every possible tension between state authority and other responsibilities. It is not just that this seems complex or difficult, but – for familiar Wittgensteinian reasons – impossible. We therefore need a different way to develop a Confucian distinction between rule of law and virtue politics. I suggest that we can find valuable contemporary lessons by returning to Zhang Shizhao and Mou Zongsan.

Lessons for Progressive Confucianism

The vast scope of current Chinese literature on my topic means that any effort to do more than offer a cursory summary would require a much longer chapter, but my goal lies elsewhere. If we cannot find the way toward a viable Confucian vision of the rule of law in current writings, can we find it if we return to Zhang Shizhao (ironically, not a Confucian himself at all) and Mou Zongsan? What do they have to teach us?

First of all, they both contribute rich resources for shoring up a valuable line of thought that has emerged in contemporary discussions: namely, the idea that communities must avoid placing too much weight on the authority that comes with virtue. Zhang argued both that claims to virtue tend to be based on socially imposed norms, and that because there is no one with perfect virtue, there can be no one with an unimpeachable claim to authority. Mou's worries about politics being swallowed by morality, and his consequent argument that moral subjectivity must partly negate itself, at least partly mesh with Zhang's perspective. Mou's explicit assertion that the pursuit of sagehood is an endless process matches perfectly with Zhang's claim that no one should have absolute or perfect authority. I would add, incidentally, that while Mou is more explicit about the "endless" nature of the process than most Confucians and Neo-Confucians, his understanding of this point is fundamentally compatible with Confucian teachings through much of its history. So one thing that we can take away from both Zhang and Mou is that our political and legal institutions, as well as the special kinds of authority they institute, must be open to all, rather than hostage to an adequate level of virtue or ideological purity.

Mentioning the word "purity" brings me to my second point, which follows from the first. Zhang's stress on openness to the disparate talents of all and Mou's positing of an independent realm of the political – governed by a constitution, but not by demands for strict virtue – mean that politics will and should be characterized by contestation and dissonance. There are various ways in which this dissonance can and should be restrained, on which more in a moment. But our multifarious perspectives, experiences, talents, and imperfections guarantee that a healthy political process will not lead to easy unanimity. To one degree or another, Liang Qichao, many of his contemporaries, and indeed many Chinese intellectuals down to the present day, have decried the dirtiness of politics and longed for a purer solution. They pine for cultural and social transformation leading to unanimity. Thomas Metzger has astutely analyzed this trajectory within Chinese political thinking, linking the discomfort with dissonance to what he calls "epistemological optimism."[52] Notwithstanding the light that Metzger's argument sheds on a great deal of Chinese political discourse, Zhang and Mou represent two contrary voices. Embracing politics and law means also embracing the conflictual world of politicians and lawyers.

Third, although both Zhang and Mou argue that the realms of morality and virtue, on the one hand, and law and politics, on the other, must be distinguished from one another, they also insist that in various ways these two realms are also continuous. There are actually two separate issues here. One aspect of continuity is the lack of a hard and fast line between personal and public. Local or even individual activity can have broad, "political" import, as Zhang especially emphasizes. The second aspect of continuity concerns the rootedness of political and legal values in morality. Mou argues that such rootedness has the critical effect of constraining what counts as legitimate political values, since political values "emerge out of," and are designed to aid in the ultimate realization of, ethical values.[53] This means – as Joseph Chan, Fan Ruiping, and others have pointed out – that the contents of Confucian laws may well reflect distinctively Confucian ethical values in certain ways.[54] In addition, I have argued elsewhere that a Confucian society's norms, and the details of the legal system itself, should be arranged such that recourse to the legal system is typically not one's first choice when faced with some sort of dispute, even though the legal system is there and available for those who genuinely need it; I call this "law as a system of second resort."[55] In contrast to all of this, Mou worried that liberalism was prone to characterize issues of public norms as only constrained by political debate rather than by any deeper values.[56] Among other dangers, this would provide liberalism with no adequate counter to Communism.

The fourth lesson we can take away from Zhang and Mou, finally, concerns the concrete ways in which virtue might be able appropriately to moderate the contestation of the politics and law. For Zhang, the key is "accommodation (*tiaohe*)." Accommodation has both institutional and personal sides to it, according to Zhang, but at its root it is the virtuous character trait of recognizing and appreciating differences, a capacity that relies on "discernment and the exercise of particularity."[57] Zhang wants us to use and develop our talents, but to do so in ways that are conscious of the different talents and needs of others. "Self-awareness (*zijue*)" is what underlies this kind of manifestation of our talents. As such, all citizens are encouraged to develop self-awareness – in part, Zhang argues, through their participation in political processes at all levels. For his part, Mou talks of the need for universal moral education, and sees no problem with the state having a role in this process of "edification (*jiaohua*)." However, in keeping with his "self-restriction" argument, the role of any public moral education must be strictly limited. Mou says that the values we should publicly advocate are the minimum and universal way of humanity.[58] Compared with the standards to which one ought to hold oneself as part of individual moral cultivation, the standards that are taught and expected through public education are loose. Mou repeatedly argues that a central political principle is that leaders must be open to, and conform to, the desires of the people, rather than imposing the leader's vision on the people in any coercive fashion.[59] Public, political, and legal contestation, therefore, will be constrained owing to the fact that citizens have been recipients of a moral education which has helped them, Mou imagines, to have developed the rudiments of basic virtues. It is also constrained, of course, by the constitution. Beyond this, Mou explicitly rejects any public restrictions on the practice of politics or law.[60]

In conclusion, both Zhang and Mou have offered us reasons to be very cautious about any political institution designed on the premise that the more virtuous should rule over the less virtuous, even though they are both very friendly to the idea that the virtuous should contribute to politics. Any discussion of the possible structure of a Confucian polity will do well to keep in mind the concerns of Zhang and Mou. For now, let us now examine another dimension of the legal field: what should Confucians say about human rights?

5

The Rights of All Under Heaven: Human Rights and Contemporary Confucianism

There is a deep tension in much of today's international legal and ethical thinking between national sovereignty and universal human rights. We value both the self-determination of individual nation-states and yet also the border-transcending rights of individual people. This tension is exacerbated because, as Jack Donnelley has observed, the state is both the "principal violator and essential protector" of human rights.[1] The immense power and reach of the modern nation-state puts individual rights in danger as never before, yet the state is also uniquely capable of enabling citizens to realize their rights. Furthermore, the international human rights regime that has developed since the Second World War is primarily a set of institutions agreed to by nation-states. From the Universal Declaration of Human Rights in 1948, to the subsequent International Covenants, other treaties, various regional documents and institutions, and UN-based committees: all these are "international" because set up among nations.

Two sets of countervailing trends are important to note. First, there are the many economic and social changes that we can roughly refer to as "globalization." This is a vastly complicated subject, but it is at least approximately true that global and social interdependence has increased dramatically. Transnational or multinational actors (like corporations and NGOs) are now important parts of everyday experience in many parts of the world. Whether these various actors genuinely count as "global" – in the sense of being of or being responsible to the whole world – is a further question. A scientist who works with other researchers from many places and is concerned with global climate change might count. A corporation with far-flung business interests and shareholders around the world might also make a claim, though the class-based nature of its objectives is an obvious constraint.

Second, and relatedly, international institutions that try to govern aspects of this increasingly "globalized" world have been gradually undermining strong claims of national self-determination. This is of course true in the economic realm (think of the WTO); for our purposes, efforts to protect human rights across national boundaries are most relevant. At the moment, one cutting-edge effort is the "Responsibility to Protect" doctrine that was first articulated by the International Commission on Intervention and State Sovereignty in 2001, and then substantially endorsed by the UN's Sixtieth Anniversary World Summit in 2005.[2] The core ideas of this doctrine are first, that state sovereignty implies responsibility for the well-being of the state's people; and second, if this responsibility is seriously neglected, then "the principle of nonintervention yields to the international responsibility to protect."[3] Where does this latter kind of responsibility come from? The document summarizes as follows:

A. obligations inherent in the concept of sovereignty;
B. the responsibility of the Security Council, under article 24 of the UN Charter, for the maintenance of international peace and security;
C. specific legal obligations under human rights and human protection declarations, covenants and treaties, international humanitarian law, and national law;
D. the developing practice of states, regional organizations and the Security Council itself.

In other words, the international responsibility to protect is really an articulation of internationally negotiated laws and practices; this responsibility comes into play when (and only when) the responsibility inherent in national sovereignty is abandoned by the state's rulers.

While the responsibility to protect is concerned with individuals no matter where they may be, it is still framed in terms of agreements among nations. Recently, the Chinese philosopher Zhao Tingyang has argued that a crucial failing in the current world lies precisely on this point: the obsession with national sovereignty obscures a broader commonality which could actually lead to solutions of world problems.[4] Drawing on ancient Chinese thinking, Zhao suggests that a framework in which individuals, families, and nations were all seen as constituents of "all-under-heaven (*tianxia*)" would enable us better to realize our moral and political responsibilities to one another. In this chapter, I will use Zhao's ideas as my point of departure toward developing a Progressive Confucian framework for human rights, which I will call the rights of all-under-heaven. This is not Zhao's own view; he neither identifies himself as a Confucian nor is he enthusiastic about current views of human rights. Once again in this chapter I will draw significantly on Mou Zongsan to help answer some of the worries that Zhao has about Confucianism and about rights.

Mou himself had little to say about human rights that was very concrete, though, so in the end I will have to take final responsibility for the position I put forward here.

The rights of all-under-heaven may sound superficially similar to the Western idea of "God-given rights," which is of course an important grounding for human rights in the West, both historically and even today, at least based on the language one finds in many contemporary Constitutions. This legacy of divine sanction for human rights is one of the great conundrums within the current philosophy of human rights, though: we find we have inherited a concept that has enormous value, but we no longer accept its justification. It goes without saying that philosophers have been working assiduously to articulate plausible justifications. For many, this means showing how a specific conception of human rights is demanded by the theory of morality which they find most plausible. A very different approach was employed by Jacques Maritain when he convened a conference of world philosophers in 1947, as part of the discussions surrounding the emerging Universal Declaration of Human Rights. Without denying the value of rational justification, he nonetheless highlights the importance of practical agreement, relating a story in which "champions of violently opposed ideologies had agreed on a list of rights . . . They said: 'We agree about the rights, but on the condition that no one asks us why.'"[5] That is, they disagree about the reasons the rights are important – some adopting a Kantian justification, others a Christian, and so on – but they still can agree on a list of fundamental rights. The core of my argument here is that contemporary Confucians have good reasons to endorse an approach to human rights that shares something of Maritain's pragmatism.[6] Drawing on the idea of self-restriction, Progressive Confucians can make a principled distinction between moral and political values. This enables such Confucians to both allow for, and indeed insist upon actual agreements on the political values which are to govern all of us – thus avoiding what Habermas has called "human rights fundamentalism." Human rights fundamentalism is much the same as Mou's idea of "morality swallowing politics": a "sham legal legitimation" is used to conceal what is really a "moral legitimation" to justify an intervention.[7] The legal legitimation is a sham, Habermas thinks, whenever there is not a genuine agreement on the relevant legal or political norms, which is independent of whether one group is morally convinced that it is in the right. In short, my argument here is not so much about the specific content or list of human rights, as about the means by which contemporary Confucians should approach the topic.

Zhao Tingyang and the "All Under Heaven" System

Upon hearing the title of this chapter, anyone familiar with the contemporary Chinese philosophical scene would likely think of Zhao Tingyang, a prominent philosopher whose *The All-Under-Heaven System: An Introduction to the Philosophy of a World Institution* was widely read and discussed upon its publication in 2005.[8] Zhao has written important books and essays on ethics, political philosophy, and philosophical methodology, and is a leader in the creative development of Chinese philosophy today. While I will ultimately part company with Zhao on the best way to develop a Confucian conception of human rights, there is much we can learn from him about how to undertake our project.

The central methodological idea that I want to embrace is Zhao's insistence on the need to "rethink China (*chongsi zhongguo*)."[9] This means to re-think the significance of China, and to do so from China's standpoint. He says, "The historical significance of 'rethinking China' lies in striving to restore China's own ability to think, so that China once again begins thinking, re-establishes its own frameworks of thought and fundamental concepts, once again creates its own worldview, values, and methodology, and . . . reflects on China's future . . . and on China's role and responsibilities in the world."[10] He contrasts "rethinking" China with "critically investigating (*jiantao*)" China, in which China is the object of analysis but not necessarily the active subject undertaking the analysis.[11] Often the frameworks used to "critically investigate" China – including most discussions by Chinese intellectuals – are imported from outside. Such discussions are not necessarily wrong or unhelpful, but Zhao worries about the potential misfit between China and the various analytical categories used to discuss it, given the origin of the categories in very different contexts. More generally, he argues that it is important to recover a sense of agency for China and Chinese philosophy. It must be "creative" and "constructive."[12] Elsewhere, specifically addressing Confucianism, he urges that Confucianism not be understood as "finished" or complete; it needs to respond dynamically to challenges. It needs to move from "local knowledge" to "universal knowledge." He writes: "Renewing Confucianism means abandoning the negative stance as 'the interpreted,' and the recovery of the positive place as 'interpreter.' Confucianism should be used to analyze all political problems and explain every society in the world. If it cannot do [this] . . ., then Confucianism cannot be a universally valid theory."[13]

Zhao is not confident that Confucianism itself can rise to the challenge of becoming universal knowledge; he says that to do so, Confucianism would have to undergo a "great theoretical breakthrough."[14] When he surveys his twentieth-century predecessors in rethinking China, in fact, he prefers those (like Liang Shuming and Li Zehou) whom he sees as drawing broadly on all aspects of the Chinese tradition, which he argues should be seen as a whole made up of various complementary aspects. Zhao is critical of Mou Zongsan for confining himself too narrowly to Confucianism, thus losing the ability to fundamentally "rethink China."[15] A more careful reading of Mou's oeuvre would have shown Zhao that despite the fact that he considered himself a Confucian, Mou draws extremely widely on Daoist, Buddhist, and to some degree Legalist concepts and values; I would argue that Mou is actually an excellent example of the approach that Zhao favors, both in Mou's creativity and his broad scope. Furthermore, I will argue later in this chapter that Mou made precisely the "great theoretical breakthrough" that Confucianism – and Zhao's own theory – need in order to articulate properly the meaning and status of human rights.

For the time being, though, let us turn to the specific contributions that Zhao makes concerning the "all-under-heaven" idea. "*Tianxia*" or "all-under-heaven" is an ancient Chinese term.[16] As Zhao uses the term, all-under-heaven has three dimensions: the physical world, the psychological world (by which he means the "general sentiment of peoples"[17]), and the institutional world (that is, a world institution). Building on ideas he sees in various early Chinese texts and on the political structure of the early Zhou dynasty, Zhao argues that a genuine world exists only when it is unified along all three dimensions implicit in the all-under-heaven concept. Some sort of world government supported by the general will of all people is required; without it, we are left with a "failed world."[18] Currently, he says, we are stuck with a political philosophy based on the idea of the nation-state, but neither this nor the concept of internationalism can provide the concept of justified "worldness" that we need, especially as globalization accelerates. An important value of Chinese philosophy is its ability to articulate a world perspective, which is rooted in the fact that unlike Greek political philosophy with its central notion of *polis*, Chinese politics was framed in terms of "all-under-heaven."[19]

An immediate objection that one might raise is that many philosophies, whatever their origins, have universalist aspirations. They aim to say true things that apply to everyone. Zhao replies: "Anybody can have a world philosophy in accordance with his own horizons . . . However, we need a world philosophy which speaks on behalf of the world. The world is absent because of our refusal to see it from its own perspective."[20] The aim of his "all-under-heaven" concept is to bring forward a framework that is designed from the outset as a way to view the world from the world. Some scholars, particularly those attending to the ways that "all-under-heaven" might be used in an International Relations context, have charged that Zhao's rhetoric masks an effort to replace Western hegemony with Chinese hegemony.[21] This might be true if Zhao's goal was simply to insist that an ancient Chinese notion – or, for that matter, his own, updated version of that notion – be accepted by everyone. This does not seem to be his intention, however. He says that a cornerstone of Chinese philosophy is a broad openness to diverse perspectives, though this is different from toleration. Toleration is a kind of acceptance of something that one more deeply rejects. The "openness" he finds in Chinese philosophy instead involves a magnanimous learning process, ultimately leading to a transformation of the underlying unity to accommodate the new element.[22] More concretely, Zhao ends a recent essay by stressing that a justifiable "world" will depend not just on "all-under-heaven," but also on rethinking and incorporating the Greek idea of rational dialogue (*agora*): "In my opinion, a suitable world could be based on two key concepts, *agora* and *all-under-heaven*, where Greek and Chinese traditions meet in harmony. Of course, both these concepts should be renewed or rewritten in keeping with contemporary ways."[23]

To this point, I find myself largely in sympathy with Zhao's method and goals, and in later sections of this chapter I will myself make use of the "all-under-heaven" concept. As critics have pointed out, though, a significant problem with Zhao's approach is the lack of any clear path toward what looks to be a quite utopian objective.[24] One manifestation of this is his overly narrow reading of the UN and associated international agreements. This is not to challenge Zhao's distinction between "international" and "global," but to suggest that it may be easier to move from existing international institutions toward a more genuinely global institution, than to reject the existing institutions and try to start from scratch. Zhao asserts that the UN is "only an organization for negotiating and bargaining each nation's interests. As a result, it can never lead to any real agreements, since everyone is defined as being a rational selfish creature intent only upon maximizing its own interests."[25] There is certainly some truth to this, both conceptually and in practice, but the "Responsibility to Protect" idea, not to mention the human rights movement more generally, show efforts to begin to rethink the nature and responsibilities of, as well as the relationships among, the UN's constituent entities (states and individuals).

If we turn to Zhao's writings specifically about human rights, we also find problems. Although I will not go into details, I again find Zhao's methodology to be quite appropriate and to ground an ability to engage in a genuinely open world conversation about human rights – one in which Chinese ideas were neither privileged nor ignored.[26] However, his own "credit" theory of human rights – according to which one begins life with a set of rights that one can lose if one does not shoulder one's just social responsibilities – is troubling, and seems clearly vulnerable to an arbitrary authority's judgment that one no longer merits one's rights. Zhao is driven to this view because he does not believe that it makes sense for rights to have priority over particular judgments of justice or injustice. In what follows, I will suggest that Mou Zongsan gives us a way to ground the priority of rights without the problems to which Zhao worries this will lead. In so doing, it also will allow a contemporary Confucian to work more constructively with existing human rights institutions toward the goal of concretely recognizing and protecting the rights of all under heaven.

Confucians and Human Rights

Human rights are a special kind of protection for some of our most basic values or interests. Theorists disagree on exactly how to articulate this special protection – Dworkin's theory that rights "trump" interests is one well-known view – but the idea that human rights are somehow distinct from and have priority over other values is central to their meaning. I mentioned a moment ago that Zhao Tingyang could not accept that human rights had priority over justice, and sought to resolve this conflict by making human rights provisional. Since Confucians have traditionally recognized but a single realm of value, which we can label as "ethical" value, they too face a challenge in explaining why there might be human rights. It is not that Confucians ignore the existence of putative conflicts among values, such as when filial devotion and public responsibilities seem to pull in different directions, but they have long argued that when situations are understood and seen correctly, a harmonious solution is always achievable. There seems to be no room in this framework for a special set of distinctly protected interests. To be sure, Confucians have said that we should benevolently care about the well-being of all-under-heaven, but this should be harmonized with other sorts of more local responsibilities. Such harmonizing is a particularistic matter, to be judged on a case-by-case basis. The idea that there are straightforward, public, unbendable constraints on each of us does not fit well into a Confucian framework.[27]

Still, many contemporary Confucians have looked for a way to endorse some version of human rights. It may be helpful to list a range of possible positions:

1. Confucianism has *recognized* human rights from the beginning. Confucians (and a hypothetical modern Confucian polity) have no difficulty endorsing human rights today.
2. Confucianism is *incompatible* with human rights, and should reject them today as parochial and problematic.
3. Confucianism did not historically develop a doctrine of human rights, but it is *compatible* with such an idea, and can endorse it today.
4. Confucianism did not historically develop a doctrine of human rights, but in order to realize its own core commitments, it is *necessary* that it now develop the resources to do so.
5. Confucianism did not historically develop a doctrine of human rights; it is necessary that it now develop the resources to do so, and the result will be *transforming* Confucianism into Western liberalism. Confucianism as a distinct philosophical position will cease to exist.

Position 1 has had its adherents. In 1947, as the Universal Declaration of Human Rights was being drafted, a major conference of world philosophers was held to explore attitudes toward human rights from around the globe. Chinese philosopher Lo Chung-shu wrote that, while the "problem of human rights was seldom discussed by Chinese thinkers in the past," nonetheless "the idea of human rights developed very early in China."[28] As immediately becomes clear from reading the balance of Lo's essay, though, he is using "human rights" very loosely, and moving quickly from the fact that early Confucianism recognized responsibilities of, for example, ruler to subject, to the conclusion that subjects had right against their rulers. This is a misreading of the texts, for reasons I have indicated already.

Henry Rosemont, an American philosopher who is both very sympathetic to Confucianism and highly critical of Western neo-liberalism, argues that Confucians should embrace Position 2. His argument has three main premises: (1) classical Confucian ethical language is very different from, and indeed incompatible with, the language of rights-based morality; (2) contemporary societies based on individualistic rights-claiming are suffering from grave problems; and (3) with certain emendations, a Confucian vision can serve as a successful alternative to the Western rights-based tradition.[29] The key question is what sorts of emendations might be necessary in order to deal with the dangers posed by modern phenomena like powerful states and global corporations – to say nothing of the problems China traditionally had with despotic rulers.[30] These are the very real problems that have led a wide range of Confucians (including Mou Zongsan) to argue that Confucianism needs a significantly different political philosophy. Rosemont's solution seems to depend heavily on a thorough-going ritualization of society, which I will discuss (and reject) in the next chapter.[31]

Many writers about Confucianism and human rights have taken Position 3, arguing that since Confucianism is compatible with human rights, if we desire to have a doctrine of human rights (for reasons that may be external to central Confucian concerns), Confucians can go along. Joseph Chan, whom I identified in Chapter 1 as a Neo-Classical Confucian, offers a notable instance of this kind of argument. Chan suggests that a justification of human rights from multiple cultural or religious perspectives may be preferable to a one-size-fits-all universalist justification, and proceeds to argue both that Confucianism and human rights are not incompatible, and that a version of human rights can be justified based on classical Confucian ideas. Chan says: "the Confucian perspective would take rights as a fallback auxiliary apparatus that serves to protect basic human interests in case virtues do not obtain or human relationships clearly break down."[32] Chan's reasoning is that if one wants to justify human rights from within Confucianism, then one can find the resources to do so without causing a fundamental conflict, but note that Chan does not say that Confucianism *needs* human rights. We can find a structurally similar argument in the writings of Kantian New Confucian Lee Ming-huei. Lee says that Confucianism has the key resources needed to develop human rights: a doctrine of universal human nature; respect for individual persons; the distinction between righteousness and profit, which Lee interprets as leading to a rights-friendly deontological approach to ethics; and a politics that is "of the people" and "for the people," if not "by the people." Lee emphasizes that he is not claiming that Confucianism had the idea of human rights all along: after all, he says, it is a modern idea in the West as well. Since it has become so widely accepted around the world, though, it would be well if Confucians can endorse it too – and perhaps along the way contribute to enriching the significance and grounding of human rights.[33]

For his part, Fan Ruiping also recognizes that classical Confucianism did not make use of a concept of human rights, and follows Chan in arguing that Confucianism can add a kind of rights language to its moral and legal framework. "Establishing Confucian rights would amount to adding a minimal self-asserting, entitlement language to the rich, other-regarding, virtue language of the Confucian framework."[34] So far, this sounds like adding a "fallback" mechanism à la Chan. Fan goes farther, though, and in so doing comes to adopt Position 4: he says that Confucianism *needs* (some version of) human rights. "Even if rights are not necessary when the virtues prevail in society . . ., they are necessary when the virtues do not prevail."[35] This makes good sense: after all, rights are designed to protect key interests – just the sorts of interests that might fail to be protected in a society without widespread virtue. Fan says that Confucian rights should be derived from a Confucian conception of virtues; the latter are more basic than are the rights. He proposes the following method for deriving rights: (1) For each Confucian virtue, determine the characteristic obligations that are entailed in exercising the virtue. For example, exercising the virtue of filial devotion (*xiao*) entails an obligation to care for one's elderly parents' well-being. (2) The entitlements entailed by these obligations – in our example, the elderly parents' entitlement to receive care – are then set down as human rights. Fan emphasizes that, in keeping with Confucian particularism, the rights emerging from such a process will be "specific, agent-relative, context-sensitive, and role-based."[36]

If rights are to be able to serve their requisite function, they must have a status that allows them to overcome tendentious claims based on virtue. Fan sees that rights must be available in cases of "virtue failure," but then owes us an account of their status that allows them to function in such a context. For two reasons, I worry that the strategy Fan adopts is not up to this challenge. First, there is a set of features critical to the power and thus importance of human rights that Fan's version of human rights lacks. In order to play their role in protecting vital interests against powerful entities like modern states and global corporations, human rights must be clear, publically known, readily enforceable, and maximally unambiguous.[37] Fan's rights are not. Instead they are highly specific and even subject, under some possible situations, to be traded-off against other goods or interests.[38] Rather than serving as a critical kind of protection on which individuals can rely, Fan's human rights seem more like one mechanism among others in a government's toolkit for seeking to realize general well-being and social order. My second concern covers both Fan's proposal and others, like Chan's, that rely on the idea of rights as a "fallback." It is certainly true that a society in which people's main mechanism of problem solving was to claim rights against one another would be deeply problematic, but not even the most committed liberal thinks otherwise.[39] So in some sense we all agree that human rights should be a fallback: they only need to be claimed in the (hopefully rare) circumstances when things have gone badly wrong and other sorts of mechanisms fail to help. The question is whether Confucians can find a way to be comfortable with what Justin Tiwald has called the "passive ways in which rights can influence the moral contours of human behavior." Tiwald points out that "the mere existence of [a] right, even when unclaimed, has a remarkable effect on group dynamics." Rights consciousness – the awareness of claimable rights – may encourage people to think of their interests as competitive with one another, warping feelings and motives in ways fundamentally at odds with what one would expect in a healthy Confucian society.[40]

My conclusion is not that Fan's (or Chan's) approach is hopeless, but I think they face significant challenges. I believe that Confucians entering into negotiations about what rights should be protected in a domestic constitution, or what rights should be recognized as human rights, would do well to take seriously the arguments that Fan, Chan, and others make concerning the contents of rights, but that we should look elsewhere for our understanding of the form and source of rights. Mou Zongsan's idea of self-restriction offers a way of understanding the value of human rights such that Confucians can embrace them without thereby loosening their commitment to a harmonious world.[41,42]

Mou Zongsan

While some have labeled Mou Zongsan a "cultural conservative" and others criticize him for turning Confucianism into an imitation of liberal democracy, I see Mou as engaged in a genuine project of "rethinking China." He operated under somewhat different constraints than Zhao Tingyang, though, because – notwithstanding Mou's broad reliance on other philosophical schools – Mou saw himself as self-consciously developing Confucian ideas, and thus was beholden to what he took to be the core commitments of that tradition. In terms of the list of positions from the last section, Mou fits in Position 4. He believed that there were shortcomings in the Confucian tradition, including a failure to understand the true status of laws and rights, and that New Confucianism needed to address this failure through conceptual and normative innovation. In the eyes of some of Mou's critics, the result of this rethinking of China is actually Position 5, but in my view this is a mistake: Mou's version of Position 4 is coherent and attractive, and well worth our while to investigate. For present purposes I am only going to sketch the argument, both because I have discussed it extensively elsewhere in this book, and because Mou in fact only takes us part of the way to my goal of a Confucian theory of the rights of all-under-heaven and I want to leave room to explore the issues that remain even after one accepts Mou's argument. Specifically, while Mou occasionally mentions "human rights," he actually focuses primarily on other sorts of "political" constraints on ethical value, like the laws and rights enshrined in a domestic constitution. One of my objectives here is to see whether Mou's position can be extended to the broader realm of the world.

In previous chapters we have already encountered Mou's self-restriction argument. Its key ideas, recall, are (i) that full virtue must be realized in the public, political world, and (ii) that without objective structures (like laws), the public goals of full virtue are inaccessible. Notice that this argument has the structure of Position 4 from above: the constitution, laws, and rights are not merely *compatible* with Confucianism; these objective political structures are *required* by Confucianism if it is to realize its own goals. Mou's argument does not depend on an independent commitment to constitutional democracy, but is a critique internal to the Confucian tradition. The fact that he draws on Hegelian language does not change this fact, just as the ways in which earlier Confucians drew on Buddhist ideas does not render their critiques external to the tradition. For further discussion of this argument, see Chapters 2 and 3. Here, let us focus on the precise meaning of his conclusion, namely, that even sages "cannot override the relevant limits (that is, the highest principles (*lüze*) of the political world), and in fact must devote [their] august character to the realization of these limits." What is the "political world," what are its highest principles, and how do we come to know what these principles are? As noted above, these "principles" are distinct from the particularistic ethical judgments sages make: the principles are general, public, and are articulated through institutions. The "political world" is appropriately governed by the kind of political authority that a proper constitution – one that institutes genuine laws and rights – will enable. These laws offer the main examples that Mou uses of "political principles," and it is important to my subsequent argument to recognize that they are domestic laws that are founded in a nation-state's constitutional process.

I will ask about state-transcending human rights in a moment, but first let us also note that Mou offers us an answer to where a given nation-state's constitution comes from. The crucial dynamic, Mou argues, is the struggle and eventual negotiation between distinct social classes. As he puts it in one place, "It is the mutual struggle by class groups to attain their rights, and the resulting specification of a constitution, that creates democratic politics.[43]" According to Mou, this process took place in the West but not in China, because in China there was no theoretical correlation between economic groups and political prerogatives. In principle, at least, the political roles (of bureaucratic minister, for example) were "variables" that could be filled by someone with any economic background;[44] an individual just had to pass the civil service exams. In actuality, Mou recognizes, this was enormously more difficult for a poor farmer's son than for a rich landowner's son, with the result that in practice, China's political system was rigidified into ruling and ruled classes. The "people (*min*)" had no kind of citizenship. The theory, though, remained one in which each person could potentially play a leading political role, and this undermined the possibility of groups debating over the rights properly accruing to group members, and thus never led to the articulation of public political rules in a constitution.[45] The upshot is that only when you have distinct groups with distinct perspectives on their interests do you get the hammering out of rights and laws, and only when you have rights and laws do you have genuine political authority. Groups are important, in part, because they push one in the direction of articulating institutionalized general principles instead of relying only on particularistic ethical judgments.

My final topic in this section is to expand on the significance of Mou's focus on the domestic. It is true that Mou does occasionally make explicit reference to "human rights," but this is invariably in a list of various values he associates with the West or with democratic institutions; he does not offer an account of how "human rights" might differ from the general account he has provided of rights in the framework of a domestic constitution. More significant for our purposes is Mou's discussion of "all-under-heaven." Mou argues that any individual unit (*geti*) will be characterized by individuality and yet Coherence is capable of being realized through the unit's praxis. Without the practices of concrete units, in fact, there is no way for Coherence to be realized. He says that individuals, families, and states are all instances of such "units." Furthermore, Mou suggests that "all-under-heaven," seen as an organized grouping of states in which "the practical lives of the states are combined," is also a concrete "individual unit" that can manifest humaneness and Coherence.[46] Mou's language strongly suggests that as we move to units based on broader syntheses, and especially to all-under-heaven, the process of synthesizing diverse perspectives will push the emerging unit toward Coherence. However, Mou emphasizes that it would be a mistake to think that one could conceptualize human life and value using only "all-under-heaven." He writes: "In the process of moral practice, the realization of moral rationality must pass through the affirmation of the family and the state before it can be expanded to all-under-heaven."[47] If one tries to simply operate at the level of all-under-heaven – as did the early twentieth-century utopian Confucian Kang Youwei, and as did the Communists – one will actually be imposing an artificial, external set of norms. One will have lost touch with actual human life and the crucial subjective meaning of our values. We can conclude two things about Mou's understanding of "all-under-heaven": first, even though it is very broad, it is not an abstraction, but a concrete universal (a "unit" composed out of the "practical lives of states"); and second, such a unit only has meaning for Mou when it emerges out of the interaction of lower-level concrete units like states and families.

Synthesis and Development: The Rights of All Under Heaven

It is time to take stock. After an introduction that laid out one of the key challenges facing current international discussion of human rights, I proposed that by working through the ideas of two Chinese philosophers – both of them committed to "rethinking China," though only one of them an avowed Confucian – we could gather the materials needed to spell out a Confucian theory of human rights, and furthermore that its central concept, the "rights of all-under-heaven," would offer a solution to the current conundrum concerning nation-states. From Zhao Tingyang we gained the methodological framework of "rethinking China" and the idea of "all-under-heaven" as a putative way of talking about the world from the perspective of the world. On the other hand, Zhao saw no way to justify the priority that human rights are thought to have over specific claims of justice, and seems committed to a utopian framework of creating a world government out of whole cloth. Mou Zongsan's distinction between ethical value and political value, together with the idea that the former was indirectly related to the latter, since ethical value could only be fully realized via "self-restriction," offered a way to understand the priority of rights claims. Mou briefly discusses a notion of all-under-heaven that is similar in some striking ways to Zhao's – particularly in the homologous relations among family, nation-state, and all-under-heaven when each is understood as a concrete "unit" – but neither all-under-heaven nor human rights play a significant role in Mou's political thinking, which focuses much more on nations and their constitutions, laws, and rights. Mou has some ideas about how constitutions might have emerged and been justified, but he gives little hint as to how his ideas might extend to an international or global context.

As we build upon these foundations, let us first attend to the idea of seeing the world from the world's perspective. What would it mean to view all-under-heaven from the perspective of all-under-heaven? Recall that all-under-heaven has three dimensions: the geographical, psychological, and institutional. We need say little about the geographical; it simply means that the scope of all-under-heaven is the entire known world. For Zhao, it seems that the psychological and institutional dimensions might be quite distinct from one another. What I mean is that one could have an institution representing the world (e.g., the Zhou dynasty "son of heaven," royal family, and retainers), without any institutional mechanism that manifests the psychological support of the people. According to early Confucian thinking, the people's support is crucial, but they "vote" with their feet: people migrate toward good rulers and flee (or resist) bad ones. If the world is peaceful and harmonious, that means that the son of heaven has legitimacy.

We saw in Chapter 3, though, that there is a serious tension in the early Confucian conception of political authority, which seems simultaneously to insist upon and yet deny the ability of individual common people to see what is good for them and for their communities. We can see this reflected in the Zhou political arrangement I have just described, since the people are only allowed to serve as a reactive sign of legitimacy, rather than having any actual input into what policies to pursue. The solution to this problem surrounding Confucian political authority, I believe, is to vest authority more completely in the people (*min*). "The people" will be the collection of all individuals, rather than a reactive mass. Each of us will be part of this authoritative entity because each of us has a unique and valuable, though of course also limited, perspective on how we can all fit together in an ideally harmonious way (that is, achieve Coherence). "The people" will therefore not be functioning as a passive indicator of the will of heaven, but as our best and indeed only access to what is genuinely valuable.

Supposing that we accept my proposed amendment to the Confucian conception of political authority, then we will need to rethink the psychological and institutional dimensions of all-under-heaven – and, in particular, the relation between these two dimensions. The "institutional" will need to encompass not just an authoritative world institution, but also the processes by which that institution and its norms become established and then maintain their authority. Here Mou can be of assistance. In the context of domestic constitutions, we saw that only when there are distinct groups with distinct perspectives on their interests will there be the hammering out of rights and laws. Negotiations between groups encourage the articulation of institutionalized general principles. We will therefore need to find a way for groups with distinctive perspectives on the world – for economic, cultural, or perhaps other reasons – to be involved in the process of global norm-articulation. Rights or laws to which they can agree would then have a claim to be authorized by all-under-heaven, for all-under-heaven. Viewing the world from the perspective of the world, in other words, requires us to arrive at the universal, world perspective through an inclusive process, rather than universalizing a single perspective. To be clear, therefore, I am arguing that a Confucian perspective on the rights of all-under-heaven tells us that these rights would not come solely or directly from pre-existing Confucian values.[48]

One of the criticisms of Zhao that I have mentioned is the lack of any path toward his ambitious goals. Is the perspective that I am offering here subject to the same criticism? Some will think that counting on an inclusive process resulting in an agreement about the rights of all people is truly naive. To the contrary, I want to suggest that the process is already well underway. While the United Nations, the Universal Declaration of Human Rights (UDHR), and the many human rights treaties that have been negotiated since the Second World War are not perfect, they do collectively represent the kind of process that a concern for all-under-heaven would demand. As mentioned above, Zhao himself is quite skeptical about the United Nations. Recall that he says that "the UN is not a world organization with substantial power to govern the world, but only an organization for negotiating and bargaining each nation's interests. As a result, it can never lead to any real agreements, since everyone is defined as being a rational selfish creature intent only upon maximizing its own interests."[49] Zhao recognizes the efforts of the UN to promote "rational dialogue," but notes that without a broader entity to which all are committed (like a world), even "understanding" cannot reliably lead to "acceptance" and agreement. Furthermore, the UN's lack of real power makes it unable to resist the dominance of a single superpower over the world.

I accept some of these criticisms as important, but believe that they are significantly overstated. Even though the UN is an organization composed of member states, it has from the beginning also been more than that. According to its Charter, it was founded in part to "to save succeeding generations from the scourge of war" and "to promote social progress and better standards of life in larger freedom." Its many committees and offices have been spaces in which collective goals can be discovered and pursued, as well as training grounds for public-spirited individuals who have the whole world in view, rather than just the interests of their country. The efforts of such individuals to articulate a "responsibility to protect" that I mentioned at the outset are surely evidence that within the confines of the UN, individuals are not understood solely as selfish creatures focused on their own interests; the very idea of "responsibility" – of sovereign states, and of the international community – clearly refers to relationships rather than just to individuals on their own. In addition, when we look at the many perspectives that mutually contributed to the UDHR and at the complex and diverse processes of communication and negotiation involved in the various existing and emerging human rights treaties, it seems clear that the current human rights regime is far more promising than Zhao's critique suggests. (It is surely relevant, for example, that the reference to a "spirit of brotherhood" in Article One of the UDHR was inserted at the request of Chinese representative P. C. Chang, who meant it to express the Confucian idea of humaneness (*ren*).)[50] Indeed, as both Zhao and Mou have said, all-under-heaven is not an abstraction but a concrete entity that emerges from the interactions of constituent groups. Theorists cannot will such a concrete universal into existence; only the coordinated interactions of individuals can do that. Insofar as Confucians are concerned with bringing an ideal like Coherence into more concrete realization, they should participate in the human rights regime. Their moral and metaphysical commitments give Confucians firm reasons for confidence in the value and intelligibility of all-under-heaven and their attendant rights.[51]

Zhao Tingyang does not write as a "Confucian," but his stress on the perspective of all-under-heaven is tailor-made to articulate what Confucians should say about human rights, in an effort to move international rights discourse forward, beyond what Confucians should see as a false dichotomy between nation and world. Confucians see great value in the responsibilities that we have to intimate and local groups (paradigmatically, families), and they also see importance in our wider networks of relationships. Seeing Coherence is precisely seeing a way to balance or harmonize these different kinds of responsibilities. And our wider networks of relationships are themselves diverse. As Mou emphasized, our nationality is significant to our moral and political identity, but so is our place within (and perspective on) all-under-heaven. We have moral responsibilities to our fellow humans, and because of the existence of political institutions on a global scale, we can also say that we share with all humans the rights of all-under-heaven.

6

Neither Ethics nor Law: Ritual Propriety as Confucian Civility

"Ritual," "propriety," and "civility" are all possible translations for a crucial Confucian idea – the Chinese term is li^1 – about which I have so far had little to say. Emphasizing the importance of ritual is at the heart of much of the work of contemporary Confucian Revivalists and Institutional Confucians, among others. Mou Zongsan and many of the contemporary Kantian New Confucians, on the other hand, have regularly come in for criticism (from Institutional Confucians, among others) for not taking ritual seriously enough. This is an instance in which I agree with criticisms of Mou, at least partly. Progressive Confucianism needs to find more room for ritual to play a constructive role than Mou was able to accommodate. At the same time, we must not exaggerate the role that ritual or civility should play in our overall philosophy: it needs to be balanced against the distinct and equally critical roles served by ethics and law. Together, the three form the tripod on which Progressive Confucianism rests.

Thomas Metzger is among the most insightful analysts of Chinese political thinking, whether traditional or contemporary. In a typically provocative style, he raises the topic of "doable virtues that any decent person could practice," and then asserts that:

> such virtues cannot even be conceptualized in Chinese without concocting a preposterous term, such as *xiangyuan de daode* (the morality of the person who seeks to seem respectable but actually lacks a commitment to doing what is right) . . . In the West, however, [doable virtues] were emphasized in a cultural context accepting the permanent moral dissonance of political life. Thus virtue in public life could be emphasized without implying the need to realize a society and a political life free of the pursuit of selfish interest. Indeed, "civility" as the public virtue of the merely decent person is not even a word that can be translated into Chinese.[2]

If Metzger is right, then it looks like our quest to learn something about civility from Confucian philosophers may be over before it begins. And there is considerable truth in what he says. Both the *Analects* and the

Mencius rail against the *"xiangyuan,"* or "village worthy," because the superficial respectability of "village worthies" undermines the possibility of further moral progress both for themselves and for others in their communities.[3] If the *xiangyuan* represents the only way that Confucians can conceptualize "doable virtue," then it may indeed be difficult to speak of anything like Confucian civility. However, Metzger himself concedes that while the works of the great philosophers did not speak of doable virtue, one finds more of an emphasis on "the virtues of the merely decent person" in popular "Confucian China."[4] In fact, I will argue that the philosophers *were* often conscious of what I will call a minimalist sense of *li* (ritual or propriety), and that this idea fits well with the notion of "doable virtue." There is admittedly the potential for confusion, as one can also find evidence for a maximalist reading of propriety, sometimes in the very same texts. It is the task of this chapter to explain and defend the "minimal" notion of ritual that I will endorse and to show how this kind of accessible "civility" – as distinct from both ethical and legal norms – contributes importantly to contemporary Confucian political philosophy.

Vicissitudes of Ritual Propriety

A concern for ritual has been central to the thought and practice of virtually all Confucians.[5] "Ritual" here does not just mean a formal ceremony, but covers all the multifarious social norms that govern how we interact with one another; in the contemporary world, we see rituals in situations as diverse as family meals, greetings between strangers, and committee meetings. According to Confucians, societies that are ritually ordered flourish; individuals whose lives are governed by ritual are humans rather than beasts. The "patterning *(wen)*" that is distinctive of ritually shaped activities enables culture, community, and civilization. Despite general agreement, though, a closer look at Confucian teachings on ritual reveals some important differences – both issues that were debated in a given era, and some general trends of change over time. In order to provide context for my subsequent arguments about the proper place of ritual propriety in a contemporary setting, it will be helpful to begin by looking at some of the key issues raised in Confucianism's long history.

Already in the *Analects* there appears to be a tension between two roles that a system of rituals might play. On the one hand, there is what I will call a *maximal* notion of ritual's role, according to which the full program of both individual self-cultivation and social perfection is encompassed by the proper enactment of the rituals. This is most famously expressed when the Master (i.e., Confucius) says: "To overcome the self and turn to ritual propriety (*li*) is humaneness (*ren*)."[6] Humaneness is the pinnacle of ethical achievement, so if one's turning to *li* thereby means one has achieved *ren*, *li* is clearly playing a maximal role. Once one has attained *li* – which, admittedly, may be very difficult and rare – there is nothing more for one to do. On the other hand, one can also detect a *minimal* role that *li* seems to play. Another famous *Analects* passage tells us that coercive, punishment-based governance will fail, but that "regulating [the masses] by ritual" will lead them to acquire a sense of shame and therefore be orderly.[7] Far from representing the acme of ethical achievement, *li* in this context is something that the masses can be taught.[8] It has a positive effect on them, but no one will be tempted to conclude that as a result of the ritual teachings they have received, all the people now count as sages.

Many views formed as the tradition developed. Building on the maximalist-sounding descriptions of *li* one finds in certain classical texts,[9] some later political thinkers took ritual as their central concept. Alan Wood explains that for someone like the early Song dynasty writer Sun Fu (992–1057 CE), "These 'rituals' were thought to be the outward manifestations of certain absolute moral principles, . . . [and therefore] violations of ritual are violations not only of the human order but of the universal order as well."[10] The major philosophers of the Neo-Confucian movement, though, tended to distinguish between rituals and the underlying Coherence[11] that the rituals were designed to elicit. For example, Zhang Zai (1020–77) asserts that, "Ritual is Coherence. You must first learn to apprehend Coherence; ritual is then the means by which you put into practice what is right [according to Coherence] . . . Rituals come after Coherence."[12] The most influential of the Neo-Confucians, Zhu Xi (1130–1200), goes further in a minimalist direction. He criticizes Zhang Zai for over-emphasizing ritual, and argues that while ritual offers one route toward personal transformation, it is not the only possible means.[13] Still, Zhu saw ritual as a very useful and broadly applicable educational mechanism, and authored the most important ritual manual of the later imperial period, *Master Zhu's Family Rituals*.[14]

The pendulum has swung back and forth between maximalist and minimalist views in the centuries since the era of the Neo-Confucians. We find a strongly maximalist perspective in the writings of many Qing dynasty (1644–1911) thinkers, who both felt that the Neo-Confucians had promoted an overly subjectivist reading of the tradition, and that this subjectivism was responsible for the fall of the Ming dynasty to the invading Manchus. A notable exponent of this movement toward ritual purism was Ling Tingkan (1757–1809), who announced: "The Way of the sages is only ritual propriety (*li*)."[15] Ling strongly distrusted the ability of average people to perceive propriety without the guidance of explicit rituals, and even worried about the ability of sages to avoid mistakes. The result is a rigorist and authoritarian ethics that demands scrupulous adherence to the rituals recorded in the ancient classics, at least as these often obscure texts were interpreted by Ling.[16]

By the time the Qing dynasty collapsed in 1911, ushering in the Republican era, ritual purism was under increasing attack. Most Confucian philosophers of the twentieth century – including leading New Confucians like Tang Junyi and Mou Zongsan – put much more emphasis on ethical ideals like humaneness than they did on ritual. As far as institutions were concerned, a major focus was on how Confucianism could be understood so as to justify a reconstructed democratic politics. To be sure, rituals were not completely absent from twentieth-century Confucian concern. Some effort went into arguing for the importance of Confucian ritual and practices as part of a program of moral education, but very much in a minimalist vein. For example, New Confucian Xu Fuguan (1902–82) put considerable emphasis on what had previously been a somewhat obscure chapter of the *Record of Rites*. In the *Biao Ji* chapter, the following insight is attributed to the Master:

> It has long been understood that complete attainment of humaneness is difficult, and only possible for a superior person. Thus the superior person does not criticize people, nor shame them, on the basis of what he alone can attain. When the sage lays down rules for conduct, he does not use himself as the rule, but sees that the people shall be able to stimulate themselves to endeavor, and feel shame if they fail, in order that the sage's words be put into practice. [Therefore the sage] enjoins ritual propriety to regulate conduct, good faith to bind it on them, right demeanor to express it (*wen*), costume to distinguish it, and friendship to perfect it.[17]

Even if one believes that all of "the people" can, in principle, become "superior people," at any given point they are clearly not yet there: this means that they cannot, then and there, live up to the high standards of humaneness to which a superior person holds him or herself. If one hopes for order, therefore, one needs to have a lower (though not negligible) and more realistic standard that one can demand of the people. According to the passage, this standard is to be understood in terms of ritual propriety. In short, it is only a minimalist sense of propriety that we can demand of one another.[18]

In the last decade or so, though, an increasing number of voices have been sounding more maximalist themes, leading some scholars to speak of a strong "fundamentalist" strain in the current Confucian revival taking place in China.[19] For example, I have argued elsewhere that Hong Kong philosopher Fan Ruiping has tied the values of his "reconstructionist Confucianism" so closely to the practices of traditional Chinese society that he risks endorsing forms of discrimination that are increasingly rejected around the world, and which have no deep justification in Confucian values.[20] At the very least, we can say that the role of ritual within contemporary Confucianism – just as within Confucianism's lengthy history – is a contested subject.[21]

Problems with Maximalism

Since the scope and significance of *li* has been contested throughout the tradition, no Confucian today should assert that the tradition offers a straightforward answer as to how one ought to interpret ritual propriety in the contemporary world. Instead, we need to engage with the differing positions and reasons one can find in the tradition, as well as with relevant arguments from outside the tradition, in order to arrive at a convincing vision of ritual propriety's contemporary role. We can begin with a critique of Qing dynasty maximalist rigorism that comes from another Qing thinker, Fang Dongshu (1772–1851). Fang is concerned that rigorists like Ling Tingkan prohibit the search for Coherence and "instead depend exclusively on rituals as the instrument of teaching. What they call rituals are nothing but the names of things, institutions that are recorded in the commentaries and annotations written by scholars of later times."[22] The problem with the rigorists, in other words, is that they try to use a purely descriptive methodology – research into what the specific rituals were – to generate a prescriptive standard for contemporary behavior. This is problematic because rituals need to be adjusted, and so there needs to be something in terms of which the adjustments are made – something like Coherence. Rituals themselves cannot be the ultimate standards. This logic applies both when the needs of a new era necessitate changes, and whenever one is faced with a particular set of new circumstances.[23] The classic Confucian text *Mencius* tells us that even though the rituals prohibit a man from touching his sister-in-law, if he were to come upon her drowning, he should of course reach out and save her.[24] This is an exercise of "discretion (*quan*)." The rituals are usually reliable guides, but judging when and how they need to be modified or suspended cannot itself be a matter of ritual.

We can see a similar problem in a well-known contemporary effort to develop a kind of Confucian ritualism, namely the work of Roger Ames, together with both David Hall and Henry Rosemont, to develop what Ames and Rosemont now call a Confucian "role ethics." At first glance, Ames's Deweyan version of Confucianism seems to be the polar opposite of Ling Tingkan's rigorism. Ames emphasizes the "creative personal dimension" of ritual practice: "ritual is a pliant body for registering, developing, and displaying one's own sense of cultural importance." As a result, "rituals cannot be construed as mere passive deference to external patterns or norms." Individual participation in ritual "is a vehicle for reifying the insights of the cultivating person, enabling one to reform the community from one's unique perspective."[25] As far as it goes, I believe that this characterization of the ways in which ritual can be shaped by an individual is very perceptive. One *can* adjust rituals, consciously or unconsciously, in an effort to reform the community. The trouble is that Ames and his collaborators want to deny that there is a source of "insight" other than ritual itself: they believe it is ritual (and ritually defined roles) all the way down.[26] But their own writings make clear their belief that contemporary Chinese need leverage on their roles and rituals that is not characterized in ritual terms. Concerning gender relations, they speak of the need for women to be "allowed the freedom to pursue the same project of self-actualization as the male." Concerning the status of minorities, they say that "the Confucian principle that has the greatest potential effect in changing things for the better is the principle of merit."[27] One may readily grant that the Confucian way to pursue these ethically valuable ends will be greatly shaped by ritual propriety, but it is hard to see how the notion of ritual propriety exhausts the categories of freedom, self-actualization, and merit.

Related difficulties can be seen in another contemporary, Confucian-influenced effort to articulate the centrality of rituals. In *Ritual and its Consequences*, a team of four scholars based in the Boston area argue that ritual should be understood as creating a shared "subjunctive" universe. By engaging in ritual activity, we treat one another "as if" it were the case that our world genuinely was structured by the values the rituals express. The authors explain: "By framing our intentions with the 'illusions' of courtesy, the frame actually pulls us in after it, making the illusion the reality. And the reality will last only as long as we adhere to the illusion."[28] There is much we can learn from this provocative book, and I will return to it later in this chapter. However, it also offers a clear case of the problems of a "ritual all the way down" approach. The Boston team uses Confucian texts as a source of its account, and these scholars recognize that texts like the *Analects* make a distinction between ritual and humaneness (*ren*). For many readers of the *Analects*, humaneness is the virtuous disposition that represents the supreme achievement of Confucian ethics; ritual propriety is centrally involved in the cultivation and expression of humaneness, but – on this minimalist reading of *li* – it is the humane disposition that is fundamental, and can serve as a source of "discretionary" correction to *li*.[29] In contrast, the Boston scholars write: "[Humaneness] is perhaps best understood as simply the way that one acts ritually when there is no ritual to tell one what to do: if one spends one's life doing rituals properly, then one gains a sense of how the subjunctive world constructed out of these rituals could be constructed in a situation without ritual precedent, or in situations where ritual obligations conflict . . . . When ritual obligations conflict, the key is to have trained one's responses such that one can act as if there was indeed a clear ritual guide."[30] It is true that one needs to develop a sense or disposition to act ritually without explicit guidance; for Wittgensteinian reasons, our actions will always outrun the explicit guidance of rules, so we need a sense of the point of the rule in order to "go on in the same way."[31] But this is quite different from the question of how to act when there is no relevant ritual rule at all, or when rituals conflict, or when – to return to Mencius's example of the drowning sister-in-law – rituals conflict with the humane response to an exigent situation. In all these cases, I simply do not know what it means to say that we should act as if there were a clear ritual guide. There is no such guide. Perhaps one's humane response may be taken up, subsequently, as a new kind of ritual guidance, but then again this may not happen. Even if it does, a community's subsequently deeming one's behavior to be ritually proper does not mean that one was following ritual in the first place. It seems hard to avoid the conclusion that *li* and *ren* are understood by early Confucians as distinct concepts.

In his recent book *Reconstructionist Confucianism*, institutional Confucian Fan Ruiping urges his own view of ritual maximalism. In response to objections like those raised above, he offers two proposals that are worth considering. First, with regard to the drowning sister-in-law case, he suggests that "in the establishment of a ritual, . . . certain defenses, excuses, and exceptions are already accepted, either explicitly or implicitly, for the applicable cases of the ritual."[32] He offers the example of the mourning ritual's prohibition of luxurious food such as meat, together with the explicit exception that if one is ill and needs such food for one's health, eating meat is acceptable. In other words, "proper Confucian deliberation on observing a ritual in a particular case does not allow complete liberty to weigh one's action on personal, subjective, or utilitarian grounds. It is rather deliberating about whether any of the defenses, excuses, or exceptions already accepted in the ritual applies to one's case."[33] There is certainly something to what Fan says here, but it will not take him as far as he wants to go. As Fan says, there are often explicitly accepted exceptions to ritual requirements: exceptions that have themselves been ritualized, as when a Rabbi reminds the congregation on Yom Kippur morning that those with health issues should not fast. However, neither the Confucian texts nor our own reflection support the idea that all appropriate exceptions should be thought about in this way. There is no indication in any of the numerous passages in *Mencius* bearing on the exercise of discretion that pre-existing exceptions are being discussed.[34] Furthermore, influential voices in the later tradition explicitly maintain that discretionary exceptions from rituals are not themselves matters of ritual, but rather the result of one's cultivated ethical responsiveness.[35] Unless we simply beg the question and assume that in every case of apt exception there was an "implicit" presumption that such exceptions are allowed, there must be more going on than Fan allows. While Fan is right that one cannot both take ritual seriously and simultaneously be at "complete liberty to weigh one's action on personal, subjective, or utilitarian grounds," we need to find a less maximalist way to capture ritual's resistance to arbitrary change.

Fan's second innovative argument concerns changes to rituals. He maintains that a moral community needs to have decision-making procedures about how their ritual-constitutive rules may be changed; he refers to these as "metarites." He adds, "the success of such special rites often relies on the distinctive role of some authoritative persons accepted in the community . . . For the Confucian community, revision of the rites may be made by Confucian sages according to the moral virtue of *ren*."[36] As in the case of his discussion of exceptions, I want to agree partly with Fan here. Sometimes rites do change in the way he describes. But more often they do not. Changes typically emerge from the complex processes of social, economic, and political life, which are then either accepted or not by authoritative voices in the community, and by the community as a whole. (Sometimes the authoritative voices and the community will be at odds.) The clearest instance of ritual change in the *Analects* is precisely this kind of case: rather than a sage revising the rites, in the *Analects*, Confucius comments on two changes that have taken place, approving of one because it still expresses, albeit more economically, the same underlying respect and disapproving of the other because it is less respectful than the earlier version.[37] We are not told whether his criticism of the latter change had any traction on his society. Finally, note that when Fan says that the Confucian sages make their decisions in terms of *ren*, he is acknowledging that a maximal view of *li* is inadequate.[38]

An American Minimalism: Calhoun's "Virtue of Civility"

To say that we should adopt a minimalist version of ritual is not to say that it is inconsequential. Even on the kind of minimalist account I have in mind, ritual propriety is still an important factor in our lives. As a starting point, all should agree that ritual rules enable a kind of personal *discipline*. Various social pressures and psychological tendencies (on which I expand in a moment) motivate us to discipline ourselves in accord with the external standards of ritual. For instance, one may not feel spontaneously motivated to dress in black for a funeral, but typically one will (even if a parent needs to insist on a child's doing so). As the early Confucian luminary Xunzi explained, disciplining ourselves through ritual shapes the ways that our desires are manifested. By ornamenting the corpse of a revered relative and keeping an appropriate distance away, one can avoid feeling revulsion (which would, in another context, be natural and appropriate when encountering a dead body). The discipline imposed by ritual rules can have other effects as well, including enforcing conformity with existing structures of power, as when one defers to one's elders at the dining table.[39] Going back at least as far as Durkheim, though, Western analysts have recognized that more is involved in ritual than discipline. In one way or another, ritual involves a kind of *expression* or *communication*. Roughly, the idea is that by wearing black or ornamenting a corpse, we express things to others: our sadness, our love, our respect.

One way in which we might develop these thoughts about "expression" is suggested in an influential essay about civility by the contemporary philosopher Cheshire Calhoun. She argues that civility is an important moral virtue because it enables the *communication* of respect, tolerance, and considerateness. It is one thing to *be* respectful; it is another thing to "display" this in a way that the "target of civility might reasonably interpret as making clear that I recognize some morally considerable fact about her that makes her worth treating with respect."[40] Calhoun emphasizes that in order to make such a display, we are required to "follow whatever the socially established norms are for showing people . . . respect."[41] Following the historical (Western) development of the idea, she takes civility to cover both "political" and "polite" realms. Keeping a "civil tongue" in political conversations, as well as an active willingness to listen to others, are examples of the former; avoiding nosiness and self-righteousness, as well as waiting one's turn are examples of the latter. In these instances and many others, Calhoun sees the acknowledgement of and respect for others' lives.[42]

As mentioned a moment ago, Calhoun argues that this communicative role of civility can only succeed because we follow existing socially established norms. She dwells for some time on the possibility that communicating respect (via civility) and treating people with respect might come apart. The most important issue for our purposes is that "in morally imperfect social worlds, we may have to choose between being civil – that is, successfully communicating our attitude of respect . . . – and behaving in ways that are genuinely respectful."[43] Is it truly respectful to open doors for women? Or are we currently stuck with social conventions based in older, more sexist values? No matter what one makes of this specific example, it seems clear that Calhoun is working with an account of social conventions (or rituals) that is minimalist. She argues that civility is an important moral virtue, because the communication of respect is so important. But it can conflict with another important moral virtue, namely the "integrity" demanded of us as "socially critical moral reasoners."[44] Whether one can both have integrity and be civil will depend on the moral decency of the shared understandings of one's society. Because learning and following the conventions of one's society cannot exhaust the project of morality, on this account, the role of these conventions cannot be maximalist.

There is something importantly right about Calhoun's idea of civility-as-communication. Civility – and Confucian propriety – seem extremely well-suited to the efficient communication of attitudes and values among people who may not know one another at all, but have a shared sense of what the rituals mean. Enacting these rituals also does more than simply communicate, as Calhoun notes. She writes that civility aims to "safeguard the possibility of a common social life together," in part by serving frequently as a precondition for others' willingness to enter or continue shared ventures with us.[45] If we cannot signal to others our openness to working with them as co-participants, then our common projects will stand in danger of collapse. To reiterate, the idea here is minimalist, because the rituals are accessible broadly and fall short of maximal moral accomplishment. Even in an informal, contemporary American household, there are recognizable rituals surrounding a family dinner. If they are ignored – if the table is not set, perhaps with candles lit or grace said, or if there is no shared conversation about the day – then the communal project of a family dinner may fail. Without propriety, there may be feeding time, but no dinner.[46] If enough rituals fail, then it even becomes difficult to speak of a "family" in more than a biological sense. Even if "minimal," then, rituals are hardly trivial.

Although Calhoun's talk of communication and signaling does get at part of what enables rituals to make possible communal projects like a family, it is time to recognize that her framework also has some shortcomings. First, in keeping with my "minimalist" theme, let us note that we can go beyond rituals. Calhoun strongly implies that following the social norms of civility is the only way that one can communicate respect, and this argument is made explicit by the philosopher Sarah Buss in a related essay. Buss claims that if one were to try to substitute "You are worthy of respect" for polite rituals like saying "please," then the new statement would simply become a different means of being polite.[47] One can see her point, but it ignores the ability of acquaintances with varying degrees of intimacy to set propriety (at least partially) aside and communicate our attitudes through direct conversation. One might say, "I am so sorry that I was late to the opening; I hope you weren't offended! I certainly meant no disrespect, but had something come up that I just had to attend to." If one is responding to seriously wounded feelings (and if one's own distraction, forgetfulness, or negligence has contributed), the conversation might take some time. There is propriety here, to be sure, but when necessary, one can reach beyond rituals themselves and address the question of respect with an increased intensity and directness. One also presses at the bounds of rituals, and may even contribute to their reshaping, when one responds creatively and successfully to a novel or especially challenging situation. This need not be a case, like those Calhoun considers, in which one's critical moral faculties show existing social conventions to be morally problematic; rather, it may simply be unclear what would count as an apt extension of the convention into the new terrain. In such a context, success comes from perceiving the ethical contours of the situation, guided by one's virtuous sensibilities.

There is a second, and more basic, problem with the idea that civility communicates: often enough, we do not really, or not fully, mean what we communicate. Sometimes this is an instance of the disconnection between current conventions (holding a door open for a woman) and genuine respect, as discussed above. Our civil action may convey respect but this would be false, because we are not (*ex hypothesi*) genuinely respectful. More frequently, our civil behavior may seem to convey a meaning that we do not fully intend or even understand. Does my firm handshake communicate a sense that we are equals, or is it just the result of what I was taught to do? Surely, it is not uncommon for most of us to engage in ritualized behavior half-heartedly, distractedly, going through the motions. Is it proper in these cases to talk of communication? The analogy with standard verbal communication seems to break down. Here we can learn from the thesis of Seligman and his Boston colleagues that rituals create a "subjunctively shared arena,"[48] a social space in which we treat one another "as if" certain values were real – and in which, as a consequence of our ritual activity, these values take on reality. Creation is the key trope, because rituals play several parallel roles in constituting our world so that the relevant values emerge. Part of this has to do with disciplining our emotions and with communication, as discussed above, but note that we can respond in a ritually apt manner regardless of communicative intent. These responses express values and commitments – again, even if it would be too strong to say we intended to communicate them – which influence the ways that we and our interlocutors see the world. We can see this if we notice what is missing in an otherwise helpful analogy between juggling and rituals. Juggling both expresses dexterity and simultaneously develops one's dexterity, just as ritual both expresses respect and develops one's disposition to be respectful.[49] This is true enough, but if we are to make the analogy with ritual work, we must further stress that the act of juggling also serves (partly) to constitute one's identity as a juggler (and thus perhaps as an entertainer or a clown), and thereby to help construct a world in which entertainment is valued.

Ethics and/versus Ritual

One might worry that in emphasizing the creative, constitutive role of ritual, I have fallen back into a maximalist view, so let us now consider the ways in which ritual, or civility, is and is not distinct from broader notions of ethical value. After all, as I argued previously, without such a distinct source of value (like humaneness) we cannot adequately explain when we ought to depart from rituals and when rituals ought to change. The social norms of civility must therefore exist in at least partial independence from full-fledged ethical assessment. Indeed, this independence allows for a community composed mainly of individuals who are strangers to one another to be maintained with relatively low overhead, as civility functions as an *accessible shorthand* for communication and places only *modest demands* on each person. At the same time, rituals are part of the process through which our identity and values are constituted, and they also lay the groundwork for further relational ethical growth.[50]

Suppose someone has died – the mother of a colleague, the uncle of a friend, or a student in your children's school. What should you do? Depending on the circumstances, you may well have a complex set of feelings and perhaps a complicated relationship with the survivor. How do you express your feelings, how much distance should you offer, how much support? On a Confucian account of our ethical responsibilities, these are weighty matters that demand a balancing of all the relevant values as we seek harmony in our world.[51] Still, all of us who are not sages will fall short in some way, miss out on a significant nuance (or more), and find that there still is room for growth in our ethical perceptivity and responsiveness. One of the great values of ritual is that it makes finding the right thing to do much easier. What do you say? "Please accept my condolences," or some variation. What do you do? Attend the wake, form part of the minyan when the family sits shiva, or whatever else is ritually apt, given their identity and traditions. If you do not know what to do, often enough you can look it up: even in the contemporary United States, there are handbooks of ritual, civility, and etiquette that simplify one's task. Of course, "Please accept my condolences" does not communicate everything one might be thinking and feeling; as a kind of shorthand, it has limits in what it can express. These limits are part of ritual's value, though, as they make participation in a ritual comparatively easy. After all, as discussed above, ritual does not simply aim to communicate. While it does have an expressive dimension, at least as important is its role in constituting us as part of a shared community. Even something as simple as "Please accept my condolences" reinforces, in a small but crucial way, our joint membership in a community of shared values. The accessibility of the social conventions of ritual is what makes this possible.

Rituals are so accessible, in fact, that they can be faked.[52] It seems plausible that one can perform them without feeling any of the emotions that are supposed to correspond, and perhaps even without experiencing any shaping of our future dispositions. Is this a problem for my view, or for the Confucian stress on ritual more generally? One possible response is simply to deny the premise and insist that a suitably observant person, given ample time, will always be able to tell what someone's behavior really shows about his or her emotional reactions. *Analects* 2:10 records Confucius as saying, "See what he bases himself on, observe what he follows, find out what he is comfortable with. Where can the man hide?"[53] I certainly think there is much to be said for this response, but it still allows that rituals might be successfully faked in the short term, and it has not offered us a definitive reason to think long-term faking will never be possible. A more thorough-going answer to the challenge will draw again on the idea that rituals create a "subjunctively shared arena." Faked ritual is still ritual, and can still have most of the effects for which we value ritual, even in the unlikely extreme case in which it is having no "shaping" effect on the person acting out the ritual.[54] For most of us, I presume, faking or forcing ritual is a regular occurrence, which does little to undermine its importance.[55]

In saying that ritual is accessible, it might seem that I am reading an egalitarian notion of civility into Confucianism where it does not belong. After all, are not the rituals described in Confucian texts often hierarchically delimited, with many of them only appropriately performable by members of the elite? My response to this is two-fold. First, distinctions of status and hierarchy are central parts of many rituals, but the rituals still marry participants into a single community even while recognizing (and reinforcing) these differences of status. As some contemporary commentators on Confucianism have pointed out, the result of rituals joining people together can therefore be to mitigate the substantive effects that their status differences might otherwise have on their lives: roughly, the idea is that the boss who engages in rituals together with his or her employees has a kind of bond with them, and is less able to simply ignore their interests.[56] Second, it is nonetheless true that contemporary social-political worlds are significantly more egalitarian than ancient China, and the rituals endorsed by contemporary Confucians will have to recognize this. One major area of change is gender relations. As some contemporary thinkers have shown, a strong critique of gender inequality can be mounted in terms of Confucian ethics itself, making the rejection of oppressive rituals all the more pressing for contemporary Confucians.[57]

This reference to the critique and revision of rituals that are oppressive brings to center stage the possibility of tension between the rituals of civility and our full-fledged ethical judgment. We might imagine a range of cases. The least fraught are those situations in which the rituals have explicit room for exceptions built-in, as Fan mentioned above. Moderate cases will be those in which one's ethical judgment pushes in one direction and the rituals push in another, though one is not tempted to therefore conclude that the ritual itself is flawed. Rituals surrounding gender relations, finally, might be instances of the most extreme situation, in which the rituals partly constitute and express values that are seriously problematic. Consider for a moment the middle range of cases. Up until now I have been focusing on the sister-in-law case from the *Mencius*, which seems a clear instance of when rituals should be overridden. But many other cases are not so straightforward. Mencius is recorded as saying:

> Suppose a man treats one in an outrageous manner. Faced with this, a
> gentleman will say to himself, "I must be lacking in humaneness and

propriety, or else how could such a thing happen to me?" When, looking into himself, he finds he has been humane and proper, and yet this out-rageous treatment continues, then the gentleman will say to himself, "I must have failed to do my best for him." When, on looking into himself, he finds he has done his best and yet this outrageous treatment contin-ues, then the gentleman will say, "This man does not know what he is doing. Such a person is no different from an animal. One cannot expect an animal to know better."[58]

There are multiple dimensions to this fascinating passage, but the one relevant to our present concern is that Mencius says one should respond initially with civility to outrageous treatment. That is, one's initial judg-ment is that one has been unjustifiably wronged, but rather than criticize the other or respond equally "outrageously," one should respond civilly and review one's conduct and feelings. Keeping to a ritually proper response gives one space to question oneself, which also has the effect of striving to maintain the possibility of shared values: in the terms of Seligman and his colleagues, one keeps alive the subjunctive world. It is striking that Calhoun concludes her essay on civility with a similar sen-timent. She writes that she finds "something odd, and oddly troubling, about the great confidence one must have in one's own judgment (and lack of confidence in others') to be willing to be uncivil to others in the name of a higher moral calling. When one is very sure that one has gotten it right, and when avoiding a major wrong is at stake, civility does indeed seem a minor consideration. But to adopt a policy of eschewing civility in favor of one's own best judgment seems a kind of hubris."[59] Certainly one must be alive to tensions between ethics and ritual – especially because they may be indications of deep-seated problems – but it need not be the case that civility should always bow to one's ethical judgment.

There is one more facet of the ritual–ethics relationship that must be faced. The central idea of a "minimalist" approach to ritual, I have been saying, is that ritual is not all there is to say on questions of value. There is a distinct perspective on value that I have been calling "ethical." One version of such a distinction is Calhoun's; she contrasts the social conven-tions on which civility is based with the "critical moral point of view" that comes from adopting a moral theory like utilitarianism or Kantianism.[60] It is unfortunately beyond the scope of the present book to say very much about how we should understand Confucian ethics, but I believe that both Classical and Neo-Confucians differed radically from Calhoun on two key issues. First, rather than distinguishing between impartial "moral" value and other forms of "non-moral" value, Confucians understand value to be fundamentally continuous. Second, rather than a rule-centered ethical theory like utilitarianism or Kantianism, Confucians develop various versions of agent-centered virtue ethics.[61] In fact, "propriety" (*li*) is, according to many texts, one of the central virtues.[62] Both of these differences from Calhoun make it look as though it will be difficult for Confucians to draw as strict a line as Calhoun does between civility and ethics.

It is true that the Confucian's distinction between civility and ethics will not be as sharp as Calhoun's, but this is an advantage. Consider, for example, the sense in which propriety is a virtue. Calhoun also wants to say that civility is a "moral virtue" – virtues are secondary rather than primary on both Kantian and utilitarian accounts – but the only way she can do this is indirectly, via the importance of communicating respect. For a Confucian, in contrast, having a well-formed disposition toward propriety is itself part of the human good. The capacity to recognize and respond to social distinctions is a critical part of our human nature. It undergirds the effectiveness of ritual, and is also one of the dimensions in which flourishing, consummate human activity takes place. Several recent commentators have emphasized the insight of Confucianism in recognizing the importance of style: for all kinds of reasons, it matters very much how we do something, not just what we do.[63] The point of minimalism about ritual is not to minimize the significance of style, but rather to mark a distinction between the role ritual plays in all our lives, as the general social expectation of civility, and the endless opportunities we have for further perfecting our individual performances of propriety. For the purposes of civility, our motivation for following ritual is relatively unimportant; it matters little where we fall on the continuum from rigid self-control to fluid spontaneity. The latter end of the spectrum is ethically superior, but the former is sufficient for achieving the goals of civility with which we are here concerned. In addition, even quite consciously controlled (or "conscientious") civility can teach one the means to greater spontaneity, either consciously or unconsciously.[64] Finally, by construing the relation between the rituals and the virtue of propriety in this way, it is easier to understand the dynamic relationship between existing rituals and the all-encompassing demands of ethics. The rituals to which we hold ourselves are necessarily less particularistic and flexible than are ethical judgments; rituals also take on a life of their own, evolving in response to socio-economic changes. If it comes to the point that rituals obstruct the development and expression of our ethical sensibilities, or if we come to see that current rituals were based on mistaken ethical views of the past, then it is time to criticize and revise the rituals.[65]

Law and Ritual

In 1903, an anonymous Chinese author published an essay called "On Rights." The essay begins: "It is my agony that in my China, with her 300 rites (*li*) and 3,000 formalities, all the people have sunk into submission. No one suspects that anything is wrong, however, and far too many still boast 'Our land is the land of propriety.'"[66] The author goes on to complain that China's "feeble civility" (*wenruo*) has lasted for thousands of years.[67] The solution is to understand and embrace "rights" and "rights consciousness" so that Chinese individuals and China itself can stand up.[68] This author's view that China needed more rights and laws, and less ritual and civility, was the predominant position throughout most of the twentieth century in China (except for the Cultural Revolution in which neither laws nor civility were seen as valuable: the Communist understanding of ethics attempted to stand alone). In one way or another, most New Confucians favored the rule of law, though its exact relation to Confucianism remained a matter of controversy. In recent decades, though, the stridency of human rights-based critiques of China has encouraged a number of Confucian voices to articulate visions in which rights and laws are less important or even absent, and rituals once again assume pride of place. The goals of this section are to briefly survey this trend, and then to argue that we can and must find places both for law and for civility.

A key point shared by most of the writers who have argued for stressing ritual at the expense of law is that Western individualist metaphysical and epistemological assumptions make law necessary, while relational or collectivist Chinese assumptions render law superfluous and even problematic. Conversely, rituals are said to be well-suited to a Chinese framework and less well-suited to standard Western ones. In a recent and particularly sophisticated version of these arguments, Sungmoon Kim maintains that notwithstanding its talk of civil virtues, Western liberalism really never gets beyond the self-controlling suppression of passions: "Since these passions are inherently indeterminate . . . [liberalism] is still vulnerable to the politics of resentment," and in the end must resort to the rule of law.[69] Kim continues, "the Confucian practice of ritual propriety fills this important liberal lacuna by providing certain criteria in dealing with otherwise indeterminate passions." His idea is that instead of sublimating passions through self-mastery, Confucianism "dissolves [the lure of self-love] by rendering the self porous to others in the ritualistic relations across multilayered life realms."[70]

Whatever we make of Kim's critical remarks about "liberal virtue,"

I believe we can endorse much of what he says about the positive function of ritual. Ritual *can* play a major role in the kind of transformation he describes. The problem is that in actual social circumstances, it does not reliably do so, which leaves people desperately vulnerable. Many of those who have tried to work out a distinctively Confucian approach to human rights have ended up endorsing views on which rights need to be "earned" or are "granted by society."[71] The problem with this is that they can be lost or taken away, and not always appropriately. Rituals can become rigid and oppressive. To adapt a saying of New Confucian Mou Zongsan's, if not protected by law and rights, the healthy practice of political contestation can become swallowed by civility. It is best if we do not have to resort to laws and rights-claims in our interactions with one another, but if these mechanisms are not available, society risks "sinking into submissiveness."[72]

The solution, therefore, is to find a way to say "yes" both to rituals and to law: they are distinct from one another and are both needed.[73] This is by no means a simple task, because for a Confucian to say this means finding Confucian reasons for endorsing the rule of law, as well as exploring ways in which the precise meaning of the "rule of law" in a Confucian context may differ from its meaning in a liberal democratic context.[74] For present purposes, though, we can set those challenges aside and simply ask whether the notion of minimalist ritual, or civility, that I have been developing needs to be adjusted in any way in order to sit comfortably alongside laws and rights. I believe the basic answer is "no": there is no particular difficulty that needs to be solved. There will always be the potential for tension between laws and civility in any given case, however, just as there is the on-going possibility of tension between ethics and civility, as Calhoun emphasized. In some contexts – say, relations within a family – we hope that law will rarely if ever intrude on our rituals, and then only in extreme circumstances.[75] Voting offers a more complicated case of balancing law and ritual. As Paul Woodruff has emphasized, voting is a ritual as much as it is a law-governed political institution.[76] If the ritual dimension dominates, it may be serving to mask imbalances of power, and thus be dangerous.[77] Part of what gives the rituals surrounding elections their force, in fact, is their association with laws before which all are equal.[78] When the combination of ritual, reverence, and impartial law is challenged, however, elections can lose much of their function, even if they succeed in identifying a unique winner through a process that can be claimed as "fair." One of the lasting impressions of the US presidential election of 2000 is the teams of lawyers deployed by each candidate, poised to challenge any inconsistency that might put their candidate at a disadvantage. While this can seem like a good thing – after all, fairness is a fundamental desideratum for elections – it also puts in the foreground an image of law as a tool to be exploited in one's interest, and undermines the significance of voting as ritual. Whenever we lean too far in the direction of law and lose track of the sustaining, constitutive role played by our rituals, we risk serious damage to the fabric of our communities and thus to our sources of meaning and value.

Conclusion: Ritual and Civility

My goal in this chapter has been to articulate and defend an interpretation of the Confucian concern with ritual (*li*) that meets several desiderata. First, it is minimal, in the sense of placing only modest demands on people and being accessible to those without advanced levels of ethical cultivation. Unlike maximal views of ritual, the view I have been developing is comfortable with the idea that ethical value goes beyond and can critique any given set of rituals. Second, ritual has a partial independence from context-sensitive ethical judgments. Because it plays a central role in the constitution of our communities, partly through the way it expresses a commitment to shared values, ritual has a viscous nature and is not easily changed. Third, ritual as we practice it meshes with the ethical virtue of propriety. Propriety is an important dimension of an ideal ethical response to a given situation. It disposes us to focus on the apt manner in which one should act, rather than simply on the intention, type of act, or outcome. In many cases, the apt manner of action is socially understood (as ritual), though the virtue of propriety should be seen as outrunning existing rituals. Finally, ritual is distinct from, but compatible with, the rule of law.

I submit that thus understood, Confucian ritual offers a robust model of civility and therefore an answer to the challenge from Thomas Metzger with which we began. Ritual propriety covers both the "political and polite," as do Western models of civility, and it is accessible to all, which is key to Metzger's idea of "doable virtue." By recognizing that this form of civility is "minimal" and so both subject to critique and a basis for further personal growth, we avoid the trap of the "village worthy," for whom the currently prevailing social norms are all one could ever want. Ritual is a rich notion, as both two millennia of the Confucian tradition and more recent Western analysts have helped us to see. By explicating civility as ritual, we have therefore learned a great deal both about the immediate functions of civility – for example, the way it helps to constitute a community's values – and about the ways in which civility contributes to, while being distinct from, the two other critical types of norms that should govern our lives, namely, the ethical and the legal.

7

Virtue, Politics, and Social Criticism: Toward Deference without Oppression

The idea of Confucian social criticism – and indeed, the whole project of Progressive Confucianism – may seem quixotic. After all, Confucianism has often been thought of as conservative rather than critical. *Analects* 7:1 tells us that the Master saw himself as one who transmitted rather than innovated, one who loved and was faithful to antiquity.[1] *Analects* 8:13 says, "If the Way is being realized in the world then show yourself; if it is not, then go into seclusion." And there have been no shortage of self-styled Confucians, from antiquity down to the present day, who did not challenge injustice in their societies, focusing – at most – on the ritual and moral purity of themselves and their families. Of course, there have been many Confucians who were critical of socio-economic injustice in their societies. Mencius has harsh words for rulers who neglect the well-being of their people; some of the followers of Wang Yangming developed his thought in a populist direction; and Huang Zongxi's critical manifesto, *Waiting for the Dawn*, shows a concern for the economic effects of bad politics and bad education.[2] In addition, the *Analects* itself is by no means opposed to social and political criticism. Consider 18:7, in which Zilu offers the following criticism – presumably, on behalf of Confucius – regarding a recluse who has withdrawn from engagement with society:

> Not to serve is to have no sense of duty. Distinctions of age and youth may not be set aside; how can duties of ruler and subject be set aside? He wants to keep his person pure but as a result he disorders the great social relationships. The gentleman's serving is merely doing his duty. That the way does not obtain: *this* he knows already.[3]

In other words, the result of an uncompromising insistence on purity is partial personal responsibility for disordering the world. Zilu is not stating that "dirty hands," in the sense of doing wrong in order to achieve a higher good, are necessary. Even if the reference to "seclusion" in 8:13 provides a kind of safety valve, the general Confucian expectation is that one will be able to act well in the dirty world. Zilu insists that our responsibility is to engage with the less virtuous. Indeed, part of being virtuous is to be motivated to engage in precisely this way.

In light of *Analects* 18:7 and other sources, I would argue that the classic Confucian texts provide little comfort for those who want to remain passive in the face of the many imperfections of our world.[4] Still, a contemporary, Progressive Confucianism must offer clear guidance as to why and how a Confucian today should engage in social critique. The aim of this chapter is to provide precisely that. While I draw on some Western philosophical and psychological theories, I will nonetheless articulate Confucian reasons and Confucian goals for progressive social criticism, without erasing the differences between Confucianism and other progressive doctrines. My first step is to show that Confucianism long ago anticipated an important finding of contemporary psychology: namely, our social and physical environments have significant effects on the ways and degrees to which we can be virtuous. Confucian insights in this regard have been limited by their particularism, however, so Confucianism has sometimes been blind to the systematic effects of large-scale social and economic arrangements. In fact, the same kind of logic that makes particular situations important also applies to the large-scale arrangements, so I argue that Confucians must actively concern themselves with their socio-economic environments. A particularly worrisome type of social arrangement is oppression – when a group is systematically immobilized or diminished – and so Progressive Confucians must stand against oppression, notwithstanding historical Confucian complacency concerning many types of oppression. Still, non-oppressive forms of hierarchy and deference are both possible and important, as any Confucian political philosophy must recognize.

Situations and Virtues

According to the *Analects* 10:12, if Confucius's mat was not straight, he would not sit on it. Why not? Was he obsessive-compulsive, or for some other reason obsessed with every last detail of ancient rituals? The text contains many other instances of scrupulous attention to the rites, but it also includes a few suggestions that undermine the idea that we can explain Confucius's behavior via his obsession with the past. In 9:3 he allows for change to a ritual, and in 3:18 we read: "The Master said, If one served one's ruler by observing every last detail of propriety, people would regard it as obsequious."[5] A more plausible explanation for Confucius's concern with his mat is suggested by the recent work of scholars who have recognized a strong resonance between Confucian teachings and contemporary social psychology.[6] Both Confucians and modern psychologists understand that human behavior has two main roots: inner sources like character traits, and external features of the particular situations in which we find ourselves. In fact, recent research has shown that we should not dichotomize inner and outer sources too strictly; "social-cognitive" approaches to moral functioning emphasize the interactions between inner and outer. For example, we understand an agent's moral functioning better when we parse a given "situation" in the terms that are salient to the agent, rather than as things "objectively" appear to a researcher.[7] Nor should we understand the inner merely in terms of character traits: current research suggests that a range of factors go into an individual's moral identity.[8]

Be all this as it may, for current purposes it will do no harm to talk of character traits and situations as the main factors determining one's ethical functioning. If we return to Confucius on his mat, it is intuitively plausible that neatness and order in one's surroundings support an inner calm and focus, and that this can have positive behavioral effects. Recent research backs up our intuition.[9] In other words, Confucius's concern that his mat be straight expresses recognition that insofar as we are concerned about appropriate behavior, we need to attend to our situations. The same point is clearly recognized by Xunzi, another important classical-era Confucian, when he explains why rituals call for corpses to be decorated with sweet-smelling flowers. He writes: "The way that death works is that if one does not ornament the dead, then one will come to feel disgust at them, and if one feels disgust, then one will not feel grief."[10] Xunzi sees that the situation – the presence or absence of flowers – exerts a powerful influence on one's emotions and, ultimately, on one's behavior. One of the most important functions of ritual, therefore, is the way that it structures situations such that people can readily respond in apt ways.[11]

So early Confucians understood the need to structure situations in order to influence behavior, and an important resource on which they drew in order to structure situations was ritual. However, Confucians were not content with relying on ritually structured situations. They sought to inculcate in each of us the virtuous character traits that would make one a "worthy," a "gentleman," or even a "sage." Sages' character traits were reliable even in the most inhospitable of situations. One example is Shun's abiding love for his parents even as they sought to harm him, as related in *Mencius* 5A:1–4. As Xunzi puts it, the goal of moral learning is to arrive at "fixity," which I submit means not being swayed by temptations or other situational features:

> Learning is precisely learning to pursue [the virtues of *ren* and *yi*] single-mindedly. To depart from it in one affair and adhere to it in another is the way of the common people ... When one has grasped virtue, only then can one achieve fixity. When one has achieved fixity, only then can one respond to things.[12]

In other words, the ultimate goal of moral education and personality development is reliable virtue. Confucians generally see this as a matter of gradual attainment that admits of degrees. Categories like "lesser Confucian (*xiaoru*)," "scholar (*shi*)," "worthy," and "gentleman" are all sometimes used to delineate levels of ethical attainment that go beyond the minimum but fall short of sagehood.[13] Insofar as ritual and situational design figure in moral education, therefore, we should seek to encourage and inhabit situations that promote the development of situation-independent traits. A detailed discussion of Confucian moral education is clearly beyond the scope of the present chapter, but many Confucians have insightful teachings concerning how to develop robust, situation-independent virtue. We must not simply mimic the sages nor go through the ritual motions, but make the sages' heartminds our own, which involves changing the ways we perceive and feel about our world.[14] Of course, simple practices can help: if one's thoughts are orderly and centered – as might be encouraged by a straight mat – then one is more likely to respond appropriately to whatever situation arises thereafter. The habits of attention encouraged by rituals can help in other ways, too, and arguably may be able to transform into deeper, more broad-based dispositions (like the "reverence" on which Zhu Xi and others put so much emphasis).[15] In sum, Confucians seem to have developed a theory that is both consistent with much contemporary psychology in its recognition of the importance of situations, and pushes beyond a reliance on situations toward full virtue.

For all the insight Confucians have manifested into the roles played by situations in our moral functioning, a central thesis of this chapter is that there are critical gaps in the traditional Confucian understanding of situations and virtue. There are key types of situations about which they say little or nothing. The situations I have in mind are different from those we have been discussing for one or both of two reasons. First, one group of situations concerns political activity, a type of activity that Confucians tend to construe so narrowly that its relevance to the vast majority of people is ignored. This blind spot is related to the way "the people (*min*)" are generally understood, on which see Chapter 3, and to the Confucian discomfort with legal and other sorts of institutions, on which see Chapter 4. The arguments of Chapters 3 and 4 have already pushed us toward recognizing that the political institutions of a Progressive Confucian polity will be very different from those of traditional Confucian China. My point here is to supplement those arguments with the thesis that the situations in which one can actively participate in shaping public goals and endeavors are of great importance to one's moral development. Sor-hoon Tan reminds us of John Dewey's take on this issue: "Human nature is developed only when its elements take part in directing things which are common, things for the sake of which men and women form groups – families, industrial companies, governments, churches, scientific associations, and so on." Tan herself adds, "A person who focuses solely on her own needs and wishes is ethically stunted, since she fails to recognize the sociality of human beings."[16] I believe that, although Tan draws on Dewey, a contemporary Confucian should say precisely the same things. After all, if a state were to make all the major decisions for its citizens, leaving them space for decisions only about personal matters, it would be infantilizing its citizens. That is, it would be denying them access to situations crucial for developing moral maturity. Genuine ethical development requires engaging with issues in all their complexity, because only by recognizing the many dimensions of each given situation can we see our way toward harmonious resolutions. Ethical maturity must involve listening carefully (and critically) to the advice of experts, rather than being subjects of an intellectual elitism.[17]

So one type of gap in Confucian recognition of the importance of situations concerns the political. The second type is best understood in social terms, though it will often have political and economic ramifications as well. In the next section I will develop the idea that oppression, which is the systematic immobilization or diminishment of a group, poses deep challenges to the moral development of individuals, and thus must be combatted by Confucians committed to the virtuous development of all. Oppression can be hard to see because of its structural and group nature. In addition, as contemporary virtue ethicist Christine Swanton has acknowledged, moralities that foreground the virtue of individuals (as Confucianism does, for all its emphasis on relationality) seem better-suited to dealing with small-scale rather than large-scale problems. Local concerns give individuals more room to make progress because such concerns tend to be more tractable, which can then have positive feedback effects, forestalling cynicism or despair.[18] Swanton adds that local successes may also help one develop capacities for dealing with larger problems, but her main point is that her virtue ethics faces challenges in extending itself in the direction of political philosophy. The same is true of Confucianism, and thus we have the gaps in attention that I have mentioned. Before exploring how Confucianism can fully meet these challenges, we need to more thoroughly articulate the main obstacle to Confucian social justice: oppression.

Oppression

Confucian Oppression

Since Confucians rightly recognize the importance of situational factors to ethics and to ethical development, once they recognize the ways that social situations can systematically undermine or limit the capacity of some individuals to develop virtue, Confucians should have a strong motive to criticize and reform the society. We must acknowledge, though, that traditional Confucianism did not follow this path. Instead, we find ample evidence that social distinctions of the kinds I will go on to argue can be oppressive were regularly endorsed. One example is the clear distinction between genders. *Mencius* 3A:4 is the *locus classicus* for the idea that one of the five ethical norms for human relationships that needs to be taught to the people is that there be "distinction (*bie*)" between husband and wife, and the idea that women are associated with the "inner (*nei*)," as opposed to the male "outer (*wai*)," came to be quite pervasive in Chinese society.[19] Now I want immediately to acknowledge that conceptions of gender and gender norms are complex and changing throughout Chinese history, and that Confucianism variously interacts with these norms – sometimes accepting, sometimes justifying, and sometimes critiquing – over time. Numerous studies have shown that simplistic images of women as mere victims are significantly misleading. One counter-narrative emphasizes a gradual shift from gender complementarity in early sources to a more dualistic and repressive "prudery" in the last millennium.[20] Other scholars contest this latter picture, pointing out that it ignores important complexities even in the late imperial period. Still, even the more nuanced picture of the norms and realities surrounding the *nei-wai* distinction in this later period offers us an excellent example of how Confucianism can be blind to systematic oppression.

As described in sources like Dorothy Ko's important *Teachers of the Inner Chambers: Women and Culture in Seventeenth-Century China*, the *nei-wai* distinction was pervasive in elite society. The gender-based division of labor was reinforced by the prohibition of women from participating in the civil service examinations and by norms calling for women to remain in their homes. Even the architecture of the courtyard home supported a firm distinction, with its inward-focused design and few – and thus controllable – openings to the street. At the same time, Ko explores the many ways in which *nei-wai* was neither firm nor impenetrable. For one thing, "despite moral precepts admonishing women to stay at home, even gentrywomen travelled a great deal, on trips ranging from long-distance journeys accompanying their husbands on official appointments to excursions for pleasure in the company of other women."[21] More significant for my purposes are twin trends that Ko describes as the "privatization" of Chinese life and the "private as public." By the first, Ko refers both to the increasing importance that domestic life, with its manifold objects and activities, came to take on in the (male) Chinese imagination; and to the increasingly prominent role that the family setting played in social and cultural activities – even including knowledge and learning.[22] There were thus many more opportunities for the lives and interests of women and men to intersect. With her phrase "private as public," Ko calls our attention to ways in which the activities of women transcended the boundaries of the inner chambers. For example, "a diligent, frugal, and chaste woman was publically recognized as a symbol of the family's moral uprightness";[23] women's poetry also circulated widely outside the home. A general theme of Ko's study is the active participation of women in creating and shaping their worlds: even footbinding, perhaps the most infamous symbol of women's oppression, comes across more ambiguously. Not mere victims, women in Ko's study come to life as agents, even though they are operating in a field characterized by significant constraints.

People do not have to be, or understand themselves to be, passive victims for them to be correctly characterized as subject to oppression. The key is the constraints: as I will elaborate below, oppression is about structural limitations on the ways in which a group can flourish or develop. If we look at the best-known texts advocating women's moral development, we will see precisely this at work. The texts tend to be marked as applicable only to women, with titles like *Women's Analects* (*Nü Lunyu*) and *Women's Classic of Filial Devotion* (*Nü Xiaojing*).[24] The latter emphasizes that wives have a responsibility to remonstrate with their wayward husbands that is analogous to the duties of sons to fathers and (male) ministers to rulers. Remonstrance, flowing from women's virtuous reactions to problematic situations, demonstrates that women are moral beings whose characters can be cultivated. Crucially, though, all the examples in the *Nü Xiaojing* remain within the scope of "inner" affairs. A queen criticizes her husband the king for rising late (and therefore neglecting affairs of court); a concubine refuses to violate propriety and ride with an emperor in public.[25]

Similarly, when the *Women's Analects* instructs women to "establish your proper self so as to become a [true] human being" – which resonates with ideas in the original *Analects* – it goes on to specify that women do this by "working hard to establish one's purity and chastity."[26] A similar message is expressed in Ban Zhao's famous (and earlier) *Precepts for Women (Nü Jie)* when she expressly limits the scope of her Four Virtues for women. As Ko summarizes, "in contrast to a man's expansionary arenas, a woman's calling lay at the stove and the spinning wheel and loom; her orientation was to be inward, and she was to be modest in personality, appearance, behavior, and movement."[27] We can see in all of these examples the limited sphere in which women were expected to operate and thus the limited kind of virtue to which they can aspire.

It is occasionally possible to detect, for example in the voices of certain women poets, a frustration or resistance to the limits imposed on women.[28] A remarkable exception is also found in the *Instructions for the Inner Chambers (Nei Xun)* written by the Ming dynasty Empress Xu. Empress Xu was deeply impressed by the example of her mother-in-law, Empress Ma (the wife of the dynasty's founder), who actively engaged in the affairs of the state, in one famous case interceding on behalf of the Confucian scholar Song Lian. The physical setting of Empress Xu's *Nei Xun* is still the inner chambers, but its moral and psychological setting is much less limited than that of other texts in this genre. In particular, she is explicit that the traditional Confucian virtues of humaneness, rightness, wisdom, trustworthiness, and ritual propriety apply to women as much as to men, and that women can become sages.[29] In the context of late imperial China, it has to be said that Empress Xu is the exception that proves the rule: it was possible for individuals to conceptualize things as she did, and in rare circumstances to act as she and Empress Ma did, but this does not change the structural fact of women's oppression in her society. Confucians *could* critique gender oppression; the point is that they almost never did.[30] Even if Confucians held that women had some potential for moral growth, the specific ways that gender was conceptualized provided only limited space for women's moral growth. As Lisa Rosenlee puts it, from a traditional Confucian perspective, women should not be perceived as mere victims, "unequivocally oppressed by men"; instead,

> . . . women are perceived not just as natural beings but also as cultural beings who, despite the structural limitations imposed on them, also strive to achieve cultural ideals through the means available to them, which are limited in comparison with the cultural resources available to men.[31]

Recognizing both the value in Confucian virtue ethics and the important ways in which such an ethics is compromised by sexism, Rosenlee therefore works in her book's final chapter to articulate a revisionist, contemporary Confucian feminism.[32]

My argument is not that core Confucian texts unambiguously call for the oppression of women. The classic texts contain considerable openness and ambiguity on these issues, which can be exploited to develop an explicitly non-oppressive vision of hierarchy and social relations, as I will do later in this chapter. Still, aspects of Confucian views (like the call for "distinction" between husbands and wives) lent themselves to the support of an oppressive social system, and Confucians did not do enough to criticize the system's various incarnations over the centuries. Much the same can be said for oppression of the social class of the "masses (*min*)." Because of the parallels and because I have already explored the relevant tensions – on the one hand, the idea that the *min* are passively reactive, like thermometers; on the other hand, the textual strand according to which "all people" can become sages – in Chapter 3, I can be quite brief here. Consider the famous invocation of the division of labor in *Mencius* 3A4:

> There are affairs of great men, and there are affairs of small men (*xiaoren*). Moreover, it is necessary for each man to use the products of all the hundred crafts. If everyone must make everything he uses, the Empire will be led along the path of incessant toil. Hence it is said, 'There are those who use their minds and there are those who use their muscles. The former rule; the latter are ruled. Those who rule are supported by those who are ruled.'

The implication here is that these distinctions are rigid and unchanging, although I will explore possibilities for flexibility below. It might be said on Mencius's behalf that he is not marking a moral distinction here: both "great" and "small," rulers and ruled, are moral beings, and in fact he goes on in this passage to discuss the importance of a basic moral education for the people (*min*) lest they "degenerate to the level of animals." I grant that Mencius sees a certain moral potential in the people and that "*xiaoren*" is not always a term of moral condemnation. Still, the general tenor of this passage is that there are distinct limitations to what "small men" can achieve, morally speaking, and I believe this is consistent with many aspects of the *Mencius*.

It cannot be denied that some Confucians over the centuries were sensitive to the problems posed by structural oppression of the masses. Some exploited the pregnant saying in the Analects that "In education there shall be no distinction of kinds" to argue for mass education.[33] As mentioned in Chapter 5, Mou Zongsan actually denied that traditional Chinese was characterized by class divisions because in principle any male could pass the civil service examinations and become a member of the governing elite, and in fact social mobility (especially downward, which is easier to measure from the available data) was more significant in China than in feudal Europe.[34] This seems to me more like an effort to explain away a problem than to grapple with it directly, however. I prefer the more direct methods of the great Ming dynasty Confucian Wang Yangming, who tried to shock his students out of their complacent acceptance of an oppressive society by telling them that "all the people in the streets are sages." Some of his students, members of the Taizhou group, took this to heart and directed their education activities to the masses.[35] So perhaps we can say that Confucians were somewhat more aware of class-based oppression than gender-based oppression, and tried to do more about it. Contemporary Confucians will have to do still more, partly because we understand the nature and harms of oppression much better today than did earlier generations.

Moral Luck

With respect to both class and gender, in short, traditional Confucianism would seem to be vulnerable to criticism. Before delving into the specific problems caused by oppression in more detail, it will be helpful to look at the general topic of "moral luck." Do Confucians accept that there are factors outside of one's control – matters of mere luck – that influence one's capacity for moral development? If so, does that mean that some people are less responsible than others for their moral failings? These questions are important because if Confucians were to deny the significance of bad moral luck – saying, for example, that we all have the same opportunities to develop our moral faculties, no matter what our circumstances – then it will be much harder to make a case that Confucians should care about oppression.

There are indeed some grounds for wondering whether moral luck is a category about which Confucians historically were concerned. Consider Confucius's well-known words concerning his favorite student, Yan Hui:

> The Master said, "Worthy indeed is this Yan Hui! One dish of food, a dipper of drink, living in a narrow alley: Others could not have borne their sorrow, yet for Hui it has no effect on his joy."[36]

Confucius says much the same about himself: "Eating coarse food, drinking water, crooking one's arm and pillowing upon it – joy may be found also in these circumstances."[37] A natural way to read these passages is as claiming that wretched circumstances do not matter to proper, even joyous, moral functioning. Passages from *Mencius* appear to reinforce such an idea. In 7A:3, we read:

> Mencius said, "Seek and you will get it; let go and you will lose it. If this is the case, then seeking is of use to getting and what is sought is within yourself. But if there is a proper way to seek it and whether you get it or not depends on the Decree (*ming*), then seeking is of no use to getting and what is sought lies outside yourself."[38]

In other words, moral betterment can be sought within oneself; it does not depend on another's bestowing it. Worldly success, by contrast, is not within one's own control. All one can do is pursue it in the proper way – which is, of course, the moral way, the same way that leads to one's moral betterment.

There is no question that these early Confucian sources insist that office, fortune, and fame are beyond one's control and unimportant for one's central task of becoming a better person. It would be reading too much into the passages, however, to conclude that they are denying any role for moral luck. Sean Walsh has pointed out that even if Yan Hui's means are modest, he still has access to food, drink, and shelter. Walsh further argues that there are many ways in which we can see recognition in the *Analects* of luck playing a role: it is important to be fortunate enough to live in a state with a good ruler, to find a good teacher, and to be surrounded by a community that observes the rituals, among other things, even if no one of these things is absolutely necessary.[39] In *Mencius* 6A7, we find agricultural analogies that make clear that moral maturation relies in part on things outside us:

> Take the barley for example. Sow the seeds and cover them with soil. The place is the same and the time of sowing is also the same. The plants shoot up and by the summer solstice they all ripen. If there is any unevenness, it is because the soil varies in richness and there is no uniformity in the benefit of rain and dew and the amount of human effort devoted to tending it. Now things of the same kind are all alike. Why should we have doubts when it comes to man?[40]

No matter how one unpacks this metaphor,[41] Mencius must hold that the context in which one matures, over which one has little or no control, makes a difference to how one turns out. Mencius's point is that humans (like barley seeds) are a "kind (*lei*)" and are thus alike, even though once the process of growth is underway, we can become very different from one another. As can be seen in the very next passage in *Mencius*, the impact of the "environment" can be quite destructive: Ox Mountain is denuded of foliage thanks to human activity.[42]

Supposing that we accept that luck can influence one's ethical development – and thus, presumably, one's ethical functioning – does this mean that we have limited responsibility for what we do? The evidence in *Mencius* concerning responsibility is interestingly mixed. On the one hand, the text sometimes sounds like it is at least partly absolving the "people (*min*)" of responsibility for acting badly when they are in desperate circumstances. Consider this passage from the end of 1A7:

> Only a Gentleman can have a constant heart in spite of a lack of constant means of support. The people, on the other hand, will not have constant hearts if they are without constant means. Lacking constant hearts, they will go astray and fall into excesses, stopping at nothing. To punish them after they have fallen foul of the law is to set a trap for the people. How can a benevolent man in authority allow himself to set a trap for the people?[43]

The ruler is being criticized here for what the people might do, not the people themselves. This is very much in keeping with the people-as-thermometer analogy I elaborated in Chapter 3: we do not blame a thermometer for registering a high temperature when it is hot out.[44] On the other hand, there are many passages that look to assign blame and responsibility not just to those who do wrong, but more relevantly, to those who fail to develop their moral characters properly. Recall that *Mencius* 7A:3 said, of developing a moral character, "seeking is of use to getting and what is sought is within yourself." Since "seeking is of use," that means that we can make progress, if we just make the effort. It is revealing that Mencius condemns those who "destroy themselves (*zibao*)" or "throw themselves away (*ziqi*)": even though he goes on to say that one cannot have a fruitful discussion with the former or work successfully with the latter, the very terms "destroy themselves" and "throw themselves away" imply personal responsibility. How, though, can we fit this idea of responsibility together with the apparent importance of moral luck?

Joel Kupperman's work on character and responsibility can be of use to us here. He contends that our actions are often the involuntary (i.e., not consciously chosen) results of an interaction between our character and our situation, and that our characters themselves are largely involuntary.

By this latter point he means that we cannot change our characters at will, and indeed sometimes even great efforts over extended periods of time will fail.[45] Nonetheless, he holds that often enough, we do have control over circumstances that will gradually reshape our characters, and as a result it is possible for one's character to change dramatically. We have enough control, that is, that "it makes sense to hold people responsible both for their characters and for actions that flow from their characters."[46] Kupperman's position is attractive because it allows us to honor both the insight (and empirical evidence, on which see below) that luck has a significant role in determining one's character and actions, and the powerful need (also backed by evidence) to hold that we can exert some control over ourselves and over the shape our societies take. Not only do we find both of these ideas in *Mencius*, but this seems to be the balance that later Neo-Confucians wanted to strike as well. Here is Cheng Yi (1033–1107):

> When Shu Xiang's mother heard Yang Siwo being born, she knew that he would certainly destroy his clan. There is nothing wonderful in this. He was endowed at birth with bad psycho-physical stuff (*qi*), so that there was a coherent possibility (*li*) that he would destroy his clan. This is why she knew it when she heard the sound of his voice. If he could have learned to conquer his psycho-physical stuff and restore his nature, this misfortune need not have happened.[47]

As A. C. Graham comments, "Wherever there is a crossroads, the path by which one has arrived does not determine which alternative one will choose."[48] One's current "psycho-physical stuff" – i.e., one's character and other physical and psychological traits – may incline one to choose a problematic direction, but the Way (*dao*) remains open to one.

Oppression and Systematic Moral Luck

I thus conclude that Confucians from throughout the tradition have been able to find room for the idea of moral luck. At the same time, I believe we have seen evidence that the Confucians – like virtually all virtue-oriented theorists in the West – have not taken moral luck seriously enough. The position that I have found in Confucians and in Kupperman acknowledges that luck plays a role in a given person's readiness for and ease of progress in moral development, but not so much of a role that individuals can appropriately abdicate responsibility for their characters or for their actions. Furthermore, the highest praise is reserved for those who act well with the ease of a sage, on the basis of a firm and mature character. The role of luck is thus recognized but then set aside, either because it is ultimately not very important or because there is nothing we can do about it.[49]

In one sense we can readily do something about luck: if one governs well or teaches well, then the likelihood is increased of one's people or students having a good situation – that is, a lucky one – in which to mature. Of course Confucians will agree; this is exactly the kind of luck that they tend to talk about, as canvassed in Walsh's essay.[50] The reason that they nonetheless do not take luck seriously enough is that they miss the fact that there are structural features of even a (by their lights) well-governed society that systematically undermine the possibilities for some inhabitants to develop morally. Inspired by the work of some contemporary feminist philosophers, I maintain that the problematic nature of oppression has not been adequately understood within traditional Confucianism, and that a central aspect of oppression's badness is the predictable, systematic way in which it limits or undermines people's character.[51] This is a kind of systematic bad moral luck that Confucians must take more seriously.

The most detailed account of the consequences of oppression from a virtue-ethical perspective comes from Lisa Tessman, to whose work I will turn in a moment. First, though, let us consider oppression more generally. Iris Marion Young's well-known analysis of oppression will do nicely for our purposes.[52] The kind of oppression with which we are concerned has three key features: (1) it is a structural feature of everyday, ingrained social practices, rather than the result of a tyrant's policy; (2) it "immobilizes" or "diminishes" its subjects; and (3) the subject of oppression is always a group. On Young's telling – which I find to resonate well with the deep Confucian emphasis on relationality – individuals are partly constituted by groups. Young details five types or "faces" of oppression which, individually or severally, are sufficient to describe the oppression of any group: exploitation, marginalization, powerlessness, cultural imperialism, and violence. In each case, she explains how being the subject of such a pattern of social practices leads to members of the group being immobilized or diminished. For example, "marginalization is unjust because it blocks the opportunity to exercise capacities in socially defined and recognized ways."[53] Young's conception of social justice, with its emphasis on enabling the development and exercise of individual capacities, is close enough to a Confucian conception that Contemporary Confucians will readily be able to adapt an analysis based on Young's understanding of oppression.

Oppression harms more than one's capacity for full moral development,[54] but I submit that it is the diminishment of moral capacity to which

Confucians should be especially attentive. Oppression has three major negative consequences on virtue or character development. First, it can make it more difficult for an individual to develop character traits that are widely recognized as virtuous. Second, it can encourage the formation of what Lisa Tessman calls "burdened virtues": these are character traits that either contribute to a better life under the oppressive circumstances or offer one the possibility of resistance to oppression, but which are in one way or another problematic. Third, in a world with oppression, those who are privileged may suffer from what Tessman calls "the ordinary vices of domination." In highlighting the kinds of moral damage that flow from oppression, we must be careful not to simplistically blame the victims.[55] Still, given that Confucians should find the enabling of moral growth for all to be a powerful motive to social activism, it is important that we cautiously examine the ways in which oppression damages its victims.

Tessman's discussion of problems with blaming the victim helps us to see one way in which discussing moral damage can go wrong: such an analysis can be used as a further tool to oppress the group in question.[56] A second potential problem is especially salient in work like mine, and can be approached in terms of Young's category of "cultural imperialism." Young explains: "Cultural imperialism involves the universalization of a dominant group's experience and culture, and its establishment as the norm"; the oppressed group's meanings are rendered invisible.[57] For our purposes, wanting to avoid this kind of oppression translates into being particularly careful not to assume that any experience different from that of privileged contemporary Americans must be inferior, undesirable, and likely the result of oppression. That is, we must not jump from observing that the experiences and values of women in traditional China were different from those of current white middle-class women in the United States, to the conclusion that the Chinese women were oppressed (and that the Confucians of their day ignored or participated in their oppression). To make such a leap without explaining wherein lies the oppression, and explaining why it counts as oppression in terms Confucians should accept, is to partake of cultural imperialism.[58]

The reasons that, notwithstanding these two dangers, we must still confront the moral damage that comes from oppression are that evidence of the damage is compelling, and precisely this kind of harm should best motivate Confucians to recognize, confront, and correct the oppressive structures. Consider first the ways in which oppression can make it more difficult to develop virtues. As discussed above, the *nei-wai* distinction clearly limited the scope within which elite, late imperial women could envision and exercise virtue. Confucians are committed to the idea that "inner sageliness (*neisheng*)" – which is to say, the development of a virtuous character – is intimately related to "outer kingliness (*waiwang*)," which refers to all kinds of action in the outer, public, political world.[59] Involvement with the public world is crucial for two reasons: first, it better enables one to develop the appropriate balance between personal and impersonal concerns; second, by engaging with more types and dimensions of value, one better learns to react harmoniously to complex situations of apparent conflict.[60] This is of course not to say that men's access to the outer world automatically leads to virtue, nor even that women's very restricted access automatically denies them the possibility of sagely virtue. The point is that because of oppressive constraints, it is more challenging for women to develop what Confucians understand to be full, human virtue.[61]

The second source of harm is more subtle: oppressive circumstances can encourage the formation of "burdened virtues." Lisa Tessman outlines a continuum of traits that might be encouraged (or even self-consciously developed), ranging from those that would be unproblematically good in non-oppressive circumstances to those that would not be chosen in a better world. Some examples she offers of the latter type of trait include unrelenting anger, sacrificial courage, and loyalty to comrades: in each case, she discusses at length why such traits are often endorsed by those living under oppression, and yet details the harms that come to those with the traits.[62] Anger, courage, and loyalty are all connected to resisting oppression. Another type of burdened trait that can be encouraged by oppression includes whatever might help one to the best available life under the circumstances; Tessman suggests denial and numbness as possibilities.[63] In the context of late imperial China, feminine chastity looks like an example of this latter kind of burdened virtue. It was explicitly lauded and, as mentioned earlier, the example of a chaste widow would sometimes project into the public world, offering the woman a tangible, if somewhat restricted, kind of public influence. Still, the burdens of this virtue seem clear, whether from the perspective of human emotions that need to be suppressed or from within the framework of Confucian ethics itself: Ko points out that the demand for widows to be chaste could lead to tensions and conflicting loyalties "arising out of the woman's multiple responsibilities as wife, kin, and daughter."[64]

The last type of moral damage resulting from oppression is what Tessman calls the "ordinary vices of domination." As the name suggests, these are harms that attend to the privileged in an oppressive society, rather than to the oppressed. Even those who do not actively participate in repressive practices, according to Tessman, may come to suffer from one or another form of these vices. At the more extreme end of the spectrum, she lists callousness, greed, and dishonesty; less dramatic forms of these "ordinary vices" include milder self-centeredness, indifference, and laziness. Tessman's argument is that most people of privilege suffer from one or more of these vices.[65] Confucians will certainly recognize these vices – most especially selfishness, which features centrally in Neo-Confucian discourse – but they nonetheless miss ways in which social structures can encourage not attending to the plight of others. Of course, nothing here is meant to say that the Confucians were worse than others in China or in the West at noticing or critiquing oppression, nor, obviously, that there are no problems in non-Chinese or non-Confucian societies. Tessman's critique is aimed at the contemporary West. For all the differences between modern, Western societies and pre-modern, Chinese societies, the argument of this section has been that structural oppression is a problem for both, and therefore that a Progressive Confucian political philosophy will have to find a way to respond to the challenge of oppression.

Solutions

The general conclusion that the chapter has been driving toward is that Confucians must be political and social activists, seeking in particular to identify and eliminate systematic grounds of oppression. There is still quite a lot to be said, though, about what this means. To begin with, while I have argued that the burdens oppression places on people provide Confucians with important reasons to oppose it, I have not spelled out the way that such reasons figure into the Confucian understanding of individual motivation. Insofar as recent Confucians have attended to the need for social criticism, they have frequently adverted to the motivating power of what they call "concern consciousness (*youhuan yishi*)." As John Berthrong says, New Confucians like Mou Zongsan and Xu Fuguan took concern consciousness to be the motivation behind the "ceaseless toil and work that the sage kings lavished on their societies," as well as the stimulus for students of Confucianism across the ages to cultivate their heartminds "for the sake of serving the world."[66] Fundamentally, concern consciousness is a way of referencing the capacity of the core Confucian virtue of humaneness (*ren*) to expand its scope so as to encompass the lives and needs of many others – even including, for later Confucians at least, the concerns of the whole cosmos. This kind of concern, though, tended to still be particularistic rather than systematic. The scope of the sage's concern might take in vast numbers of individuals, as when *Mencius* 1B:3 tells us, "If there was one bully in the empire, King Wu felt this to be a personal affront,"[67] without noticing the insidious, systematic signs of oppression. Recognizing oppression – seeing it correctly, which is to say seeing it as wrong – is thus an affective/cognitive capacity that helps to channel humaneness the right ways. This is why we need to supplement talk of humaneness and concern consciousness with the categories of systematic moral luck and oppression. One solution that I have identified, then, is this: when the motivational capacities of humaneness and concern consciousness are combined with the capacity to recognize oppression, Confucian agents will be much more reliably motivated to engage in social criticism. Confucian ethics must find additional room for the category of oppression; Confucian programs of moral education must emphasize the signs and harms of oppression; and Confucian participants in politics must be on the lookout for ways in which the political and legal systems may support oppression. On these bases, we should expect that such a society informed by Progressive Confucianism will be better able to approach the ethical ideals for which Confucians strive.

For three reasons, I believe that even while contemporary Confucians identify and criticize oppression, they should not reject all forms of hierarchy and deference, both of which are sometimes mistakenly identified with oppression. By "hierarchy," I simply mean any social structure that marks systematic differences of status so that some are "higher" than others. Functional divisions (in particular, distinct economic or political functions) need not be hierarchical in this sense, although status differences will often track functional differences. Differences of power form a third dimension that is independent, in principle, from both status and function, though of course it will often be bound up with one or both of these. Deference, which often goes hand-in-hand with hierarchy, means that people in one position will defer to those in another. The first reason for holding on to some forms of hierarchy and deference is that they are, I baldly assert, inevitable in human societies. I offer this consideration not so much as a major argument in favor of my position, but rather as a stimulus to reflection: there are hierarchies of many kinds throughout all contemporary societies, and we would do well to learn from their diverse forms, functions, and potential values. Second, the understanding of human relationality in terms of hierarchy and deference is so pervasive in Confucian writings that it is difficult to imagine that a doctrine rejecting hierarchy could ever count as Confucian.[68] Status distinctions are crucial to the Confucian understanding of ritual, and Confucians have also argued in various ways that the making of hierarchical distinctions, and reacting to such distinctions with deference, are both natural and normative for humans.[69]

Third, and most crucially, deference and hierarchies can be extremely valuable, and they can be realized in non-oppressive ways. In order to spell out and defend these two claims, it will be helpful to note that while deference and hierarchy often come together, hierarchy is not always a necessary setting for deference. In many situations a guide, teacher, or other kind of leader may emerge from a group without bearing any ante-cedent marker of higher status in the relevant dimension. Consider the contrast between following an official tour guide – he may be carrying a flag – and following someone who stands out in an emergent situation, someone who simply "seems to know what she's doing," and so we defer. Another way in which hierarchy and deference can come apart is when, in a specific type of situation, the apt thing is for one status-equal person to defer to another, or even for a status-superior person to defer to someone with an inferior status. An example of the former might be holding open a door: whoever reaches the door first holds it for the others, expressing a modest form of deference. In conversations, we tend to defer to whom-ever has the floor, although a good committee chair may endeavor to ensure that a shy or soft-spoken committee member gets a say – even if that involves seeing that a more senior member defer to a more junior one. It might be tempting to say that in each of these cases, what we are actually faced with is the momentary and fluid shifting of status, so that deference and hierarchy always perfectly track one another. Although I do think that it is important that hierarchies be seen as malleable, we should nonethe-less resist simply conflating apt deference with the existence of hierarchy. Hierarchies are expressed through markers of status and therefore have a somewhat viscous nature. A key aspect of their value lies in their ability to call attention to expected patterns of deference; our lives would not go very well if we were continually waiting for someone to step forward and say, "Follow me!" In this sense, the markers of hierarchies can be seen as a specific type of ritual: useful as a communicative shorthand (see Chapter 6).

Deference itself is central to many aspects of well-lived human lives. First, it communicates and enables an openness to learning and growth. By deferring to a teacher, we create a space in which we can become more or better than we currently are. This is consistent with recognizing that the processes of learning and growth will involve reflection, probing, and questioning; Zhu Xi's thoughts on how to read are eminently relevant here, as is Confucius's statement recorded in the *Analects* 7:22, "When I am walking in a group of three people, there will surely be a teacher for me among them. I pick out the good parts and follow them; the bad parts, and change them."[70] Deference never properly calls for rigid submission. A second and related value of deference is allowing us entry into what Lisa Rosenlee calls "the complex web of human relations in which the knowledge of the past is passed on from the elderly to the young."[71] Deference to the cultural tradition(s) that form one's heritage is closely related to deferring to teachers. Third, deference expresses a recognition of one's finite and fallible nature. Although Confucianism is perfectionistic and the ideal of sagehood is understood to be accessible, in principle, to actual people, the accessibility of sagehood goes alongside the idea that none of us is in fact a sage. Confucius repeatedly denied that he was.[72] Fourth, deference communicates both to oneself and to others the centrality of relationality to one's identity and well-being. By deferring and being deferred to, one enacts one's roles within relationships and groups. The fifth aspect of deference is its connection to non-coercive authority. In Chapter 3 I discussed Hannah Arendt's three-fold distinction among coercion, authority, and persuasion. As she sees it, authority is a demand for obedience based on hierarchical superiority, which is different both from the "external" threat of violence that supports coercion and from the egalitarian order within which persuasion finds its home.[73] As discussed in that chapter, I believe that a contemporary Confucian politics will have to make a central place for persuasion in the legitimizing of authority, but it is not the case that all forms of hierarchy and deference should disappear. Even in a state like the US, the normal course of things is for individuals regularly and appropriately to defer to legitimate authorities. Several of the features I have listed contribute to what can be labeled the sixth value of deference, namely, its contribution to fluid – and even graceful or beautiful – social functioning. When looked at on a broad scale, this fluid social functioning results in the dynamic social stability that Confucians call harmony. Finally, seventh, deference is one means of expressing respect. This respect can, on a Confucian understanding, be of two kinds: we respect people both because of the roles they occupy and because of their basic capacity to exercise moral agency (which capacity I discussed in Chapter 3 in terms of a sensitivity to Coherence).

I understand the value of hierarchy to lie in its ability to call attention to expected patterns of deference. On any plausible version of contemporary Confucianism, it should be uncontroversial that each of the seven aspects of deference is valuable. Confucians will in fact want to make the stronger claim that deference's distinctive contribution to the realization of each of these values shows that any ethic or ideology without a place for deference is thereby problematic. While I am sympathetic to this argument, I will not pursue it here because it would distract me from my main goal, which is showing that deference and hierarchy need not be oppressive. The most important point to realize in this regard is that, on the basis of all that I have just said, relations of hierarchy and deference are properly understood as occurring between individuals, not groups. One person aptly defers to another on the basis of a fit between the latter's role, experiences, learning, or skills, and the particular circumstance in which the two find themselves. I defer to Elaine in the courtroom because she is the judge, but not in the grocery store – or at least, not for that reason. If Elaine is older than me, I may defer to her in the grocery store as well. When people of one social group – identified by gender, ethnicity, religious affiliation, and so on – defer to members of another across situation-types, though, this smacks of oppression. I can see no reason why such cross-situational deference would be needed to achieve the valuable aims of deference, and the systematic inferiority imputed to the deferential group seems extremely likely to display one of the "faces of oppression" discussed by Young. Nor do "the young" or "the elderly" count as exceptions, since it is the relative age between two individuals that makes the difference, not someone's membership in a self-identified group of "the young."

In one sense, then, I have solved my problem: hierarchy and deference cannot be oppressive because they do not apply to group relations, yet oppression (in the sense of the term I have been using) necessarily applies to groups. Thus, no oppressive hierarchies. However, this is surely too easy. For one thing, status hierarchies are almost inevitably entangled with differences in wealth and power; I will explore pros and cons of such entanglements in this chapter's concluding section, below. Second, there is a looser sense of oppression according to which even individual-based relations of deference can be deeply troubling. The values of deference can be undermined if the relationship is characterized by any of the following six defeaters. The first, *rigidity*, occurs to the degree that participants resist recognizing changes to situations, statuses, or capabilities. Identifying superior status with membership in a particular group would be an extreme version of rigidity. *Coercion* is a second defeater, since at least when it is explicitly invoked, it denies the connection between deference and authority, and will tend to alienate one from the other valuable aspects of deference.[74] Third is *sacrifice*, by which I mean giving up a significant value without thereby realizing some other important end that one also endorses. Valuable deference relations do not demand sacrifice in this sense.[75] The fourth defeater, *omnivalence*, refers to situations in which one individual is hierarchically inferior (or superior) across all contexts, even if he or she is not inferior (or superior) to the same others in every one of these contexts. Deference is healthier when one is able to balance deferring and being-deferred-to. *Indefeasibility* is a clear problem, and applies when the superior's judgment is difficult or impossible to challenge. The sixth and final defeater, *emptiness*, occurs to whatever extent the occupant of a status-incurring role fails to embody the virtues and responsibilities owing to that role. Deference to an empty shell of a teacher, parent, or ruler has little or no value. All these defeaters will typically be matters of degree, so mixed cases – some disvalue but some value; perhaps a difficult judgment on whether continued deference is merited – are certainly possible.

If non-oppressive hierarchy and deference are only possible to the extent that the defeaters are not present, then our final step is to identify values and institutions that Confucians should encourage in order to minimize the presence of the defeaters in any given relationship. There are at least five supporter values. *Reverence* for shared ideals, before which we all fall short, is key.[76] This commitment to shared ideals will help inoculate us against several of the defeaters. Second, *imagination* and *openness* to alternative perspectives or ways of framing issues will be extremely healthy, since such openness will make it easier for all parties to see when growth and change are possible (as opposed to rigidity). Valuing *dialogue* – which means both questioning and responsive answering – has similar effects to imagination and openness. It is also worth noting that all three of the supporters mentioned so far reinforce the idea of one's own limits and fallibility, in the face of which it makes sense to be open to additional perspectives on Coherence. We thus might speak of *fallibilism* as a value in its own right. Fifth, I mentioned above that one of the values supported by deference was respect, both for people-in-roles, and for people-as-moral-agents. Insofar as one respects another, this will also help one to resist the defeaters, so *respect* can be both cause and effect of healthy deference. These values should form an important part of the Confucian ethical curriculum, since they will be key to the success of distinctively Confucian social arrangements. Finally, while Progressive Confucianism calls for both domestic legal rights and global human rights – either or both of which might be appealed to in order to resist oppression – protecting oneself through a rights claim will necessarily undermine the values sought via deference, so insofar as a robust ethical culture can be cultivated without its being oppressive, the society and its individuals will be better off.

Conclusion: Entanglements

It might be helpful at this point to list the main conclusions for which I have been arguing throughout this chapter:

1. Confucians have long understood the influence of situations on virtues.
2. Recognizing the role of situations and moral luck, Confucians should (but historically did not) recognize the significance of systematic moral luck.
3. Oppression is a particularly troubling kind of systematic bad moral luck, whereby the possibilities for ethical growth on the part of the oppressed are variously undermined.
4. Confucians should therefore be committed to the exposure and eradication of oppression.
5. Hierarchy and deference, which are often connected to talk of oppression, should be understood by Confucians as individual rather than group relations, and as bearing important values.
6. The values of hierarchy and oppression can be lost if hierarchical relations are characterized by any of the five defeaters, and so Confucians should combat the defeaters through direct critique and via the cultivation of the supportive values identified at the end of the last section.

In this concluding section of the chapter, I want to acknowledge two types of entanglements that make the task of Confucian social critique even more complicated. The first, which I will only treat briefly here, is the question of whether a Confucian ethical education, with its emphasis on particular moral perception, rituals, and harmony, will do a good job of enabling one to perceive oppressive structures in which one may very well be entangled. The second issue concerns entanglements between status distinctions, on the one hand, and wealth and power, on the other. Facing this issue will also offer an opportunity to reflect on a Progressive Confucian view of distributive justice.

Oppression can be hard to see. One reason for this is its structural nature, as discussed above: large-scale patterns can only be detected if one has the right experience and vantage-point. It is also important to remember that oppression is not the dramatic wrong-doing of a tyrant, but the everyday attitudes and structures of our lives. Insofar as oppression is "normalized," it is also rendered almost invisible. Confucianism stresses cultural education, yet what help is this in the face of culturally unacknowledged forms of oppression? According to feminist philosopher

Diana Meyers, a program of moral education like that of Confucianism will compound an independently existing tendency not to acknowledge one's victimization, with the result that good Confucians will "find it nearly impossible to see that employers, teachers, or peers at work or at school are oppressing them."[77] In Chapter 6 of *Sagehood*, I discuss Meyers's criticism and her suggested solution at some length. I argue there that we must avoid the mistake of thinking that the Confucian commitment to harmony is tantamount to desiring not to "rock the boat." Meyers is right to suggest that non-sages have important contributions to make to our moral ecology, even if her argument fails to convince that those with "rancorous emotions" will be more perceptive than sages.[78] The upshot is that while identifying oppression will sometimes be a challenge, Confucian education should be up to the task, especially when fortified by the explicit recognition that "oppression" is a category about which we should be concerned, and by the somewhat less-traditional "supportive values" I have already mentioned.

What, then, of entanglements among status, wealth, and power? The first thing that needs to be said is that Confucians have typically called for considerable alignment of these three dimensions. High social and moral statuses were supposed to go together, and should properly be accompanied by at least some degree of material wealth and political power. Since I have already had quite a bit to say about power (especially in its guise as "authority") in the present chapter and in Chapter 3, I will not dwell on that topic here. Instead, let us focus on the distribution of wealth and its consequences. While this is a complex topic on which different Confucians have had somewhat different views, we can roughly summarize the reasons for which they have argued that status and wealth ought to align as follows. First, material finery can serve an expressive role, helping to communicate status distinctions. Second, it offers a distribution scheme for apportioning limited goods. Those of lower status get less than those above, but (if the scheme is going to work) the portions of those above will be limited as well.[79] It might also be thought that wealth can actually assist in motivating deference or long-term improvement (and thus increased status), though consistent Confucian criticism of being motivated by personal benefit makes this a tricky issue. At the very least, material comfort might be able to appropriately support one's remaining in an onerous position of authority. It is also clear that significant material deprivation makes deference and other virtuous behavior much more difficult, as discussed earlier in relation to moral luck.

Studies of Confucian attitudes toward distributive justice, both historically and in the contemporary period, make it clear that while Confucians are not radical egalitarians, they do tend to support one or another kind of limitation on imbalanced distribution. We can find in classical Confucian writings the materials out of which principles of "sufficiency" and "priority for the worst off" can be constructed.[80] Sor-hoon Tan has found evidence in various early Confucian sources that inequalities of virtue and merit are not supposed to be translated directly into equivalent inequalities of distribution.[81] The Analects contains a statement according to which "it is a problem when wealth is unequally distributed (*bujun*)," though a recent essay shows quite powerfully that this idea of "equality" may be best understood along the lines of Aristotle's notion of "proportional equality."[82] For instance, according to the Han dynasty Confucian Dong Zhongshu, "Let the rich be rich enough to show their wealth yet not be pretentious; let the poor have enough to take care of their lives without being worried. This is the standard for being even (*jun*)."[83] Many modern Confucians, finally, have found socialism quite attractive.[84]

My discussion of the potential defeaters for valuable hierarchy and deference sheds some additional light on these Confucian views of distributive justice. Modest differences in wealth can serve the functions listed earlier just as well as dramatic differences, but dramatic differences are much more likely to cause problems. Large differences in wealth will tend to make hierarchy both more rigid and more omnivalent – for example, with teachers deferring to their rich students, rather than the other way around. Another worrisome example from contemporary America is the reliance of political leaders on financial support from the super-wealthy (including large corporations): expected and appropriate kinds of deference are reversed, as all bow to the mighty dollar. Rigid and omnivalent status differences entail group-based rather than individual role-based hierarchies, which – as discussed earlier – make oppression much likelier. Some degree of entanglement between status and wealth is inevitable and perhaps even beneficial, but contemporary Confucians must follow their forbearers in keeping economic inequality in check, lest it lead to oppression.

Conclusion: The Shape of Confucian Virtue-Ritual-Politics

Twentieth-century New Confucians like Mou Zongsan endorsed what they called the "Learning of the Heartmind and Nature (*xinxing zhi xue*)," which emphasized the ethical, metaphysical, and psychological dimensions of the Confucian tradition. As I have discussed above, Mou consistently argued that this ethics-focused Learning of the Heartmind and Nature also required a new politics, and self-restriction is meant to explain the relation between ethics and politics. Unfortunately, many critics of New Confucianism have seen this "new politics" as simply the grafting of Western liberal democracy onto Confucianism, with the seemingly mysterious idea of self-restriction providing the hocus-pocus to make the combination seem tenable. In addition, neither Mou and his contemporaries, nor more recent Kantian New Confucians, have done very much to explain how New Confucian politics would be distinctively Confucian. The result has been to cede much of the field in political philosophy to Institutional Confucians who argue that their emphasis on creative development of Confucian social and political institutions offers a firmer ground for contemporary Confucian political thinking. As discussed in my Introduction, a variety of Neo-Classical and Synthetic positions have also begun to emerge that try to balance the ethical and political/institutional dimensions of Confucianism in different ways.

Progressive Confucianism endeavors to capture the actual importance of self-restriction to our understanding of the dependencies among three types of values: ethical, political, and ritual. The main objective of this Conclusion is to build on points that have been made throughout the book in order to emphasize the distinctive way that Progressive Confucianism balances these three dimensions. Ethical norms are highly specific, deriving from one's balanced, virtuous perception of all the values relevant to a particular situation. Political norms encompass laws, domestic rights, and human rights. They are publically codified and adjudicated, and their implementation is backed up by state power. Ritual norms are codifiable to a greater degree than ethical norms; as emphasized in Chapter 6, one of the key aspects of rituals is their offering us an accessible "shorthand" for communicating with one another. Yet rituals are grounded in and enforced by society rather than state, and regularly apply in many intimate contexts where political norms intrude only as a last resort. According to Progressive Confucianism, healthy human societies (and flourishing individuals) need all three of these dimensions to be largely independent from one another. If rights were instead to be seen as a type or offshoot of ethics, then there would be a risk of ethical subjectivity "swallowing" rights; if rights and rituals are conflated, then we risk losing crucial bonds between us that rituals help to support, as all of us simply become "atomistic" individuals relating to one another through law and rights. One general way of articulating the goal of Progressive Confucian political philosophy is that it aims at harmonizing these three dimensions of value. It is tempting to draw an analogy to a three-legged stool, since each of the three types of norms are necessary for a robust and progressing individual or society. The problem with this analogy, though, is that none of the three dimensions are fully independent from one another. They rely on and feed back into one another, sometimes via critique. The three dimensions exist in a kind of dynamic tension whereby each has the potential to both support and to resist the others.

Culturalism, Pluralism, and Political Philosophy

Throughout this book we have encountered these three types of value. The primary focus has been on political values and institutions, of course, but interactions with ethical or ritual concerns have come up repeatedly. For the most part, though, the nature of these relationships has remained quite abstract. A second goal of this Conclusion is to see what can be said in a book of this kind about the actual shape that a Confucian virtue-ritual-politics might take. In order to make progress on this question, we first need to think about the contexts in which it might be raised. Are we imagining a thoroughly Confucian state and society? Or a scenario less distant from contemporary reality, in which Confucians play some role in the political process and some role in social institutions, but are not dominant? Even granting that many Confucian values will be at least partly shared by non-Confucians – and setting aside the possibility that among the Confucians themselves there may be significantly differing understandings of goals or values – the possibility of pluralism poses an interesting challenge to Confucian political philosophers today. Gan

Chunsong, a contemporary Chinese philosopher, argues that among the twentieth-century New Confucians and their contemporary heirs, there is a tension between pluralism or even cultural relativism, on the one hand, and "centralism (*zhongxin zhuyi*)" or universalist philosophy, on the other. Is there a multiplicity of legitimate value systems in the world, or just one (perhaps one on which we are gradually converging)? Is Confucianism, as representative of Chinese culture, something just to be preserved in China or for Chinese, or is it something of crucial importance to the world, as true for Americans as it is for Chinese? In the idea that Confucianism is one kind of "spiritual resource" among many others in the world – as seen for example in the work of contemporary Confucian Tu Wei-ming – Gan sees a retreat from the more ambitious program of earlier New Confucians like Mou Zongsan.[1] A strong form of pluralism that we can call "culturalism" is clearly at work in some of the thinkers whom I have identified as Institutional Confucians; indeed, some explicitly justify their proposals through their alleged ability to save or revive Chinese culture.[2] This kind of thinking admittedly is not friendly to pluralism within the borders of a nation devoted to Chinese culture, but embraces pluralism with respect to other nations and cultures.[3]

What, then, of Progressive Confucianism? As political philosophy rather than any kind of culturalism, Progressive Confucianism aims to articulate truths about how people should best organize their societies, and these truths should apply everywhere.[4] Still, many aspects of Progressive Confucianism suggest that in a pluralistic domestic context, its adherents will be ready and willing to serve as coalition partners with adequately like-minded non-Confucians in both political and social projects. As practitioners of Rooted Global Philosophy, Progressive Confucians endeavor to learn from their encounters with other philosophies. We see this in Mou Zongsan's encounter with Hegel and Kant, and we see it in the present book's engagement with non-Confucian philosophers like Zhang Shizhao (Chapter 4) and Zhao Tingyang (Chapter 5), and with feminist thinkers in Chapter 7. The account of authority offered in Chapter 3 emphasizes taking seriously all perspectives on Coherence, and there is no reason why the views of non-Confucians should be excluded from this framework. The final section of Chapter 7 has emphasized the importance of several "supportive values," among them dialogue and fallibilism, which also tend to support respectful, open participation in pluralistic politics. In a similar vein, recall that one lesson I drew concerning the rule of law in Chapter 4 was that embracing politics and law means also embracing the conflictual world of politicians and lawyers. None of this is meant to suggest, of course, that when faced with a pluralistic political environment, Progressive Confucians will simply abandon their commitments. They will seek to educate and persuade, emphasizing aspects of our shared human experience (like the importance of rituals, perhaps) that are not adequately salient from the vantage points of others in government or society. Confucius himself offers a memorable example of someone who works resolutely to make progress in a very difficult environment: Confucians today can take inspiration from his model.

Rituals, Education, and the State

With these thoughts about pluralism in mind, let us turn to consider the relations among ethics, politics, and ritual in more detail. To begin with, I have characterized my understanding of ritual as "minimalist," but rituals are still crucial to fluid, well-functioning groups and societies, and play important roles in individual education. As discussed in Chapter 7, one of the main ways in which we structure situations so as to increase the likelihood of both appropriate behavior and personal ethical growth is through ritual. Ritual is also linked to the idea of hierarchy, defended in Chapter 7 as signaling when deference is expected. Of course, an important theme of both Chapters 6 and 7 has been that existing rituals and hierarchies can go wrong in a variety of ways, and so we have to be able to draw on both ethical and political resources to critique problematic rituals. What, though, if our problem runs in the opposite direction? That is, what if ritual practice in a society is too weak, such that healthy social interactions are not adequately promoted? In somewhat different ways, both contemporary, post-Maoist China, and the contemporary United States, might be seen as exemplifying this problem. If such a diagnosis is accurate, would a Confucian political philosopher advocate the use of political resources – say, legal intervention of some kind – to support ritual practice?[5]

Institutional Confucians like Jiang Qing and Kang Xiaoguang are quite clear in their advocacy of a state-supported Confucian church that would, in turn, both teach and advocate Confucian rituals.[6] One key to the justification of such an approach is its alleged role in protecting "Chinese culture," as discussed and criticized in Chapter 3. I suggest that if we look to the historical relation between the Chinese state and Confucian rituals for inspiration, we will find a more promising point of departure – in part because it is more consistent with domestic pluralism – than the Institutional Confucian church-based approach. Historically, there were two main ways in which the Chinese state supported Confucian rituals: directly, in the form of large-scale state rituals and state support for Confucian temples, and indirectly, since the state-sponsored educational curriculum included Confucian texts that lauded the importance of ritual.[7] Both approaches can be adapted to the contemporary world of Progressive Confucianism. For example, no matter whether they are participants in a pluralistic polity or members of a thoroughly Confucian society, Progressive Confucians will emphasize the ritual character of political campaigning and elections. "Ritual" does not mean formulaic and empty: as emphasized in Chapter 6, rituals help us to establish our identities and articulate our values, even with strangers. Since Progressive Confucianism is in some important ways new, it will push for some invention of new public rituals, in order to best ensure that the rituals express its goal of a non-oppressive, inclusive quest for virtue.

As for the role of ritual in a modernized version of Confucian state-sponsored education, this is an issue best treated together with the question of state-sponsored ethical education. There is a vibrant debate within Western political philosophy over whether it is appropriate for states to support a particular set of values by including them in state-sponsored educational curricula. Many liberals have argued that states should be "neutral" between different visions of what a good life entails. One opposing argument to liberal neutrality comes from communitarians, who believe that a shared grounding in a particular tradition and its values is essential for communal flourishing. A different and less radical response to liberal neutrality has been developed by philosophers who are sympathetic to liberal values but who believe that neutrality is a much stronger constraint on states than is necessary or appropriate. These philosophers favor a limited amount of state "perfectionism": that is, in certain ways states can work to "perfect" their citizens by advocating particular values. According to this approach, which I will follow Joseph Chan in calling "moderate perfectionism," some degree of state perfectionism is both necessary for a well-functioning state and society, and does not bring with it unacceptable costs. In particular, values like individual autonomy are not sacrificed, because moderate perfectionism endorses only widely shared values, does this in non-coercive ways, and contains independent protections for autonomy.[8]

It is still something of an open question whether moderate perfectionism can fully accommodate core liberal commitments,[9] but our concern here is not with liberalism. I introduce the idea of moderate perfectionism because it seems to nicely capture the approach to moral education favored by New Confucians like Mou Zongsan or Tang Junyi, and I believe it fits well within the parameters of Progressive Confucianism. Mou argued that some of the tenets and texts of Confucianism should be taught in public schools, but emphasized that the values we should publicly advocate are limited to the "minimum and universal way of humanity," by which he seems to have meant basic virtues like humaneness, righteousness, propriety, wisdom, and faithfulness.[10] In addition, Mou's consistent position that ethics must "restrict itself" in accordance with laws and rights matches well with George Sher's argument that since systems of laws and rights are adequate to protect against oppressive paternalism, it is gratuitous to demand what Sher calls "prophylactic neutrality" when neutralism brings with it the cost of losing the good done by perfectionist moral education.[11] We can see a roughly similar attitude in Mou's contemporary, Tang Junyi. Tang himself was quite confident of his own access to true "wisdom," but he was opposed to any coercive imposition of these truths.[12] Tang repeatedly emphasizes the complexity and difficulty of moral truths, as compared to the many sources of human fallibility (including his own "miniscule ability" as a thinker). Thus even his own synthesis could not be regarded as the "end of philosophy"; a complete philosophical grasp of our moral reality would require an "endless series of developments." Furthermore, Tang has a rich Confucian commitment to the centrality of self-criticism and the adoption of a benevolent and open attitude toward others, both of which reinforce the modesty implied by our fallibility. Tang therefore combines a perfectionist aspiration with a commitment to tolerance and pluralism. As Thomas Metzger has put it, "refusing to regard his philosophy as a kind of terminal truth, [Tang] avoided claiming that his categories necessarily overrode other ways of categorizing the aspects of human life."

Both Mou and Tang, in short, push us toward moderate perfectionism, but I find Mou's self-restriction approach to be preferable to Tang's emphasis on tolerance for two reasons. First, the role Mou gives to laws more readily lends itself to institutionalization; Tang's approach seems to depend more heavily on individual commitments to fallibilism and tolerance. Second, Tang's view suggests a degree of pathos, since unfortunate human limitations keep us from designing societies in ways that can insist on truly realizing virtue. When we turn in a moment to my Mou-inspired account of the "passive influence" of rights on our ethical development, we will see that this pathos can be avoided. Before doing so, let me say more about what Progressive Confucian moderate perfectionist education might look like in practice. With regard to content, I imagine four areas would be included: first, the biographies and some associated writings of selected Confucian exemplars; second, basic virtues (as mentioned above);

third, the supportive values identified in the final section of Chapter 7; fourth, the details and practice of selected civic rituals. Exactly which exemplars and which rituals, and whether this all would be in addition to or incorporated within standard subjects like math, science, history, and so on, are questions that can only be answered when more local context is filled in. In pluralistic societies, Confucian exemplars, texts, and rituals will share pride of place with others, and part of the pedagogy will have to include some attention to the similarities and differences among them. Finally, the topic of how one should teach these topics is large and complex. Local context will again be important, but more important still will be a creative synthesis of traditional Confucian pedagogical insights and contemporary research (as seen, for instance, in the *Journal of Moral Education*).

Rights, Ethics, and the Psychology of Self-Restriction

Another dimension of the relations among ethics, political values, and rituals within Progressive Confucianism is the concern that the recognition that we have rights against one another will undermine important relationships and lead to a stunted ethical existence. As mentioned in Chapter 5, Justin Tiwald has pressed this worry forcefully, suggesting that our awareness of our claimable rights may encourage us to think of our interests as competitive with one another, warping feelings and motives in ways fundamentally at odds with what one would expect in a healthy Confucian society. In response, I believe that the idea of self-restriction gives us the starting point for understanding how ethical and political consciousnesses can healthily relate to one another. We need to distinguish between two kinds of cases: those in which substantial violations of rights have been committed, and thus one invokes legal remedies; and those in which little or no violation has taken place, yet one still relates to another legalistically. In the first kind of case – perhaps your violent, adult brother has harmed your mother during an argument, or stolen substantially from a joint business – it is not your seeking to protect your mother's or your own rights that undermines the relationship between you and your brother: it is his own character and behavior. And note that filing an arrest warrant or a lawsuit need not indicate that the only possible relation, ever after, between you and your brother is adversarial. Sometimes what is needed is precisely a public sign that things have gone badly wrong and need to be redressed, after which perhaps relationships can gradually be rebuilt.[13] At any rate, Progressive Confucianism sees no harm, and much value, in the existence of rights in cases like these. One will of course feel badly at what has happened, but the badness has not been exacerbated by the invocation of rights.

So much for cases in which a serious rights violation has taken place. What about when one resorts to legal remedies whenever trivial violations occur? This could indeed be a problem, reflecting a failure of one's own character and probably resulting in a harmful undermining of one's relationships. Suppose I forget once too often to return the tool I borrowed from you, and as a result you charge me with theft. My thoughtlessness might partly undermine our friendship, but even if we can say that my behavior contributes to your resort to law, surely you have over-reacted. If the particular design of a legal system, or even the mere existence of a legal system at all, encourages people to think of one another simply as potential targets of legal action, then anyone hoping that relational ethical ideals can be combined with a principled commitment to public "political" values faces a steep challenge.[14]

One kind of response focuses on institutional design. In *Sagehood*, I argued that contemporary Confucianism needs to encourage citizens to think of law as a "system of second resort." The idea is that laws and legal procedures are structured in such a way as to encourage morality and even moral growth, but without falling into the trap of "last resort" avoidance.[15] I still think this is correct, and encourage interested readers to consult my discussion there of structuring incentives within a legal system and, in particular, of encouraging alternative forms of dispute resolution. However, the challenge as I have posed it here has a deeper side to it: what if the mere existence of a legal system and of rights, no matter how structured, leads to a problematic emphasis on competitive, personal interests?

The answer to this deeper challenge lies in the psychology of a sage. Sages do not think of self-restriction as a compromise with flawed reality, but rather embrace it as a necessary means to the attainment of virtue for one and all. Sages are not Pollyannas; they understand that the path toward harmony and virtue is – and always will be – an arduous one, full of obstacles. But sages will not agree with Winston Churchill's sentiment that "democracy is the worst form of government except all those other forms that have been tried." Sages see that rule of law and democracy – using the term simply to stand for broadly participatory politics, of the kind that Progressive Confucian endorse – are the right kinds of political arrangements for imperfect creatures like us, ever striving for better, more virtuous lives. It makes no more sense to regret the need for laws, rights, and democratic decision-making than it does to regret that we humans are not angels or automatons. Progressive Confucians see that as long as humans remain humans, perfectible yet fallible, self-restriction via constitution, laws, rights, and democratic process remains central to our ideals.[16]

Readers might be troubled by the talk in the last paragraph of sages. What about all of the rest of us? I put the point in terms of the "psychology of a sage" for two reasons. First, I want to emphasize that even in the ideal case of a sage, self-restriction is still part of that very ideal. According to Progressive Confucianism, sages do not aspire to be kings. Second, as I stress repeatedly throughout *Sagehood*, Confucians understand the distinction between sages and non-sages to be a difference of degree, not kind. What goes for sages goes for the rest of us, just not as fully, consistently, or strongly. To whatever degree we are individually able to measure up to the standard of sagehood, we too will embrace self-restriction.[17]

Embracing self-restriction does not mean to abandon viewing the world in ethical and ritual terms. As I have been discussing throughout this Conclusion, we are continually harmonizing all three perspectives. Learning at what points political norms and legal machinery are appropriately invoked is, according to Progressive Confucianism, one important aspect of ethical growth. As I said above, one who looks too often to the law shows a flawed character, but so does one who looks to the law too rarely. Both legal protections and political participation (aimed, perhaps, at changing some laws) are vital to a polity whose goals are avoiding oppression and developing virtue. Lacking Mou's insight into the value of self-restriction, traditional Confucians have tended to deride the world of law, seeing it as necessarily self-centered. This is a mistake. An overly submissive, self-abnegating character is just as out of balance as an overly self-centered one. In earlier work, I have argued that the explicit recognition by seventeenth- and eighteenth-century Confucians of the importance of legitimate self-concern helped to pave the way for Chinese rights discourse in the nineteenth and twentieth centuries [Angle 2002]. It is notable that the most famous argument from early twentieth-century China in favor of "rights consciousness" is put in a way that draws on Confucian values, rather than insisting on an opposition between rights and Confucianism.[18] It is no part of my argument to maintain that learning to balance one's consciousness of ethical, legal, and ritual concerns will always be easy; I have already discussed some difficult kinds of cases in Chapters 4 and 6. But few of us are really tempted to charge an absent-minded friend with theft: most of us are able to handle most situations quite fluidly.

A Wandering Soul?

One final issue concerning the shape of Confucian virtue-ritual-politics is the historical lack of an independent institutional base for Confucianism, vis-à-vis political power. Theodore deBary has written eloquently about this in *The Trouble with Confucianism*. Concerning Confucians in the Han dynasty, he says: "The actual weakness of the Confucians . . . seems to have lain not in a failure of advocacy, but in their indisposition or inability to establish any power base of their own." With reference to Confucians in the Tang dynasty: "As Confucian scholar-officials they remained exposed to the vicissitudes of a system that took advantage of their disciplined talents while keeping them in a position of extreme dependency and grave insecurity."[19] As mentioned above, Confucian temples were not designed to provide such an independent base, but rather, especially by late imperial times, were mainly a site for state rituals. Rituals themselves did serve to some degree as checks on imperial power, but it is an exaggeration to accord them "constitutional" status, at least if "constitution" means anything like what Mou Zongsan and I have been using it to mean.[20] DeBary has noted the degree to which seventeenth-century Neo-Confucian Huang Zongxi recognized the potential for Confucian academies to serve as an independent institutional home, providing checks on the exercise of political power, and adds elsewhere that during the late Ming period, academies did in fact promote "active discussion of public issues." However, deBary adds that "after the official suppression of such political criticism at the end of the sixteenth century, [academies] ceased significantly to exercise this function as a public forum."[21]

Historian Ying-shih Yu has characterized Confucianism beginning in the twentieth century as a "wandering soul," devoid of an institutional base.[22] In one sense, this is a kind of freedom, but even if the traditional institutional structures often coopted Confucians, they also allowed for the expression, development, and influence of Confucian ideas. What options might there be in the contemporary world? For Jiang Qing and Kang Xiaoguang, the answer is a Confucian church, modeled on Christian institutions and indeed based on a notion of Confucian religion (*rujiao*) that itself has been transformed along the lines of the Western category of "religion."[23] Others, either with different goals or because of the political limitations imposed in today's China, have set their hopes on the various revivalist organizations and websites to which I referred in Chapter 1. In Taiwan, New Confucians of both the Kantian and the Critical variety exist mainly in academic organizations, where their influence is quite small. If a Confucian Church fits poorly with Progressive Confucianism's ritual minimalism, then it is going to have to look for Confucianism's institutional independence elsewhere, perhaps in some combination of civil society, grassroots, and academic organizations. In the West, powerful social-political-philosophical movements like liberalism and Marxism have flourished without becoming religions, though these analogies suggest that thinking of a Confucian political party might make sense. The truth is that it is impossible to foretell what shape a future Confucian, or Confucian-influenced, polity might take. And in any event, as I have emphasized throughout the book, it is not the case that the only way contemporary Confucian political philosophy can be relevant is via a Confucian state. I believe we are entering an era in which political philosophies rooted in a range of non-European traditions will be increasingly vibrant, debated, and influential. This should be exciting for all those willing to approach political philosophy from a rooted and yet global stance.

Notes

1 Introduction: Contextualizing Progressive Confucianism

1 My goal has been to be representative rather than comprehensive; it would not be hard to expand the list of countries and languages in which Confucian philosophy is pursued today.

2 It bears noting, though, that Chinese communism is clearly influenced in various ways by China's Confucian heritage. For example, many scholars have commented on the implicit and explicit resonances with Confucianism in Liu Shaoqi (1898–1968)'s 1939 lectures, *On the Cultivation of a Communist Party Member* [Liu 1964]; for some discussion, see [Munro 1977]. For a study that looks into the Confucian (and other) sources of Mao's own thinking, see [Wakeman 1973].

3 Both Liang and Zhang were also influenced by anti-materialist trends in post-First-World War European thought. See [Alitto 1979] and [Jeans 1997].

4 "Contemporary New Confucianism" is *"dangdai xin ruxue"* in Chinese. This is sometimes rendered into English as "Contemporary Neo-Confucianism," in part to signal the indebtedness of Mou and Tang to the distinctive Confucian movement of the eleventh through eighteenth centuries that is called "Neo-Confucianism" in English. (In Chinese, this latter movement is usually called *"Song-Ming Lixue,"* or "The Coherence-Learning of the Song through Ming Dynasties.")

5 In the balance of this book, I will refer to the ideas of Mou, Tang, Xu, and their students simply as "New Confucianism." For a fascinating account of the emergence of "New Confucianism" as a movement, see [Makeham 2003].

6 This paragraph is purposely selective; a fuller account of mid-twentieth century Confucianism would include figures like Feng Youlan, Qian Mu, He Lin, and others. [Cheng and Bunnin 2002] is a good source on some of these individuals, and see also [Bresciani 2001].

7 It can also have the opposite effect. In current Chinese slang, to "be harmonized" can mean to be disappeared by agents of the government. Thinking of "harmony" this way, no matter how distant it is from a genuine Confucian position, certainly undermines interest in Confucianism as a progressive option for China.

8 See [Yu 2006] and [Bell 2008, 163–74].

9 See [Billioud & Thoraval 2008] for one aspect of current Confucian religiosity.

10 See below for more information on Confucian revivalism; for the text of an Open Letter criticizing the church plans, see http://warpweftandway.wordpress.com/2010/12/23/confucians-react-to-planned-christian-church-in-qufu/.

11 See http://www.rjfx.net/dispbbs.asp?boardID=4&ID=13064&page=1, and also http://warpweftandway.wordpress.com/2011/04/23/confucius-on-tiananmen-square/.

12 [Makeham 2008].

13 [Liu 1995, 293].

14 For extensive discussion of the emergence of "Chinese philosophy" as a category in China, see the essays collected in [Makeham 2012]. Also relevant is Joachim Kurtz's study of the emergence of the category of "Chinese logic" in this same period [Kurtz 2011].

15 Although see this discussion of Jacques Derrida's statement, upon a visit to China in 2001, that "China does not have any philosophy": [Defoort and Ge 2005, 3].

16 Quite a number of the key essays in this debate have been translated in *Contemporary Chinese Thought* vol. 37, nos. 1–3, and see also the "Editors' Introduction" to these translations [Defoort and Ge 2005].

17 Feng Youlan's claim that the Neo-Confucian ideas of *li* and *qi* are like Aristotle's form and matter is often cited. See [Fung 1953, 547]. Similarly, the Marxist insistence that philosophers are either materialists or idealists obscures more than it reveals.

18 As we will see below, one of the best-known Confucians today, Jiang Qing, left his university post to found an old-style Confucian academy wherein he tries to teach to the whole person.

19 Just to be clear: by "argument" I simply mean the giving of reasons to defend or justify one's position. I accept that the roles of argumentative techniques like distinction-making and the offering of counter-examples, and of dialogue more generally, are often different within different philosophical cultures, though they also change over time within the Chinese (or more broadly East Asian) Confucian tradition. See [Angle 2009, 172–6] and http://warpweftandway.wordpress.com/2011/09/12/zhuangzi-and-the-possibility-of-philosophical-culture/.

20 "Philosophy as a Way of Life" is the title of Pierre Hadot's groundbreaking book on this aspect of Hellenistic philosophy [Hadot 1995]. In various ways the nature of the transformative goals of course differ, both among Western schools of thought and between Confucianism and these Western schools. See [Angle 2009, 22–3].

21 See [Shusterman 1997].

22 Possibly relevant to this issue is Eric Schwitzgebel's research on the moral behavior of ethics professors, which seems to be no better—and possibly worse—than their peers in other subfields; see [Schwitzgebel 2009].

23 See [Angle 2007] and [Angle 2009, 6].

24 Openness is a matter of degree, and scholars debate about how genuinely open Mou really was. Rooted global philosophy does not demand that one always put one's commitment to one's home tradition itself into question, though: developing one's tradition via serious engagement with other traditions is all that is required.

25 This is not to say they have no interest in such projects. A few years ago, Guo spearheaded a defense of Confucianism against the charge that its emphasis on the value of family helps to explain contemporary China's problem with corruption; [Guo 2007] is one representative piece in English. Chen Lai has also sometime ranged more broadly; see the essays in [Chen 2009].

26 There are a variety of terms that can loosely be translated as "Confucianism," three of which are compounds of two characters, the first of which being "*ru*," which roughly corresponds to "Confucian-"; this is then combined with "learning" (*ruxue*), "school" (*rujia*), or "teaching" (*rujiao*). Each term has certain distinct connotations, with "*rujiao*" emphasizing the institutional and religious-practice sides of the tradition. Admittedly, the full story of "*ru*" is more complicated; some scholars maintain that for much of the pre-modern period, it is better translated as simply "scholar," though today the connections to Confucianism are unambiguous. For one (controversial) account, see [Jensen 1997].

27 Yuandao's website is http://www.yuandao.com/; Chen is helpfully discussed in [Makeham 2008, esp. ch. 9]. For other sites, see "Confucian China (*Rujia Zhongguo*)," http://www.rujiazg.com/, and "Confucian Revival Forum (*Rujiao Fuxing Luntan*)," http://www.rjfx.net/.

28 "Institutional Confucianism (*zhidu ruxue*)" is the title of a recent book by the contemporary scholar Gan Chunsong, and some of Gan's observations can help to flesh out what I mean by the term. Gan agrees with the philosophers cited as Institutional Confucians in the main text that New Confucians like Mou Zongsan consciously distanced themselves from traditional Confucian institutions, partly as a defense mechanism against Western-inspired criticisms, and thus retreated to something Gan characterizes as purely "academic Confucianism" [Gan 2006, 9]. Gan says that as an alternative approach to New Confucianism, Institutional Confucianism should look at practice as well as at texts for its sources, and it should emphasize finding ways to put its values and ideas into practice in contemporary society. At the same time, he emphasizes that taking institutions seriously does not mean any kind of fundamentalism: institutions need to change with the changing times [Ibid., 11–12]. One of Gan's

main contributions is a critical historical assessment of efforts early in the twentieth century to institutionalize Confucianism.

29 [Jiang 2003].

30 This is not to say that Jiang believes ethics and self-cultivation to be unimportant. Rather, because of the crisis of political legitimacy he perceives in China today, he believes that Confucians must currently emphasize the political, institutional side of the tradition. He disagrees with Mou Zongsan's claim that reflection on how to realize the "inner" ethical ideal can lead us to insights concerning the nature of "outer" politics: see my discussion in Chapter 2. I thank Daniel Bell for some helpful discussion of these issues.

31 [Jiang 2010, 14].

32 [Jiang 2010]. I discuss these ideas in somewhat more detail in the Conclusion.

33 See below, page 53, for further discussion of Jiang's proposals; and see also [Elstein unpublished-b].

34 For a very helpful essay on Kang, see [Ownby 2009].

35 [Kang 2005, xiv].

36 [Fan 2010, xi].

37 [Fan 2010; 106n2; 108n8].

38 The "Post-New Confucian" thinker Lin Anwu, on whom see below, refers to this group as "Apologist New Confucianism (*hujiao de xinruxue*)." See [Lin 1998, 31] and the discussion in [Makeham 2008, 181].

39 See discussion and references in [Angle unpublished-c, Section 4]. The general idea that Confucianism is deontological finds many supporters among philosophers in Taiwan, especially, though Lee is much the most explicit in his use of Kant to develop Confucianism, as discussed in the main text; see also [Lee 2001].

40 [Lee 2005a].

41 [Lee 2005b, esp. 85–7] and [Lee 2005c, 117–19]. Lee develops his case for the compatibility of an "ethic of conviction (*Gesinnungsethik* or *cunxin lunlixue*)" and an "ethic of responsibility (*Verantwortungsethik* or *zeren lunlixue*)"—terms that he takes from Max Weber—in numerous essays, including both those cited earlier in this note and also [Lee 2005a].

42 While he certainly does not eschew metaphysics and does not greatly explore political philosophy, Cheng Chung-ying of the University of Hawaii's writings that touch on political philosophy might fit in the "Critical New Confucian" category"; see [Cheng 1991].

43 See [Lin 1998], [Lin 2004], and especially [Lin 2008]. To be clear, I am intending "Critical New Confucianism" in a broader sense than Lin's own usage, which connects the category narrowly with his own specific interests, for instance in the Qing dynasty Confucian Wang Fuzhi and in Phenomenology [Lin 1998, 31]. [Makeham 2008, chs. 8–9] is a very helpful discussion of Lin's project in English.

44 [Makeham 2008, 187].
45 [Tang 2008, 190].
46 See (among other works) [Chan 1999] and [Chan 2007]. Bai's major work to date is [Bai 2009].
47 See [Bell 2006].
48 See, for example, [Hall & Ames 1999] and [Tan 2004]. Neville's explicitly Confucian work focuses primarily on topics outside political philosophy, though see both his emphasis on ritual and his social theory in [Neville 2008].
49 See, for example, [Huang 2005] and (in English translation) [Huang 2008]. He has more recently been focusing on explicitly political topics, as in [Huang 2009b].
50 [Bell 2010].
51 [Metzger 2005].
52 And *vice versa*: it often seems that Bell's ideas might equally be thought of as Confucian Leftism, and be attractive to a socialist who has come to find Confucianism independently attractive. For some discussion, see [Angle 2012].
53 [Metzger 2005, 118].
54 Among other things, I do not endorse the near identification between Confucian moral heartmind and Kantian free will that is central to Lee Ming-huei's reading of Mou. Lee may be right about Mou, but I do not think this is the best reading of the tradition as a whole, and I do not think that this particular understanding of Confucian ethics and metaphysics is necessary for self-restriction to make sense. See Chapter 2.
55 Quoted in [Tang 2008, 176].
56 Quoted in [Tang 2008, 176].
57 [Bai 2010].
58 Nor will I be defending my claims about the "general framework" of Confucian ethics. I doubt that any Confucian, past or present, would deny the significance of the five virtues I mentioned in the main text (although this group of five was not canonical during the classical period), but how central virtues are in the conceptualization of Confucian ethics is a matter of considerable contemporary debate. As mentioned in the Preface, I articulate and defend a specific reading of Neo-Confucian ethics in [Angle 2009].
59 "On the part of all people" will be controversial for some Confucians, but see the argument in Chapter 3.

2 Self-Restriction: The Indirect Link Between Ethics and Politics

1 [Mou 1991, 140].
2 [Mou 1991, 127].

3 [Mou 1991, 59]. This translation of *ziwo kanxian* was first used by David Elstein; see [Elstein 2011]. In [Angle 2009] I translated *ziwo kanxian* as "self-negation," following Mou's own lead: see [Mou 1983, 278]. However, given that Mou uses the explicitly Hegelian language of "negation" (rendered into Chinese as *fouding*) in order to explain what *kanxian* means, it now seems wiser to follow Elstein's more literal translation. See also below on the justification of "restriction."

4 [Mou 1975, 122].

5 See *Shuogua* ("Explaining the Trigrams") [Lynn 1994, 121 and 123]; and *Xugua* ("Providing the Sequence of Hexagrams") [Ibid., 105]. The former text adds that "*Kan* is water, is the drains and the ditches, is that which lies low, is the now-straightening and now-bending, and is the bow [and] the wheel" [Ibid., 124]. For some helpful discussion, see [Tang 2008, 121].

6 See [Mou 1954, 27–8]. The book was first published, in 1947, as two separate journal articles; for details, see [Lee 2008, 287n6]. As Chan notes, he also uses *kanxian* in his book *A Critique of the Cognitive Mind*, which he completed writing in 1949 [Chan 2011, 114].

7 [Mou 1991, 46–8].

8 [Ibid., 47].

9 [Ibid., 58–9].

10 One of Mou's most controversial doctrines is that through the former consciousness, humans are capable of "intellectual intuition." For some background and discussion of these ideas, see [Chan 2009, esp. 142–50]; [Billioud 2012]; and [Bunnin 2008].

11 There is of course more to be said about what counts as a virtuous perception or reaction, how this relates to the attunement and care that I mentioned in Chapter 1, how these individual reactions to particular circumstances harmonize with one another and with multiple dimensions of value, and so on. Mou offers one kind of answer, based around his idea of intellectual intuition; I offer a different answer in [Angle 2009]; and other Confucian philosophers have developed still other alternatives.

12 [Mou 1983, 278].

13 [Ibid., 128].

14 See [Yu 2006] and [Yu 2004]. I discuss Yu Ying-shih's arguments in [Angle 2009, ch. 10].

15 I discuss one important strand of these resonances between Confucianism and modern psychology in Chapter 7; see also [Angle unpublished-b].

16 For further discussion, see Chapter 6 on the balance between rituals and ethical critique; Chapter 7 on the "inner"-"outer" distinction in traditional Confucianism, and its partial critique by Progressive Confucianism; and the Conclusion.

17 Adapted from [Brooks & Brooks 1998, 89].

18 Theodore deBary has particularly emphasized the idea of "getting it for oneself" in his many writings on Neo-Confucianism; see, for example, [deBary 1989].

19 These ideas are not explicit in Mou's writings, but I take them to follow from and fill out his position. They are partly alluded to in the famous 1958 "Manifesto to the World's People on behalf of Chinese Culture," of which Mou was a co-author. See [Mou et al. 1989, 33] and, for an English translation, [Chang 1962, 472].

20 [Jiang 2003, 46–52].

21 In a 1954 monograph on Wang Yangming's theory of innate good knowing (*liangzhi*), Mou argues at length for an interpretation of Wang's notion of "extending (*zhi*)" one's good knowing according to which as part of this process, one provisionally restricts one's good knowing in order to know objects, thus grasping how to control them. This cognitive knowledge is then subsumed into the good-knowing response to a situation, such that— if one's good knowing is not obscured by selfishness—one's response cannot help but be correct. The key for now is that Mou clearly is offering this as an interpretation of Wang's teaching [Mou 1954, 27–8]. Mou offers his interpretation as a gloss or commentary (*an*) to two passages from Wang's *Record for Practice*: [Wang 1983, 37 (§6) and 182 (§139)]. We see the same thing in Mou's much later, explicitly Kantian-influenced account of cognition in *Phenomena and Things-In-Themselves*. Mou claims to find in a brief passage from the "Great Commentary" to the *Book of Changes* the idea that the moral heartmind "extends itself dialectically," via self-restriction, in order to appropriately handle the objects in situations it encounters [Mou 1975, 122–3]. The passage Mou cites is: "*Qian* is the strongest thing in the entire world, so it should always be easy to put its virtue into practice. Thus one knows whether or not there is going to be danger. *Kun* is the most compliant thing in the entire world, so it should always be simple to put its virtue into practice. Thus one knows whether or not there are going to be obstacles" [Lynn 1994, 93–9]. Mou's stress is on the idea of knowing "dangers" and "obstacles."

22 [Mou 1991].

23 One example of this is when he cites Confucius's statement that "To love knowledge without loving learning has the defect of diffuseness" [*Analects* 17:8] by way of illustrating the problems that come when one denies the importance of self-restriction and thus denies room for independent scientific inquiry [Mou 1991, 58].

24 [Mou 1991, 141].

25 [Mou 1991, ch. 9].

26 [Jiang 2003, 84].

27 Jiang also points out that Wang's political solution to the issues of his day, which involves relying on the good knowing of heroic sages, differs

dramatically from Mou's democratic politics [Jiang 2003, 86]. While true, this is less relevant to the immediate question, because I am already granting that in the case of political uses of *kanxian*, Mou acknowledges his departure from earlier voices in the tradition.

28   While Jiang does not consider it explicitly, the same can be said for Mou's later references to the *Book of Changes*; see note 78, above.

29   See [Jiang 2003, 66–72] and [Ibid., 91].

30   See, in particular, [Zheng 2000, 87]. Even Tang Zhonggang, who is in many ways critical of Mou, would agree that notwithstanding his uses of Western philosophy, Mou remains fundamentally a Confucian [Tang 2008]. For a particularly clear discussion of Buddhist influence on the idea of self-restriction, see [Clower 2010, 119n90].

31   [Tang 2008, 64 and 109].

32   My focus here is not on the scientific case, but the following example is worth noting. At one point, Mou says that "The Buddha has all types of [ethical] wisdom, but Buddha would not and could not make an atomic bomb" [Mou 1975, 121]. He goes on to say that scientific knowledge is necessary in order to overcome various physical obstacles to our ethical flourishing. Mou does not make explicit what attitude an enlightened but self-restricted scientist might have toward atomic weapons; perhaps it depends on the particular international context. It seems reasonable to think, though, that in many circumstances the scientific pursuit of atomic weapons would be unethical, and scientists should not be so firmly "attached" to discovering the truth they miss this. More generally, we can sum up by observing that Mou says quite explicitly that while science has a kind of independence from ethical values, it simultaneously remains (indirectly) connected to these values. "Whatever is true all ought to be related. [Distinct true perspectives] ought to mutually enhance one another in order to bring out the most beauty/good (*mei*), and restrict and balance one another so as to avoid deficiencies (*bi*)" [Mou 1991, 58].

33   [Mou 1991, 23 and 49].

34   [Mou 2005, 184].

35   [Mou 1991, 59]. In the contexts of science and empirical cognition, Mou also uses temporal vocabulary, such as saying that in the process of self-restriction, good knowing "halts," or that once one has mastered the relevant empirical conditions about an object, one can "return" to oneself [Mou 1954, 28].

36   [Wang 1996, 407].

37   For example, see [Wang 1996, 407] or [Peng 2010, 192].

38   [Wang 1996, 411]. Wang puts this in terms of innate good-knowing (*liang-zhi*), but the point can be generalized as I have done in the main text.

3 Rethinking Authority and Rejecting Authoritarianism: Giving the People their Voice

1 See [Mou 1991, esp. ch. 1]. In this chapter I will often simply use "authority" to mean "legitimate political authority." For discussion of these terms, see below.

2 Institutional Confucian Jiang Qing argues that according to the "Gongyang" strand of the tradition, there are actually three sources of legitimacy: Heaven, earth, and man. For some discussion of his contemporary development of these ideas, see both the current chapter and the book's Conclusion.

3 [Philpott 2010].

4 The *Mencius* 5A:4, citing a line from the *Book of Odes*, declares that there is "no territory under heaven which is not the king's."

5 For some incisive comments on issues raised in this paragraph, my thanks go to Loubna El-Amine. Political scientist Victoria Hui writes that "In the multistate era, [states or] *guo* waged wars against one another, made and broke alliances as they saw fit, and set up diplomatic offices to handle matters of war and peace. In this environment, ancient China developed the art of war and the markers of territorial sovereignty light years before Western practices" [Hui 2005, 5]. I agree that this is true in practice, but these practices did not significantly inflect the universalist Confucian theory discussed in the present essay. Interestingly, several contemporary writers on Confucian political thinking do employ the category of sovereignty, though not in ways that—in my view—enhance the clarity of their theorizing. Jiang Qing asserts that only Heaven has sovereignty (*zhuquan zai tian*), while Kang Xiaoguang and Bai Tongdong both say that sovereignty belongs to the people, but the right to rule belongs to the worthy (*zhuquan zai min, zhiquan zai xian*). See, respectively, [Jiang 2010, 123]; [Kang 2005, xxxi]; and [Bai 2010, 21].

6 In particular, I start from the early Confucian conception of *political* or *public* authority. For a stimulating discussion of the rather different contours of the more personal "authority of a master," see [Elstein 2009].

7 There is some scholarly disagreement about the date of the Zhou conquest, but many accept 1046 BCE.

8 "*Tian*" and "*Shang Di*" or "*High Lord*" are both used, seemingly interchangeably, at this point in the text; see [Allan 1984]. As an example, see [Legge 1985, 475].

9 [Allan 1984, 530–1]. Previously, this means of divination had been used by Shang rulers to learn whether the timing was propitious for various activities.

10 [Mengzi 2008, 123–4], slightly altered.

11 *Mencius* contains considerable evidence for this claim. 2A:5 lists a variety

of ways in which one should treat various groups of people well, and concludes that "If it is like this, one will have no enemies in the world. One who has no enemies in the world is the agent of Heaven (*wei tian li*). It has never happened that someone is like this yet fails to become King" [Mengzi 2008, 45]. For other relevant passages, see 2A:4, 2B:8, 2B:13, 4A:7, 5A:6, and 7B:14.

12 [Mengzi 2008, 26], slightly altered.

13 For an excellent treatment of the exact circumstances in which a ruler can be overthrown and by whom, see [Tiwald 2008], which argues convincingly that there is a more significant role for procedural constraints in Mencius's view than is often noticed.

14 *Mencius* 1A:7 [Mengzi 2008, 14].

15 [Mengzi 2008, 20].

16 See *Mencius* 2A:6 and 6A:6.

17 *Mencius* 4B:32 (my translation) and 6B:2 (from [Mengzi 2008, 159]), respectively. There is interpretive disagreement over whether Yao and Shun had something different by nature. Mencius twice says that "*Yao Shun, xing zhe ye.*" Van Norden renders this, "Yao and Shun always treated it as their nature," which makes sense in light of 7B:24's statement that the gentleman treats the moral sprouts as "nature." On the other hand, D. C. Lau and Yang Bojun render this same sentence as "Yao and Shun had it as their nature"; in context, the idea is that others had to work to attain it. See [Mencius 1970] and [Yang 1984]. While there is more that could be said on this topic, including bringing the *Analects* and *Xunzi* into the picture, I think there are good reasons to favor Van Norden's reading.

18 See [Munro 1969], *Mencius* 6A:16 and 6A:17, respectively, and [Bloom 1998].

19 Bloom writes: "Politically speaking, the concept of human dignity may not be either subversive of monarchical rule or necessarily conducive to democratic government per se, but few would deny that it provides a firm basis for critique of cruelty, oppression, and misrule in both its active and passive forms. It is surely consistent with, though not generative of, many democratic ideas and values that would evolve in subsequent centuries" [Bloom 1998, 110].

20 In her Princeton University dissertation-in-progress, Loubna El-Amine is arguing that what I am calling a tension results from the early Confucians conceiving of political and ethical goals in somewhat distinct terms and as addressed to somewhat different audiences [El-Amine 2012]. In addition, she proposes taking politics and its goal of order as primary; from this perspective, the importance of ethical virtue is limited to its contribution to lasting order. El-Amine thus offers an intriguing explanation for the tension with which I am concerned, though I do not think the tension is thereby dissolved. If she is right, then we understand it historically and

in terms of the goals of ancient theory, but it persists as a problem for contemporary Confucian philosophers seeking to build on these early foundations.

21 [Hall & Ames 1987, 139–141, 146].

22 For an alternative account of the *ren* versus *min* distinction, see [Gassmann 2000], which argues that *ren* and *min* mark off distinct social groups based in clan relationships. In my view, Gassmann starts from questionable grammatical premises and then leaps to a radical conclusion that is not supported by his evidence.

23 I say this even though Mencius certainly demonstrates empathy for the plight of the poor and the powerless: he is sometimes quite graphic in his descriptions of their suffering as he tries to draw the attention of rulers to issues of their collective well-being.

24 Developing Liang Qichao's original insight, contemporary scholar Yuri Pines has argued that "a widespread identification of the lower strata [i.e., *min*] with morally impaired 'petty men (*xiaoren*)' may explain [the classical Confucian authors'] negative views of their political activism"; see [Pines 2009, 210]. I agree that conflation of social and moral categories that we sometimes see in texts like the *Mencius* helps to reinforce the view of the *min* that I have been discussing, though I believe that their merely reactive, mass nature is more fundamental.

25 Sor-hoon Tan explores some similar terrain in her *Confucian Democracy*, including drawing on Hall and Ames. Rather than arguing that the Confucian tradition needs to revise its understanding of authority, she pushes a Dewey-inspired reading of the *Analects* and *Mencius* according to which a solution to the tension is already implicit in the texts. While I find much to like in her destination (about which I will comment further below), I am not persuaded by the route she takes to get there. See [Tan 2004, 136–56].

26 As mentioned in Chapter 1, [Ownby 2009] is a helpful account of Kang's intellectual and professional development.

27 [Arendt 1977, 92–3]; cf. [Wood 1995, 5].

28 [Kang 2005, 126–7].

29 Theorists debate about whether such obligations are merely *prima facie*, subject to further considerations like justice. For an introduction to these debates, see [Christiano 2008].

30 [Kang 2005, xxxiii].

31 [Ibid.].

32 [Kang 2005, 138]. Jiang's own development of this idea, especially in his institutional proposals, is fascinating and worthy of attention in its own right; I discuss it briefly in the book's Conclusion, and see also [Elstein unpublished-b]. These proposals are circulating in manuscript form [Jiang 2010], and a version was published in Taiwan in 2004. A partial English

translation, with critical commentary and responses from Jiang, is due to be published soon: see [Jiang 2012].

33 [Kang 2005, xxx, 184].

34 [Kang 2005, 190].

35 [Kang 2005, xlviii, 190].

36 [Kang 2005, xlvii]. In a new essay titled "Outline of Confucian Constitutionalism (*Rujia xianzheng lungang*)," Kang makes the related argument that a constitution expresses the highest values of a "nation (*minzu*)," and the continuity needed for a "nation" to exist depends centrally on the nation's culture. Therefore, the national culture (which he says is primarily Confucianism in the Chinese case) must be the main source of the constitution. See [Kang 2011].

37 [Kang 2005, 181].

38 [Kang 2005, 178].

39 See [Tu 1991].

40 [Kang 2005, 182].

41 Daniel Bell wonders whether Kang's Unity Argument can be salvaged by adding the qualification that Confucianism not be promoted as state religion in areas dominated by non-Han groups, like Tibet and Xinjiang [personal communication]. Certainly some of the centrifugal forces about which Kang is worried are non-ethnic, and thus such a narrowed focus might still serve a useful unifying role. But it is far from obvious that Han Chinese in central areas of China will perceive the institution of a national Confucian religion as anything but a coercive, external imposition.

42 [Kang 2005, xxxiv].

43 [Kang 2005, 132–5].

44 [Kang 2005, xxxv].

45 [Kang 2005, xxxvii].

46 The idea that the people are agents capable of forming independent judgments sneaks into Kang's reasoning at many places. For example, he suggests that rather than having the state decide on one interpretation of Confucianism, a society can rely on the people's choices (of which of the various interpreters of Confucianism, preaching in different "churches," they attend and support financially); this will act as an intellectual "market" [Kang 2005, 190].

47 For the late-classical Confucian Xunzi, in fact, *Tian* does not in any way dictate what we humans should do; instead, it is up to us to learn how best to shape ourselves and our environments in response to *Tian*'s constant cycles.

48 This translation is controversial. I discuss it at length in [Angle 2009, ch. 2], and it is the main subject of debate in a published exchange about the book; see [Tiwald 2011b], [Angle 2011], and [Tiwald 2011c]. About the same time I published [Angle 2009], Harvard intellectual historian

Peter Bol published [Bol 2008] in which he had independently arrived at
the decision to translate *li* as "coherence." (Note that since the publication of [Angle 2009] I have begun systematically capitalizing the "C" in
"Coherence," as discussed in [Angle 2011].) In a recent review of Bol's
book, philosopher P. J. Ivanhoe is highly critical of using "coherence"
to translate *li*, arguing that it is in various ways misleading and that it is
inferior to the older translation ("principle") [Ivanhoe 2010]. His central
argument is: (1) coherence is simply one quality that *li* has, so it is a mistake
to substitute the quality for the concept itself, and (2) the kind of normativ-
ity provided by coherence is too vague, plural, and/or relative. "Principle"
is better because it allows one to capture the idea that there is a unitary
rightness to *li*. He says that when a Neo-Confucian argues that "a widow
should remain chaste," this is a "principle," not merely coherence. Any
number of views about widows might be coherent, but Neo-Confucians
choose one by appealing, Ivanhoe says, to "a higher moral *principle*"
[Ibid., 474, emphasis in original]. My reply to all this comes in two parts.
First, Ivanhoe has nicely illustrated precisely wherein I find the problem
with "principle" to lie. Western philosophers understand well enough
what it means to appeal to a higher moral principle—something like the
Golden Rule, Kant's categorical imperative, or the utilitarian principle. *Li*
is nothing like this. Neo-Confucians do articulate principles as generally
accurate summaries of what *li* tells us about a particular class of circumstances (e.g., many held that a widow should remain chaste), but *li* is not a
supreme principle from which a host of specific principles follow. Second,
while Ivanhoe is right that *li* is not whatever we happen to find coherent—as I have consistently tried to emphasize—thinking of *li* as Coherence
enables us to get a partial understanding, at least, of what it really is.
Seeking *li* is seeking ever-broader and more inclusive ways that things can
fit together, especially as guided by our emotional registering of interconnections. Ivanhoe concludes his case against "coherence" by wondering
if perhaps Bol is using "coherence" in a "novel and highly loaded sense."
If this is the case, Ivanhoe says, then it isn't so much a translation as the
coining of a new English word, which troubles him. Were Ivanhoe to be
convinced that "principle" is too problematic, he would prefer to simply
leave it romanized (as "*li*") rather than to coin a new word. We are coming
closer to agreement here, because I certainly acknowledge that my use of
"Coherence" (and, I suspect, Bol's "coherence") is not supposed to be flat-
footedly equivalent to the standard English word "coherence." My wager
is that by using "Coherence" combined with a suitable explanation, we get
a better result (measured by readers' understandings) than by using either
"principle" or simply "*li*."

49 For further thoughts along these lines, with some references, see [Angle
2009], especially Chapters 5, 9, and the Conclusion.

50 [Mou 1991, 127]. For more discussion, see [Angle 2009, ch. 1].

51 On the need to balance intimates and strangers, see [Slote 2001, ch. 3]; [Tessman 2005, ch. 4]; and [Angle 2009, ch. 5].

52 As Christine Swanton puts it, the core "plight" driving ethics is that "in addressing the demands of the world, each of us, even the most virtuous of us, is limited in his or her perspective" [Swanton 2003, 250]. In the present regard we can see that much the same is true of broader political contexts as well.

53 [Ci 1999].

54 The issue of state-sponsored moral and civic education is an important one to Confucians; see the book's Conclusion for discussion.

55 See [Bell 2008, 151–4] for some related thoughts.

56 This is as good a place as any to signal my appreciation of the argument made in [Tan 2010], which resonates in key respects with the views I have presented in this chapter. Tan distinguishes between "authoritative" and "authoritarian": the former is based on excellence; the latter, on coercion. She argues convincingly that the views attributed to Confucius in the *Analects* support an authoritative rather than authoritarian approach. She also sees the danger of slipping from one to the other, and urges that, in order to resist such slippage, politics in a modern Confucian state be to a significant degree "autonomous" [Ibid., 147–8]. She does not develop this idea of political autonomy at much length and does not connect it to Mou's idea of self-restriction, but I feel that her argument fits extremely well into the framework presented in this chapter.

57 [Tu 1996, 29–30].

58 For a relatively early version, see Part III of [Bell 2000]. I will draw on his subsequent refinements in [Bell 2006, ch. 6].

59 [Bell 2006, 171–9]. Bell argues that a weak upper house may be more feasible, but a strong one may be more desirable.

60 [Ibid., 160–1]. Bell makes explicit the "dual commitments" to democracy and meritocratic, "Confucian" rule at [Ibid., 162].

61 [Jiang 2010]. I have mentioned Jiang's three-fold legitimacy concept above, in Chapter 3, in the context of Kang Xiaoguang's effort to apply it to his own authoritarian ideas. For an astute discussion of Jiang's political proposals, see [Elstein unpublished-b].

62 [Elstein unpublished-b, 14–15].

63 Elstein discusses (and expresses skepticism about) Jiang's response to this type of criticism, namely that Jiang is drawing on the "structural" aspects of democracy rather than its "substantive" values [Ibid.]. Throughout his essay, Elstein raises telling challenges to numerous aspects of Jiang's proposal.

64 See [Bai 2009, 43, 47, and 73], although note that on p. 47, Bai says that it is speech which takes "good government" as its goal that is protected, not speech more generally.

65 [Bai 2009, 55–6]. Rawls discusses five facts concerning democratic society in [Rawls 1999], so Bai terms his addition the "sixth fact."
66 [Ibid., 61].
67 One astute commentator on the difficulties with identifying virtue and talent is Zhang Shizhao; see Chapter 4. Other contemporary critical discussions include [Sen 2000] and [McNamee & Miller 2009].

4 Debating the Rule of Law and Virtue Politics: Zhang Shizhao, Mou Zongsan, and Today

1 This and the following two paragraphs draw substantially on [Angle 2009, §10.2.4].
2 There are also other Chinese terms that correspond to one or the other of these meanings of *fa*: for example, *lü* refers unambiguously to legal codes, while *zhi* or *zhidu* refer unambiguously to systems or institutions.
3 [Huang 1993, 97].
4 [Xunzi 1979, 263]. Knoblock renders *fa* as model, and translates: "There are men who can bring order about, but there is no model (*fa*) that will produce order" [Xunzi 1988–94, vol. 2, 175]. Knoblock's explanation of "*fa*" is helpful: "The word *fa* is used in a wide variety of sense in this book. It means the model of rule established by Yu, as well as the provisions of law and ritual Yu created as a pattern for his successors, the methods and techniques Yu used in his archery, a law code based on moral principles, and the technique of ruling by reliance on law and its sanctions advocated by such men as Shen Dao and Shang Yang" [Xunzi 1988–94, vol. 2,, 171].
5 [Zhu & Lü 1967, 234].
6 [Zhu 1991b, 138], slightly modified.
7 [Luo 1987, 88 and 86].
8 [Levey 1991, 572]; see also [Bol 2008] on the many types of "alternative" institutions advocated by the Neo-Confucians.
9 [Levey 1991, 545].
10 For a translation, see [Huang 1993]. Which includes deBary's extended introduction to the work. Others who anticipated Huang in various ways include Chen Liang, Ye Shi, and Wang Tingxiang; Gu Yanwu is a contemporary of Huang's whose views are also extremely important. Mou Zongsan's discussion of the limitations of Chen and Ye is quite illuminating: according to Mou, in an effort to come up with concrete solutions to the problems of their era, they ended up compromising with the rulers and advocating solutions too reliant on sage-heroes. Mou says that later thinkers like Huang Zongxi, despairing of short-term solutions and thus writing for the ages, are able to see deeper and offer more radical answers [Mou 1991, ch. 9].
11 [Huang 1993, 99], slightly altered; see also [Huang 1985, 7].

12 On legal specialists, see [Ocko and Gillmartin 2009, 72] and [Macauley 1998].

13 Both the litigants and the magistrate stood to learn and grow as a result of their encounter. Here is the Ming dynasty Confucian Wang Yangming (1472–1529): ". . . When you interrogate a litigant, do not become angry because his replies are impolite or glad because his words are smooth; do not punish him because you hate his effort to solicit help from your superiors; . . . do not decide the case carelessly on the spur of the moment because you are busy with your own affairs. . . . To do any of these is selfish. You need only follow what you know in yourself. You must carefully examine yourself and control yourself, lest your mind become in the least prejudiced and distort who is right and who is wrong" [Wang 1963, 197–8, slightly modified].

14 This is not to say that there were no procedures. There were, and they were taken seriously. Ocko and Gillmartin write: "Whether a trial involved Hakka boatmen in Guangdong, peasants in Jiangbei, or guest merchants in Chongqing, the process was the same" [Ocko and Gillmartin 2009, 70]. But elements of the legal codes themselves, as well as the larger cultural understanding of their role, ensured that substantive justice was paramount [Ibid., 71].

15 Neo-Confucians would put this in terms of perceiving "Universal Coherence (*tianli*)"; see discussion in Chapter 3, as well as [Angle 2009, ch. 2].

16 Quoted in [Jenco 2010b, 95].

17 [Ch'en 1972, 170–1].

18 [Jenco 2010a].

19 See especially the arguments of Wu Guanyin and Du Yaquan in [Jenco 2010a].

20 The arguments of Liang and some others for cultural change anticipate the agenda of the New Culture Movement that would break out a year later.

21 [Jenco 2010b, 95].

22 From [Zhang 2000, vol. 3, 230]. Here and below, while I have consulted Zhang's original writings, my translations follow very closely those in [Jenco 2010b], which is the major source for this section.

23 [Jenco 2010b, 97].

24 [Zhang 2000, vol. 3, 267].

25 [Jenco 2010b, 91].

26 [Zhang 2000, vol. 3, 431].

27 [Ibid., 429].

28 [Ibid., 230].

29 Li Dazhao, writing in 1916, as quoted in [Jenco 2010b, 92].

30 Quoted in [Lee 2008, 288–9].

31 [Mou 1991, 1].

32 [Ibid., 23 and 49]. Elsewhere, Mou commends certain early "legalist" thinkers for gesturing toward an idea of objective law, though he adds that this idea immediately became enmeshed with an emphasis on techniques of manipulation (*shu*), and the idea of independent, public, objective law never fully emerged [Mou 1983, 67].

33 For extensive discussion of this idea, see [Angle 2009].

34 The balance of this paragraph draws on [Angle 2009, 216–17].

35 See Peerenboom [2002, 33]. The same arrangement has also been called "ad hoc instrumentalism" by those who insist that for a means of governance to count as "law," the ruler's commitment to it must be "consistent and principled," even if law is still deployed to serve the ruler's own ends [Winston 2005, 316]. That is, for some theorists there is already a minimal moral content in "rule by law," while others call ad hoc instrumentalism "rule by law," and distinguish principled commitments to law as a "thin" theory of "rule of law" [Peerenboom 2002, 65].

36 [Peerenboom 2002, 69–70]. These issues are rendered still more complex when one overlays the English-language theories with Chinese discussions, because the relevant Chinese terminology is also somewhat ambiguous. *Fazhi* 法治 can mean either rule by law or rule of law. *Yifa zhiguo* 以法治國 clearly expresses an instrumentalist orientation, though whether it refers to purely ad hoc instrumentalism, or to principled rule by law, has been left unclear. *Yifa zhiguo* 依法治國, finally, more clearly implies that the government is bound by law, and is thus the least ambiguous rendering of "rule of law." See [Peerenboom 2002, 64].

37 For a full list, see Winston [2005, 320f] or Peerenboom [2002, 65–7]. Fuller [1969, 46–91] is the locus classicus for many of these ideas, and contains extended discussion of the moral implications of each criterion.

38 For further discussion of civil disobedience, see the end of Chapter 2.

39 [Keith 1991, 112].

40 [Peerenboom 2002, 6–7].

41 See [Hao 1999, 412]. There was sporadic academic discussion of "rule by virtue" or virtue politics (*dezhi*), mostly in connection with early Confucian models of governance, though [Li Yushi 1996] explicates the views on "using virtue to rule (*yide zhiguo*)" of the important, Confucian-inspired, twentieth-century intellectual Liang Shuming (1893–1988). A few academic discussions of the potential for positive mutual interaction between *fazhi* and *dezhi* precede Jiang Zemin's statements; see in particular [Shan 1998], which draws on both Chinese traditional thinkers and Western scholars like Lon Fuller [Fuller 1969] to discuss ways in which a modern, constructive relationship between *dezhi* and *fazhi* would have to differ from, though it could draw on, traditional Chinese ideas.

42 Cited in [Luo & Xia 2001]; translation partly based on [Keith and Lin 2003, 631].

43 The Chinese Academic Journal Database lists 1,920 articles with "use virtue to govern the country *(yide zhiguo)*" in their title; all but six date from 2001 or after. See http://chinanew.eastview.com/, accessed 7 July, 2009.
44 Western analysts have noted the contribution that claims about the "quality" of party members make toward the legitimacy of one-party rule. See, e.g., [Guo 2003].
45 Li Lanfen's book-length treatment is particularly inclusive [Li 2008].
46 [Li 2008, 58–9].
47 [Wang 2003].
48 Parts of this paragraph and the next one are drawn from [Angle 2010b].
49 [Fan 2010, 24–5].
50 [Fan 2010, 37].
51 [Ibid., 38].
52 [Metzger 2005].
53 For more details on the interrelationship between ethical and political values, see Chapter 2, and for the specific way in which proper political values help to realize virtue, see Chapter 3.
54 See [Chan 1999] and [Fan 2010, 36–7].
55 [Angle 2009, 218–21].
56 He called this "pan-politics-ism *(fan zhengzhi zhuyi)*." See [Lee 2001, 64].
57 [Jenco 2010b, 207].
58 [Mou 1991, 126].
59 [Ibid., 124 and 164].
60 I discuss Mou's idea of state moral education at some length in the book's Conclusion.

5 The Rights of All Under Heaven: Human Rights and Contemporary Confucianism

1 [Donnelly 2003, 35].
2 [ICISS 2001; Evans 2008, 44].
3 [ICISS 2001, xi].
4 An alternative approach is offered by Luke Glanville, who argues that ancient Chinese concepts of sovereignty anticipate many aspects of the currently emerging idea of sovereignty as responsibility. Glanville's work is stimulating, but relies too much on a reading of early Confucian political theory – as articulating the right of the masses to rebel, for example – that I have rejected in Chapter 3. See [Glanville 2010].
5 [Maritain, 1949, 9].
6 Maritain's attitude was more complex than I have made it sound, because he continues to insist that "it matters essentially" which justification is in fact true [Ibid., 11]. His reason for this seems to be that it matters greatly

that we should adopt true moral beliefs (moral values being the terms in which each person is presumed to articulate his or her own justification of human rights).

7 [Habermas 1998, 200].

8 He has revised, elaborated, and defended these ideas in various subsequent publications, including [Zhao 2009a] in Chinese and [Zhao 2009b] and [Zhao forthcoming] in English.

9 [Zhao 2005, 6]

10 [Ibid., 7].

11 Thanks to Phil Hand for his helpful comments on the meaning of *jiantao* 检讨.

12 [Ibid., 11].

13 [Zhao 2008, 175].

14 [Ibid., 165–6].

15 [Zhao 2005, 8].

16 For some discussion, see [Chan 2008] and [Nylan 2008, esp. nn. 9 and 80]. [Luo 2007] offers an astute reading of the meanings of *tianxia* and "world (*shijie* 世界)" during the crucial transitional era at the end of the nineteenth and beginning of the twentieth centuries. As Luo explains, traditionally one can find both broad (world) and narrow (China) meanings of *tianxia*. As the twentieth century dawned, it is well-known that Chinese thinkers made efforts to articulate a concept of "nation (*guo* and *guojia*)." Rather than see this as employing a narrow reading of *tianxia*, though, Luo argues that two contradictory sorts of transformation of *tianxia* into "world" are taking place. On the one hand, utopian thinkers like Kang Youwei try to articulate an expansive, universalist "world" within which Chinese and all people will find their just home. On the other hand, Chinese also want a place in the "world" as that category is defined by powerful Western nation-states, from which China at the time was essentially excluded. I believe that we can see Zhao Tingyang as heir to both these trends; his work is really an effort to find a single concept of *tianxia* that solves both of these distinct challenges.

17 [Zhao 2009b, 9].

18 [Ibid., 5].

19 [Ibid., 7].

20 [Ibid.].

21 See [Callahan 2008]. Callahan pays little attention to Zhao's philosophical arguments and gestures toward openness and dialogue (on which I will elaborate in a moment), focusing instead on the ways in which "all-under-heaven" rhetoric might be used to develop Chinese "soft power." Little wonder, then, that Callahan finds in Zhao a hegemonic agenda. Callahan is also a good example of another criticism of Zhao. Callahan writes that Zhao's "argument is based on a cavalier use of a few key passages from

Chinese thought, which upon closer consideration actually do not support his *Tianxia* worldview" [Callahan 2008, 753]. But this is to misunderstand Zhao as offering an interpretation of past ideas. To the contrary, Zhao is explicitly engaged in a creative, constructive enterprise that builds on, but is not strictly beholden to, past texts and authors. For further helpful discussion of these matters, see [Zhang 2010].

22 [Zhao 2005, 13].

23 [Zhao 2009b, 17]. Zhao's emphasis on openness suggests that Daniel Bell's criticism that Zhao implicitly downgrades other cultural and moral systems to "second-class status" may be unfair [Bell 2008, 25].

24 See [Zhang 2010] for one version of this criticism. [Zhao 2009a] endeavors to add detail to the basic argument, but still remains quite abstract.

25 [Zhao 2009b, 16].

26 [Zhao 2006a, 17–20].

27 For further discussion, see Chapter 3.

28 [Lo 1949, 186]. This loose way of identifying "human rights" talk, or of confusing ethical values that might support human rights with human rights themselves, is fairly common; see, e.g., [Lauren 1998].

29 See [Rosemont 1988] and [Rosemont 1998].

30 Of course, questions might be raised about the other two premises as well. For a challenge to the idea that Confucianism's emphasis on relations and roles makes it incompatible with human rights, see [Tiwald 2011a].

31 This is not to say that rituals do not have an important role in Confucian political philosophy; see Chapter 6 for details. I also want to acknowledge that rituals have and can continue to play helpful roles in restraining the powerful, as emphasized in [Chu 1998] and [Hahm 2003]; see also the concluding section of this chapter.

32 [Chan 1999, 228].

33 [Lee 2005b]. Lee does not invoke the "fallback" idea, so it is slightly unclear how he might see human rights interacting with Confucian ethical values. However, since Lee is a close follower of Mou Zongsan, he would surely endorse Mou's idea that our commitment to human rights is a kind of "self-restriction," on which see more below.

34 [Fan 2010, 58]. There are a few things with which I would take issue here: I think the self- versus other-regarding distinction fits poorly with Confucianism, and also question Fan's reading of liberal morality as largely devoid of content beyond general human rights.

35 [Ibid.].

36 [Ibid., 58–60; see esp. 60n28].

37 Some rights, especially those to minimal levels of economic wellbeing, may be difficult to enforce in certain contexts, but at least the goal should be clear.

38 [Ibid., 61].

39 Even Joel Feinberg's well-known argument that rights-claiming can serve as a source of dignity or self-esteem does not call for rights-claiming to be our main mode of interaction [Feinberg 1970].

40 [Tiwald 2011a].

41 Part of the case for this claim is made out in the balance of this chapter, but see also the discussion of the psychology of self-restriction in the book's Conclusion, where I address the issue of the "passive influence" of rights consciousness more directly.

42 I have not said anything about Position 5. I know of no Confucians who take this position, though there are some scholars of Confucianism who have come to this conclusion—see [Ci 1999]—and any number of liberals or others who conclude that since human rights and Confucianism are incompatible, we should choose human rights.

43 [Mou 1992, 257; see also Mou 1991, 130].

44 [Mou 1992, 47].

45 See also [Ibid., 257].

46 [Mou 1992, 59]. For some helpful discussion, see also [Chan 2008, 79–81].

47 [Ibid., 61].

48 This Confucian perspective, in other words, differs significantly from cosmopolitan liberal views, which arrive at human rights via the universalization of a specific conception of moral values. See [Zhao 2006b] for some relevant discussion. My Confucian perspective is also different from John Rawls's "Law of Peoples." Even though Rawls specifically aims to be more respectful of other peoples' traditions, the Law of Peoples is generated from within a liberal standpoint: other societies may qualify as "decent," but they are not consulted on the formulation of universal norms [Rawls 1999]. Bhikhu Parekh's "Non-Ethnocentric Universalism" [1999] bears some similarities to the view I here endorse; one significant difference is that I am here offering Confucian reasons for Confucians to endorse the rights of all-under-heaven, whereas Parekh tries to offer a theory that comes from all, or perhaps no, particular perspectives.

49 [Zhao 2009b, 16].

50 [Chang 2001, 209].

51 My emphasis here has been on the relation between Confucianism and both the concept and the process of human rights. The general tenor of my remarks in this chapter, as well as my reference a moment ago to P. C. Chang's participation in the drafting of the original UDHR, have been meant to suggest that Confucians will largely endorse the contents of existing human rights agreements, though I am certainly open to the idea that Confucian perspectives may highlight certain shortcomings in existing lists and formulations of rights. For some discussion, see [Chan 1999] and [Bell 2006, 76–8].

6 Neither Ethics nor Law: Ritual Propriety as Confucian Civility

1 Though pronounced the same, this is a completely different word from the *li* that I translate as "Coherence."

2 [Metzger 2005, 705].

3 *Analects* 17:13 and *Mencius* 7B:37. For considerable discussion, see [Angle unpublished-a].

4 Metzger mentions the work of scholar Patricia Ebrey, though he does not elaborate. He presumably has in mind works like [Ebrey 1984] and [Ebrey 1991].

5 The details are of course more complicated. For example, if one follows the Brooks's reconstruction of the composition of the *Analects*—which I accept in general outline—then ritual is not an explicit concern of the earliest layers of the text [Brooks & Brooks 1998]. For a contrasting view that sees ritual as central to the early practice of the Confucian school, see [Eno 1990].

6 *Analects* 12:1.

7 *Analects* 2:3.

8 As I read this passage, it is telling us that *li* is here envisioned as enacted by both rulers and by the people, in complementary and responsive ways. My thanks to Bill Haines for pushing me to clarify my thinking here; see our conversation at: http://warpweftandway.wordpress.com/2010/10/08/minimal-versus-maximal-ritual.

9 In addition to *Analects* 12:1 that I discussed already, other key passages would include the statement in *Xunzi* 19 ("Through *li*, Heaven and earth join in harmony . . .") and the *Zuo Zhuan*'s "*Li* is the constant principle of Heaven (*tiandi zhi jing*) . . ." [Duke Zhao 25; cf. Legge 1985, 708].

10 [Wood 1995, 103–5].

11 The Chinese term I translate as "Coherence" is, like "ritual," pronounced "*li*" but is an entirely different word. Other common translations are "pattern" and "principle." The idea of Coherence is explained in Chapter 3.

12 Quoted in [Bol 2008, 238]. For more on Zhang Zai's understanding of ritual, see [Kasoff 1984, 81–2 and *passim.*].

13 [Angle 2009, 146].

14 For a translation, see [Zhu 1991a], and Ebrey's monograph on the subject is invaluable [Ebrey 1991]. Bol's discussion of the *Family Rituals* is also helpful, as is his broader discussion of the role of rites and institutions for the Neo-Confucians [Bol 2008, 239–41 and *passim.*]. For considerable discussion of the roles that ritual plays in individual "lesser learning," according to Zhu, see [Angle 2009, ch. 8].

15 [Chow 1994, 191].

16 [Chow 1994, 196–7].

17 [Wang 1980, 853]; cf. [Legge 1967, 336].

18 For more on Xu's understanding of ritual as the means by which virtue politics can be realized in society, see [Xu 1980, 52] and [Elstein unpublished-a].

19 [Huang 2009a].

20 [Angle 2010a].

21 Debate about the meaning and relevance of Confucian ritual is not limited to China; for example, Robert Neville offers an interpretation of the meaning of ritual, and an argument for its relevance to Boston, in [Neville 2000].

22 Quoted in [Chow 1994, 201].

23 The *Analects* may admit of two different readings on this matter. Passages that explicitly mention changes of ritual do not make equally explicit the standard by which changes should be judged, and some (e.g., 3:9, 3:14, 2:23) might be read to suggest that there is no underlying standard: one just follows the vicissitudes of ritual evolution. However, in 9:3 the Master makes clear that some changes are acceptable while others are not, and implies that the standard is whether the new ritual successfully expresses the apt underlying moral emotion. See also the suggestion in 3:3 and 3:4 that apt moral feelings underlie rituals, as well as the Master's condemnation of a false ritual in 3:1.

24 *Mencius* 4A:17.

25 [Hall & Ames 1999, 205].

26 I find much of Ames's account very attractive, including the idea that one can only learn and develop key ethical sensibilities within family and role contexts. But as these sensibilities develop, one can then rely on them as independent sources of ethical authority to critique the roles and rituals, and as guidance when no role or ritual is there to guide. In Ames's most recent work, he notes the need for "more abstract regulative ideals such as courage or justice that provide direction for what is a legitimate claim for consideration and inclusion" [Ames 2011, 268], but because he insists on seeing virtues as "principles" that are antecedent to experience—of which he is very suspicious—he cannot find a satisfactory way to build into his account a notion of virtue that is capable of critiquing roles and rituals in the needed way [Ibid., 159].

27 [Hall & Ames 1999, 201 and 202].

28 [Seligman et al. 2008, 22].

29 As discussed above, "discretion (*quan*)" is Mencius's term; it is not found in the *Analects*, but the *Analects* contains a number of passages that highlight the insufficiency of *li* on its own. See 3:3, 15:18, and 15:33.

30 [Seligman et al. 2008, 35].

31 No rule can tell us how to apply itself to a given situation; that would require a further rule. At some point these explicit rules must come to an end. One influential discussion of these ideas is [McDowell 1979].

32 [Fan 2010, 182].

33 [Fan 2010, 182]. Fan also notes that the Song dynasty Confucian Li Gou (1009–1059) proposed a different defense of what I am calling ritual maximalism, namely that when one stretches out one's arm to save one's sister-in-law, one *is* following the appropriate ritual: in a dangerous context, a completely different ritual applies. Fan criticizes this approach for begging the question, as one can always claim to be observing a new ritual as an excuse for not following the standardly applicable ritual [Ibid., 182n19]. I believe that a similar response may be telling against Fan's own view, as I go on to discuss in the main text, above.

34 The only possible exception to this generalization is 4A:26, describing the sage Shun's decision to take a wife without first asking his parents' permission. (He knew that they would wrongly deny him permission.) We read: "[Mencius] said, 'Among the three unfilial things, to have no posterity is the worst. Shun's taking a wife without informing his parents was in order to avoid having no posterity. Gentlemen regard it as if he had informed them.'" This might fit one of Fan's models of apt exception, when one does not follow some rules of a ritual in order to complete the ritual as a whole (see his insightful discussion of the case of Confucius burying his mother [Fan 2010, 183]).

35 [Angle 2009, 124].

36 [Fan 2010, 206].

37 *Analects* 9:3. Confucius approves of changing the material of a ritual cap from hemp to (less expensive) silk, but resists a change in where one bows before a lord.

38 "Maximal" is my term, not Fan's, and while for the reasons discussed in the main text I believe Fan leans rather strongly in a maximalist direction, he also places considerable emphasis on *ren* in other contexts, and so is not a pure maximalist about ritual.

39 See *Xunzi* 19 and 23. For a critical perspective on the relation between ritual and power, see especially the work of Maurice Bloch, helpfully discussed in [Van Norden 2007, 103].

40 [Calhoun 2000, 259]. Calhoun throughout speaks of "respect, tolerance, and considerateness"; I abbreviate this throughout as simply "respect."

41 [Calhoun 2000, 260].

42 For both political and polite civility, Calhoun sees both a general consistency over time with respect to the central values she emphasizes, and also some changes. She mentions that eighteenth-century etiquette manuals in the United States, which stressed "deferential displays of respect for rank," were ultimately not suitable to American ideals and were pushed aside. [Ibid., 258].

43 [Ibid., 262].

44 [Ibid., 274].

45 [Ibid., 272 and 266].

6 6

9

46 [Woodruff 2001, 19].
47 [Buss 1999, 802].
48 [Seligman et al. 2008, 26].
49 [Van Norden 2007, 106n58]; Van Norden credits P. J. Ivanhoe with the example.
50 We tend to think of ethical growth as a solitary process, and it certainly has individual-based dimensions. But the Confucian emphasis on relationality helps us to see growth as taking place within the contexts of relationships as well. Some strands of modern therapy (e.g., couples' therapy, family therapy, the idea that some people enable others' problems) recognize this.
51 See [Angle 2009].
52 I thank David Elstein for helpful discussion of the issues raised in this paragraph.
53 Translation from [Brooks & Brooks 1998, 111].
54 Even in the case of an actor saying "Please accept my condolences" in a play, we might argue that the actor is helping to articulate norms of a community—even if the actor has no feeling of grief whatsoever. Admittedly, this is a complicated case (what do we say about plays set in different cultures that act out unfamiliar rituals?).
55 Daniel Bell has pointed out to me that faked ritual can also sometimes have unintended and problematic "shaping" consequences, as when the forced memorization of political slogans nurtures an attitude of political cynicism.
56 See [Jiang 2003, 322] and [Bell 2008, ch. 3]; Bell argues that we find a recognition of this idea in Xunzi. Calhoun makes the related (though weaker) point that norms of civility can have positive effects even in imperfect social worlds, since they are sometimes the only constraints on the privileged's expression of contempt toward the disesteemed [Calhoun 2000, 274–5].
57 See, e.g., [Chan 2000]. Other contemporary Confucian theorists resist these revisionist arguments; see [Jiang 2003, 215–29] and [Fan 2010, 170 and 32]. For reasons why Progressive Confucian need to critique oppression and yet should support non-oppressive but still hierarchical rituals, see Chapter 7.
58 Mencius 4B:28.
59 [Calhoun 2000, 275].
60 [Calhoun 2000, 263].
61 See [Angle 2009] for discussion of both these points.
62 For example, see *Mencius* 2A:6.
63 See, e.g., [Olberding 2009] and [Van Norden 2007, 354].
64 [Angle unpublished-a].
65 Along these lines, Chapter 7 focuses on the need to criticize systematic

oppression, which often is encoded in rituals. For a helpful discussion of "incivil" criticisms of authority figures in classical Confucianism, see [Kim 2011]. Incivility (which Kim differentiates from "uncivility") is based in ethical judgments. Kim writes that "the defining characteristics of Confucian incivilities are summed up as deferentially remonstrative and respectfully corrective (usually in the familial relations) but they are sometimes uncompromising and even intractable (especially in the political relations)."

66 [Anonymous 2001, 15].

67 [Ibid., 16].

68 These themes became common in the early twentieth century. The best-known articulation of "rights consciousness" is by Liang Qichao; see [Liang 2001]. For extensive discussion, including the ways in which various strands of Confucian thinking are interwoven into the rights discourse of the period, see [Angle 2002].

69 [Kim 2009, 397]. Strikingly, Kim maintains that an ideal liberal persona will be polarized between inner passions and outer behavior, and thus "very similar" to the "village worthy (*xiangyuan*)" abhorred by Confucius [Ibid., 395]. For other examples of arguments that bear structural similarities to Kim's, see [Ames 1988], [Hall and Ames 1999], and [Jiang 2003, e.g. 291–5].

70 [Kim 2009, 397 and 399].

71 For example, see [Hall and Ames 1999, 231–3]. Although not explicitly Confucian, Zhao Tingyang's "credit" theory of human rights has similar features; [Zhao 2006a]. I believe Hall and Ames are incorrect to say that a pragmatist would hold that rights are "granted by society." Rights are implicit in social practices; they need to be made explicit and laws need to be passed in order to ensure their protection, but society does not "grant" the rights in the first place. For a related view I find quite congenial, see [Li 2001].

72 I thus think there is a place for what Hahm Chaihark calls the "constitutionalist dimension" of ritual to help discipline political leaders [Hahm 2003, 47], but it must be balanced against the need emphasized here for law. In addition, as I noted in Chapter 4, allowing space for law means allowing space for lawyers and legal contestation, which will entail some pressure toward undisciplined, messy contestation. Chapter 4 allows that Confucian educational and personality ideals will mitigate this messiness to some extent, and the same can be said for ritual propriety. Still, the message of this chapter is that contemporary Confucians must look for a way to harmonize all three dimensions of value (ethics, politics/law, and ritual) rather than leaning too far in any one direction: see the concluding section.

73 Peerenboom and Fan both agree with this general sentiment, though

neither of them delivers satisfactorily, in my view, on the need for Confucian reasons for the rule of law. See [Peerenboom 1998, 251] and [Fan 2010], and the discussion of Fan in Chapter 4, above.

74 See Chapter 4.

75 [Tiwald 2011a] evokes the problems attendant with explicitly law- and rights-governed family interactions.

76 Woodruff writes, "Voting is a ceremony. It is an expression of reverence— not for our government or our laws, not for anything man-made, but for the very idea that ordinary people are more important than the juggernauts that seem to rule them" [Woodruff 2001, 21–2].

77 This and the next few sentences come from [Angle 2009, 203–4].

78 This is not to say that voting schemes in a Confucian polity must necessarily endorse one person-one vote. All must have a voice, but it is possible that the voices will not all be equal. See this book's Conclusion for further discussion.

7 Virtue, Politics, and Social Criticism: Toward Deference without Oppression

1 There is extensive scholarly debate about what exactly terms like "transmit" and "innovate" mean in this context; for one recent discussion, see http://warpweftandway.wordpress.com/2011/09/18/transmitting-述-innovating 作-and-philosophizing-in-confucius/.

2 For Mencius, see *Mencius* 1A:3 and 1A:4 (among other passages). [DeBary 1970] is one classic discussion of populism in the Yangming school, and see [Huang 1993] for Huang Zongxi.

3 Translation from [Brooks & Brooks 1998, 175], slightly altered.

4 I will not attempt to offer here a unified reading of the *Analects*; the evolving text may express more than one viewpoint. What is important is the message that later Confucians, including today's readers, can find in the text.

5 Translation (and interpretation) from [Brooks & Brooks 1998, 83]. Edward Slingerland reads it differently; see [Confucius 2003, 24]. [Olberding 2009, 14 and 21] speaks indirectly to this interpretive dispute and supports the reading that the Brooks and I prefer: she notes that if one is too perfect, one invites cynicism.

6 For some examples, see [Hutton 2006], [Sarkissian 2010], and [Slingerland 2011]. Hagop Sarkissian first drew my attention to the significance of *Analects* 10:12 that is discussed in the main text.

7 [Snow 2010] summarizes some of the key research, and elaborates on its implications for virtue ethics.

8 For a summary of some relevant research, see [Angle unpublished-b].

9 [Schnall et al. 2008].

10 *Xunzi* 19.5a; see [Xunzi 1998–94, vol. 3, 65]. My translation draws on an unpublished translation by Eric Hutton.

11 For related discussion, see Chapter 6 on the disciplinary function of ritual.

12 *Xunzi* 1.13; see [Xunzi 1988–94, vol. 1, 142]. My translation is based on Eric Hutton's unpublished translation.

13 See [Angle unpublished-a] for considerable discussion and further references.

14 See [Angle 2009, ch. 8] and [Angle unpublished-b].

15 [Angle 2009, ch. 8].

16 [Tan 2004, 121].

17 For more discussion, see [Angle 2009, ch. 11].

18 [Swanton 2003].

19 Pauline Lee argues that the *nei-wai* distinction is, according to classical Confucian sources, "graduated rather than oppositional" and is characterized by "permeability" [Lee 2000, 118]. I accept both points, which fit well with the evidence I will detail below. Gender-based differences in degree of access to the outer, more public *"wai"* dimension, though, were dramatic enough to underwrite the concerns I elaborate below, as one can see quite clearly from Lee's work on the Ming dynasty Confucian Li Zhi (e.g., see Li's criticisms of girls' education [Ibid., 126–7]).

20 [Wawrytko 2000] is one example of such a narrative. [Wang 2003, xi] notes that her collection of women's writings ends in the thirteenth century, "before the oppression of women was fully implemented."

21 [Ko 1994, 12].

22 [Ibid., 151–4].

23 [Ibid., 157].

24 Both of these texts were composed during the Tang dynasty (618–907 CE).

25 [Cheng 1999, 827].

26 [Song 1999, 827–8].

27 [Ko 1994, 145].

28 One example is Luo Qilan, a disciple of Yuan Mei, who wrote a poem about a dream in which she becomes a military figure only to wake up and discover she has bound feet [Idema & Grant 2004, 612–17]. See also a play written by Wu Zao, in which she dreams of turning into a man [Mann & Cheng 2001, 239–52]. My thanks to Ellen Widmer for discussion of these issues and help locating sources.

29 [Xu 1999].

30 One iconoclastic Confucian who did critique the oppression of women is Li Zhi (1527–1602). As Pauline Lee explains, "Li argues that women suffer intellectually, morally, and spiritually because of socially prescribed gendered differences in methods of self-cultivation" [Lee 2000, 126]. In her recent book, Lee expands on this theme, showing that Li Zhi believed that women's "life possibilities [were] wholly and severely fettered by the way

that the social world [had] been constructed." Still, Lee acknowledges that Li did not even begin to consider the possibility of structural changes to Chinese society that could have positively affected this situation [Lee 2011, 32].

31 [Rosenlee 2006, 4].

32 Rosenleee is not alone in pursuing this goal. The prominent Confucian Tu Wei-ming has for many years called for a serious Confucian reflection on "the feminist critique of tradition" [Tu 1996, 18]. Contemporary scholar Sin-yee Chan has contributed to this internal critique of Confucianism; see [Chan 2000].

33 *Analects* 15:39.

34 The classic study is [Ho 1962].

35 [DeBary 1970].

36 *Analects* 6:11; cf. [Brooks & Brooks 1998, 33].

37 *Analects* 7:15; cf. [Brooks & Brooks 1998, 41].

38 Translation from [Mencius 1970, 182].

39 [Walsh unpublished].

40 Translation from [Mencius 1970, 164].

41 For the debate between active cultivationist and natural growth readings of *Mencius*, see [Im 1999].

42 See *Mencius* 6A8. My focus here is on the role that luck can play in one's ethical or moral (using those words synonymously) development. Another kind of luck attends to how well one's life goes overall, which for many Greek thinkers was also of vital ethical import.

43 Translation from [Mencius 1970, 58].

44 Admittedly, the issue of responsibility and the *min* in *Mencius* is not quite this simple. [1B4] can be read as saying that if the people "speak ill of those in authority" as a result of not being allowed to share appropriately in the goods of the realm, it would be "wrong (*fei*)." (I say this tentatively, because in light of the *min* versus *ren* distinction discussed in Chapter 3, it may be significant that the text refers to a "person (*ren*)" speaking ill, not to the people collectively speaking ill. The rest of the passage, though, refers to the people collectively.) Nonetheless, the main emphasis in this passage is on the responsibility of the ruler.

45 On this issue, see also [Tessman 2005, 25], who criticizes some feminists for being overly sanguine about voluntarist personal transformation.

46 [Kupperman 1991, 63].

47 Translation from [Graham 1992, 28], slightly altered.

48 [Graham 1992, 22]

49 Kupperman makes an interesting version of the "there is nothing we can do about it" point when he says that his account of the self (see [Kupperman 1991, ch. 2]) "suggests that we cannot unproblematically speak of a you who would have developed a sharply different character. To say you are

lucky to have the character you do is a little like saying that you are lucky to be yourself rather than someone else" [1991, 141].

50 [Walsh unpublished].

51 In putting the problem in these terms, I do not mean to rule out the possibility – indeed, the likelihood – that there may be other good reasons to oppose oppression; my thanks to Emily McRae for emphasizing this.

52 [Young 1990, ch. 2].

53 [Ibid., 54].

54 [Tessman 2005, 26]

55 [Ibid., ch. 2].

56 For example, Tessman cites analyses the emphasize the "criminality" seen in the character of African-Americans, attribute this either to deficiencies in "black culture" or to unintended outcomes of policies aimed at ending inequality, and conclude that "there are no injustices to blacks as a group that need to be rectified" [Tessman 2005, 45].

57 [Young 1990, 59].

58 I thank contributors to a discussion on the Warp, Weft, and Way blog for helping to make the nature of this danger perspicuous. See http://warpweftandway.wordpress.com/2011/03/18/is-confucian-feminism-so-easy/.

59 For discussion of the relations between *neisheng* and *waiwang*, see [Angle 2009, ch. 10].

60 Both of these aspects of Confucian ethics are explored in [Angle 2009]; see Chapters 5 and 6, respectively.

61 Recent psychological research on the effect of social setting on moral development is extremely relevant here. One such study concludes, "For adolescents, the resources available to construct a moral identity vary systematically with neighborhood environment. Adolescents living in America's poorest neighborhoods experience stress, child saturation, and institutional scarcity at levels that make the formation of moral identity more difficult" [Hart & Matsuba 2009, 228].

62 [Tessman 2005, 164 and *passim*].

63 [Ibid., 166].

64 [Ko 1994, 163].

65 [Tessman 2005, ch. 3].

66 [Berthrong 1998, 188].

67 [Mencius 1970, 63].

68 In saying this, we must be careful not to include extraneous connotations of the English word "hierarchy" in the concept applied to Confucianism. The *Oxford English Dictionary* makes clear that the earliest uses of "hierarchy" had theological meanings, including "Each of the three divisions of angels" and, by the sixteenth century, priestly or ecclesiastical rule. From at least the seventeenth century, though, the term has been in regular use

to refer simply to "A body of persons or things ranked in grades, orders, or classes, one above another." My thanks to participants in the discussion of these issues on the Warp, Weft, and Way blog.

69 Xunzi asserts that the making of status distinctions (*fen*) is central to human identity; see *Xunzi* 9; *Mencius* 2A:6 says that "one without the feeling of deference (*cirang zhi xin*) is not human."

70 Translation from [Brooks & Brooks 1998, p. 42]. For Zhu Xi on reading, see [Angle 2009, ch. 8].

71 [Rosenlee 2006, 157–8].

72 See *Analects* 6:30, 7:26 and 7:34. Even sages are portrayed in the classics as engaging in deferential practices like asking questions of others; see [Angle 2009, ch. 9] for discussion.

73 [Arendt 1977, 92–3].

74 See [Hall & Ames 1987, 181]. As Emily McRae has helped me to see, a backdrop of coercion exists in many of the contexts in which I want to say that apt deference is possible. Courtrooms, families, and military units all may be sites of coercion. While it will sometimes be unclear or indeterminate whether one is genuinely deferring to authority or simply obeying to avoid punishment, the distinction between deference and avoiding punishment is nonetheless robust and important, as recognized in *Analects* 2:3.

75 Consider a soldier deferring to his superior's order to undertake an extremely risky mission. He may end up giving his life, but if he sees his action as helping to maintain or realize other important values, it will not count as "sacrifice" in the sense I am using here. Contrast this with a case in which the soldier's orders aim at screening his superior's corrupt behavior: here sacrifice is being demanded and the deference is compromised.

76 See [Woodruff 2001] and the development of this idea in a specifically Confucian context in [Angle 2009].

77 [Meyers 1997, 203].

78 [Angle 2009, ch. 6].

79 Both of these reasons are clearly expressed in Xunzi's famous discussion of ritual distinctions at the outset of his *Li Lun* chapter.

80 [Chan 2012].

81 [Tan unpublished].

82 *Analects* 16:1 and [Li 2012].

83 Cited in [Li 2012].

84 [Angle 2012].

8 Conclusion

1 See [Gan 2006]. Gan makes a similar argument regarding the emphasis in the work of Liu Shuxian, another heir of the New Confucians, on the slogan "Coherence is one; its manifestations are many (*li yi fen shu*)." It should be

noted that neither Tu nor Liu abandons the idea that Confucianism has grasped important and universally applicable truths, but Gan is right that their beliefs about the scope and applicability of these truths seem much less ambitious than for previous generations of New Confucians.

2 See [Jiang 2003], [Jiang 2010], and [Kang 2005]. Fan subtitles his book "Rethinking Morality After the West," but his focus is more on the ideas that East Asian countries should embrace after they have purged problematic Western ideologies, rather than on arguing that Western peoples should adopt Confucianism.

3 Of course, Chinese culture itself is pluralistic. Even if we artificially exclude the many developments of Chinese culture in the last one hundred years, it cannot be denied that there exists a huge range of non- or even anti-Confucian elements in Chinese culture. And in fairness, the Institutional Confucian Jiang Qing does make some concessions to this reality, offering some representation to alternative religions and cultures in one of the three houses of his proposed Confucian legislature. See [Jiang 2010], discussed briefly above in Chapter 3.

4 Relevant here is Bai Tongdong's distinction, mentioned in Chapter 1, between the universal openness of political philosophy and the particularist focus encouraged by Jiang Qing's viewing Confucianism (that is, *rujiao*) through the lens of religion. See [Bai 2010].

5 My thanks to Kai Marchal for raising this question.

6 [Jiang 2010]; [Kang 2005].

7 Thomas Wilson's work on Confucian temples is particularly instructive. He notes the differences and yet ambiguity between rituals at imperial Confucian temples and those of the Kong family (Confucius's surname is Kong) at their ancestral temple in Qufu; by the fifteenth century, he says, state and family cult were partly fused but never entirely reconciled. Wilson adds that "Because only state-school students and examination-degree holders were permitted to observe or participate in the local rites, the Kong temple was ritually demarcated from all other temple cults, which solidified the Confucian gentry as a community that was culturally marked, in part, by mastery of the classical language of the sages" [Wilson 1996, 564]. Still, in no sense can we talk about a Confucian "church" with clergy or congregation.

8 Within the literature on perfectionism, I have found [Chan 2000] and [Sher 1997] to be most helpful. For more discussion, see [Angle 2009, section 11.3].

9 For example, see [Metz 2001] for an argument that Chan's moderate perfectionism violates Kantian respect for persons.

10 [Mou 1991, 179 and 126].

11 [Sher 1997, ch. 5].

12 [Metzger 2005, 255–61].

13 The *Mencius* contains several stories concerning the ancient sage Shun's undying love for his father, notwithstanding his quite despicable father's repeated attempts to harm him. According to Progressive Confucianism, Shun would have been better off in an era that recognized self-restriction and the rule of law, though the existence and functioning of these institutions would not have conflicted with his love and filial devotion to his father.

14 Confucianism is of course not alone in trying to combine these values, but I will focus here on the responses that Progressive Confucianism can make to the challenge.

15 [Angle 2009, 216–21].

16 I noted above that there is a tinge of pathos in Tang Junyi's way of restraining his perfectionism via toleration: it should be clear now that self-restriction, as I understand it, does not have them same air of compromise. A similar comparison might be made with Martha Nussbaum's Aristotelian approach to the rule of law; for Nussbaum, a public domain structured by laws remains something of a necessary evil. See my discussion in [Angle 2009, 208–9].

17 Putting this point in terms of "individual" ethical cultivation is actually slightly misleading, because ethical achievement is always relational, as I discussed in Chapter 3.

18 See [Liang 2001], and the discussion in [Angle 2002, ch. 6]. Not possessing the idea of self-restriction, though, Liang tends to conflate rights consciousness with ethical consciousness. It is also worth noting that Liang is certainly critical of many aspects of traditional Chinese culture and also of certain important themes in Confucianism. On "rights consciousness," see also Chapter 6.

19 [DeBary 1991, 49].

20 See [Chu 1998], [Hahm 2003], and my discussions in Chapter 6 and in [Angle 2009, 185–6].

21 [DeBary 1991, 54]. For Huang Zongxi, see [Huang 1993, 104–10], and DeBary's comments at [Ibid., 65–7]. DeBary goes so far as to suggest that Huang was aiming at a kind of "parliament of scholars" that could "serve a function in helping to offset other concentrations of power" [Ibid., 83].

22 For references and discussion, see [Makeham 2008, 2].

23 Gan Chunsong hopes that contemporary Institutional Confucians will learn from the failures of Kang Youwei and others to establish a Confucian church early in the twentieth century [Gan 2006].

Bibliography

Alitto, Guy S. (1979). *The Last Confucian: Liang Shu-ming and the Chinese Dilemma of Modernity*. Berkeley: University of California Press.

Allan, Sarah. (1984). Drought, Human Sacrifice and the Mandate of Heaven in a Lost Text from the "Shang shu". *Bulletin of the School of Oriental and African Studies*, 47:3, 523–39.

Ames, Roger T. (1988). Rites as Rights: The Confucian Alternative. In Rouner, Leroy S. (ed.), *Human Rights and the World's Religions*. Notre Dame: University of Notre Dame Press, 199–216.

——(2011). *Confucian Role Ethics: A Vocabulary*. Honolulu: University of Hawaii Press.

Angle, Stephen C. (2002). *Human Rights and Chinese Thought: A Cross-Cultural Inquiry*. New York: Cambridge University Press.

——(2007). 中國哲學家與全求哲學 [Chinese Philosophers and Global Philosophy]. «中國哲學與文化» [*Chinese Philosophy and Culture*], 1:1.

——(2009). *Sagehood: The Contemporary Significance of Neo-Confucian Philosophy*. New York: Oxford University Press.

——(2010a). Rethinking Confucian Authority and Rejecting Confucian Authoritarianism. «中國哲學與文化» [*Chinese Philosophy and Culture*].

——(2010b). Review of *Reconstructionist Confucianism: Rethinking Morality After the West* by Ruiping Fan. *Dao: A Journal of Comparative Philosophy*, 9:3, 353–57.

——(2010c). A Reply to Fan Ruiping. *Dao: A Journal of Comparative Philosophy*, 9(4), 463–64.

——(2011). Reply to Justin Tiwald. *Dao: A Journal of Comparative Philosophy*, 10(2), 237–9.

——(2012). Contemporary Confucian Perspectives on Social Justice. In Palmer, Michael (ed.), *Companion to Religion and Social Justice*. New York: Blackwell.

——(unpublished-a). Is Conscientiousness a Virtue? Confucian Answers. In Angle, Stephen C., & Slote, Michael (eds), *Confucianism and Virtue Ethics*.

——(unpublished-b). Seeing Confucian "Active Moral Perception" in Light of Contemporary Psychology.

——(unpublished-c). The *Analects* and Moral Theory. In Olberding, Amy (ed.), *The Dao Companion to the Analects*.

Arendt, Hannah (1977). What is Authority? In *Between Past and Future*. New York: Penguin, 91–141.

Bai, Tongdong 白彤东 (2009). «旧邦新命：古今中西参照下的古典儒家政治哲学» [*New Mission of an Old State: Classical Confucian Political Philosophy in a Contemporary and Comparative Relevance Context*]. Beijing: Beijing daxue chubanshe.

——(2010). 心性儒学还是政治儒学?新邦旧命还是旧邦新命?—关于儒学复兴的几点思考 [Moral Confucianism or Political Confucianism? Old Mission for a New State or New Mission for an Old State? Some Reflections on the Revival of Confucianism]. Unpublished.

Bell, Daniel A. (2000). *East Meet West: Human Rights and Democracy in East Asia*. Princeton, NJ: Princeton University Press.

——(2006). *Beyond Liberal Democracy: Political Thinking for an East Asian Context*. Princeton: Princeton University Press.

——(2008). *China's New Confucianism: Politics and Everyday Life in a Changing Society*. Princeton: Princeton University Press.

——(2010). Reconciling Socialism with Confucianism? Reviving Tradition in China. *Dissent, Winter 2010*, 91–102.

Berthrong, John (1998). *Transformations of the Confucian Way*. Boulder, CO: Westview.

Billioud, Sébastien (2012). *Thinking Through Confucian Modernity: A Study of Mou Zongsan's Moral Metaphysics*. Leiden: Brill.

——, & Thoraval, Joël (2008). *Anshen liming* or the Religious Dimension of Confucianism. *China Perspectives*, 3, 88–106.

Bloom, Irene (1998). Fundamental Intuitions and Consensus Statements: Mencian Confucianism and Human Rights. In *Confucianism and Human Rights*. New York: Columbia University Press, 94–116.

Bol, Peter K. (2008). *Neo-Confucianism in History*. Cambridge: Harvard University Asia Center.

Bresciani, Umberto (2001). *Reinventing Confucianism: The New Confucian Movement*. Taipei: Ricci Institute for Chinese Studies.

Brooks, E. Bruce, & Brooks, A. Taeko (1998). *The Original Analects: Sayings of Confucius and His Successors*. New York: Columbia University Press.

Bunnin, Nicholas (2008). God's Knowledge and Ours: Kant and Mou Zongsan on Intellectual Intuition. *Journal of Chinese Philosophy, 35:4*, 613–24.

Buss, Sarah (1999). Appearing Respectful: The Moral Significance of Manners. *Ethics, 109*, 795–826.

Calhoun, Cheshire (2000). The Virtue of Civility. *Philosophy and Public Affairs, 29:3*, 251–75.

Callahan, William A. (2008). Chinese Visions of World Order: Post-hegemonic or a New Hegemony? *International Studies Review, 10*, 749–61.

Ch'en, Jerome (1972). *Yuan Shih-k'ai*. Stanford, CA: Stanford University Press.

Chan, Joseph (1999). A Confucian Perspective on Human Rights for Contemporary China. In Bauer, Joanne R., & Bell, Daniel A. (eds), *The East Asian Challenge for Human Rights*. Cambridge: Cambridge University Press, 212–40.

——(2000). Legitimacy, Unanimity, and Perfectionism. *Philosophy and Public Affairs, 29:1*, 5–42.

——(2007). Democracy and Meritocracy: Toward a Confucian Perspective. *Journal of Chinese Philosophy, 34(2)*, 179–93.

——(2008). Territorial Boundaries and Confucianism. In Bell, Daniel A (ed.), *Confucian Political Ethics*. Princeton: Princeton University Press, 61–84.

——(2012). Early Confucian Perspectives on Social Justice. In Palmer, Michael (ed.), *Companion to Religion and Social Justice*. New York: Blackwell.

Chan, N. S. (2011) *The Thought of Mou Zongsan*. Leiden: Brill.

Chan, Sin Yee (2000). Gender Relationship Roles in the *Analects* and the *Mencius*. *Asian Philosophy, 2:1*.

Chang, Carsun (1962). A Manifesto for a Re-appraisal of Sinology and Reconstruction of Chinese Culture. In *The Development of Neo-Confucian Thought*. New York: Bookman Associates, 455–83.

Chang, P. C. (2001). Chinese Statements During Deliberations on the UDHR (1948). In *The Chinese Human Rights Reader: Documents and Commentary, 1900–2000*. Armonk, New York: M.E.Sharpe, 206–13.

Chen, Lai (2009). (Edmund Ryden, trans.) *Tradition and Modernity: A Humanist View*. Leiden: Brill.

Cheng, Chung-ying 成中英 (1991). 現代新儒學建立的基礎 : '仁學'與'人學'合一之道 [The Foundation for the Establishment of Contemporary New Confucianism: The Way of Uniting 'Humane Learning' and 'Human Learning']. In 《當代新儒學論文集 : 內聖篇》 [*Collected Essays on Contemporary New Confucianism: Inner Sagehood Volume*]. Taibei: Wenlu chubanshe,

Cheng, Chung-ying, & Bunnin, Nicholas (2002). *Contemporary Chinese Philosophy*. Malden, MA: Blackwell.

Cheng, Madame (1999). Classic of Filial Piety for Women. In deBary, William Theodore, & Bloom, Irene (eds), *Sources of Chinese Tradition, vol. 1*. New York: Columbia University Press, 824–27.

Chow, Kai-wing (1994). *The Rise of Confucial Ritualism in Late Imperial China: Ethics, Classics, and Lineage Discourse*. Stanford: Stanford University Press.

Christiano, Tom (2008). Authority. *The Stanford Encyclopedia of Philosophy, Fall 2008 Edition*.

Chu, Ron Guey (1998). Rites and Rights in Ming China. In DeBary, Wm. Theodore, & Wei-ming, Tu (eds), *Confucianism and Human Rights*. New York: Columbia University Press, 169–78.

Ci, Jiwei (1999). The Confucian Relational Concept of the Person and its Modern Predicament. *Kennedy Institute of Ethics Journal, 9(4),* 325–46.

Clower, Jason (2010). *The Unlikely Buddhologist: Tiantai Buddhism in Mou Zongsan's New Confucianism.* Leiden: Brill.

Confucius (2003). (Slingerland, Edward, trans.) *Analects, With Selections from Traditional Commentaries.* Indianapolis: Hackett.

DeBary, William Theodore (1970). Individualism and Humanitarianism in Late Ming Thought. In DeBary, William Theodore (ed.), *Self and Society in Ming Thought.* New York: Columbia University Press, 145–247.

———(1989). *The Message of the Mind in Neo-Confucianism.* New York: Columbia University Press.

———(1991). *The Trouble with Confucianism.* Cambridge: Harvard University Press.

Defoort, Carine, & Ge, Zhaoguang (2005). Editors' Introduction: The Legitimacy of Chinese Philosophy. *Contemporary Chinese Thought, 37:1.*

Donnelley, Jack (2003). *Universal Human Rights in Theory and Practice, 2nd ed.* Ithaca: Cornell University Press.

Ebrey, Patricia Buckley (1984). *Family and Property in Sung China: Yuan Tsai's Precepts for Social Life.* Princeton: Princeton University Press.

Ebrey, Patricia Buckley (1991). *Confucianism and Family Rituals in Imperial China: A Social History of Writing about Rites.* Princeton: Princeton University Press.

El-Amine, Loubna (2012). The Confucian Conception of the Political. Ph. D. Dissertation (Princeton University).

Elstein, David (2009). The Authority of the Master in the *Analects. Philosophy East & West, 59:2,* 142–72.

———(2011). Mou Zongsan's Political Thought. *Contemporary Political Theory,* Online First.

———(unpublished-a). Recovering the Confucian Spirit: The Political Thought of Xu Fuguan.

———(unpublished-b). Jiang Qing: China's New Traditionalist.

Eno, Robert (1990). *The Confucian Creation of Heaven: Philosophy and the Defense of Ritual Mastery.* Albany: State University of New York Press.

Evans, Gareth (2008). *Responsibility to Protect : Ending Mass Atrocity Crimes Once and for All.* Washington, DC: Brookings Institution Press.

Eylon, Yuval (2009). Virtue and Continence. *Ethical Theory and Moral Practice, 12,* 137–51.

Fan, Ruiping (2010a). *Reconstructionist Confucianism: Rethinking Morality after the West.* Dordrecht: Springer.

Feinberg, Joel (1970). The Nature and Value of Rights. *The Journal of Value Inquiry, 4.*

Fingarette, Herbert (1972). *Confucius—The Secular as Sacred.* New York: Harper & Row.

Fuller, Lon L. (1969). *The Morality of Law*. New Haven: Yale University Press.

Fung, Yu-lan (1953). *A History of Chinese Philosophy*. Princeton: Princeton University Press.

Gan, Chunsong 干春松 (2006). 制度儒学 [*Institutional Confucianism*]. Shanghai: Shiji chuban jituan.

Gassmann, Robert H. (2000). Understanding Ancient Chinese Society: Approaches to *Ren* and *Min*. *The Journal of the American Oriental Society, 120:3, 348–59*.

Glanville, Luke (2010). Retaining the Mandate of Heaven: Sovereign Accountability in Ancient China. *Millennium: Journal of International Studies, 39(2), 323–43*.

Graham, A. C. (1992). *Two Chinese Philosophers*. La Salle: Open Court.

Guo, Baogang (2003). Political Legitimacy and China's Transition. *Journal of Chinese Political Science, 8:1&2, 1–25*.

Guo, Qiyong (2007). Is Confucian Ethics a 'Consanguinism'? *Dao: A Journal of Comparative Philosophy, 6(1), 21–37*.

Habermas, Jurgen (1998). Kant's Idea of Perpetual Peace. In *The Inclusion of the Other*. Cambridge, MA: MIT Press.

Hadot, Pierre (1995). *Philosophy as a Way of Life: Spiritual Exercises from Socrates to Foucault*. Cambridge, USA: Blackwell.

Hahm, Chaihark (2003). Constitutionalism, Confucian Civic Virtue, and Ritual Propreity. In Bell, Daniel A, & Hahm, Chaibong (eds), *Confucianism for the Modern World*. Cambridge: Cambridge University Press, 31–53.

Hall, David L., & Ames, Roger T. (1987). *Thinking Through Confucius*. Albany: State University of New York Press.

—— & ——(1999). *The Democracy of the Dead: Dewey, Confucius, and the Hope for Democracy in China*. Chicago: Open Court.

Hao, Yufan (1999). From Rule of Man to Rule of Law: an unintended consequence of corruption in China in the 1990s. *Journal of Contemporary China, 8:22, 405–23*.

Hart, Daniel, & Matsuba, M. Kyle (2009). Urban Neighborhoods as Contexts for Moral Identity Development. In Narvaez, Darcia, & Lapsley, Daniel K. (eds), *The Development of the Moral Personality*. New York: Cambridge University Press, 214–31.

Ho, Ping-ti (1962). *The Ladder of Success in Imperial China: Aspects of Social Mobility, 1368–1911*. New York: Columbia University Press.

Huang, Yushun 黄玉顺 (2005). 从"西方哲学"到"生活儒学" [From 'Western Philosophy' to 'Life Confucianism']. 《北京青年政治学院学报》 [*Journal of Beijing Youth Politics College*], 14(1), 42–7.

——(2008). On 'Viewing Things' and 'Viewing Nothing': A Dialogue between Confucianism and Phenomenology. *Frontiers of Philosophy in China, 3(2), 177–93*.

———(2009a). 儒学复兴的两条路线及其超越——儒家当代主义的若干思考 [The Two Directions of the Confucian Revival and their Transcendence: Reflections on Contemporary Confucianism]. «西南民族大学学报 (人文社科版)» [*Journal of Southwest Nationalities University (Social Science Edition)*] 209, 192–201.

———(2009b). 中国正义论纲要 [An Outline of a Chinese Theory of Justice]. «四川大学学报 (哲学社会科学版)» [*Journal of Sichuan University (Social Science Edition)*] 164: 32–42.

Huang, Zongxi (1993). (DeBary, William Theodore, trans.) *Waiting for the Dawn*. New York: Columbia University Press.

Huang, Zongxi 黃宗羲 (1985). 明夷待访录 [Waiting for the Dawn]. In «黃宗羲全集» [*Complete Works of Huang Zongxi*]. Hangzhou: Zhejiang Ancient Text Press,

Hui, Victoria Tin-bor (2005). *War and State Formation in Ancient China and Early Modern Europe*. Cambridge: Cambridge University Press.

Hutton, Eric L. (2006). Character, Situationism, and Early Confucian Thought. *Philosophical Studies, 127*, 37–58.

Idema, Wilt L., & Grant, Beata (2004). *The Red Brush: Writing Women of China*. Cambridge: Harvard University Asia Center.

Im, Manyul (1999). Emotional Control and Virtue in the Mencius. *Philosophy East & West, 49(1)*, 1–27.

ICISS, International Commission on Intervention and State Sovereignty (2001). *The Responsibility to Protect: Report of the International Commission on Intervention and State Sovereignty*. Ottawa: International Development Research Centre.

Ivanhoe, Philip J. (2010). Review of Peter K. Bol, *Neo-Confucianism in History*. *Dao: A Journal of Comparative Philosophy* 9(4), 471–5.

Jeans, Roger B., Jr. (1997). *Democacy and Socialism in Republican China: The Politics of Zhang Junmai (Carsun Chang), 1906–1941*. Lanham, MD: Rowman & Littlefield.

Jenco, Leigh K. (2010a). Rule by Man" and "Rule by Law" in Early Republican China: Contributions to a Theoretical Debate. *Journal of Asian Studies, forthcoming*.

———(2010b). *Making the Political: Founding and Paradox in the Political Theory of Zhang Shizhao*. New York: Cambridge University Press.

Jensen, Lionel M. (1997). *Manufacturing Confucianism: Chinese Traditions and Universal Civilization*. Durham: Duke University Press.

Jiang, Qing 蔣庆 (2003). «政治儒学 ： 当代儒学的转向、特质与发展» [*Political Confucianism: The Changing Direction, Particularities, and Development of Contemporary Confucianism*]. Beijing: Sanlian Shudian (Harvard-Yenching Academic Series).

———(2010). «政治儒學•續編 ——王道政治與儒教憲政 ： 未來中國政治發展的儒學思考» [*A Sequel to Political Confucianism – Kingly Politics and Confucian*

Constitutionalism: Confucian Reflections on the Future Development of Chinese Politics]. Unpublished.

——(2012). (Bell, Daniel, and Fan, Ruiping, eds) *A Confucian Constitutional Order*. Princeton: Princeton University Press.

Kang, Xiaoguang 康晓光 (2005). 《仁政：中国政治发展的第三条道路》[*Humane Government: A Third Road for the Development of Chinese Politics*]. Singapore: Global Publishing Co.

——(2011). 儒家宪政论纲 [An Outline of Confucian Constitutionalism]. 《儒家邮报》 [*Confucian Newsletter*], n.p.

Kasoff, Ira E. (1984). *The Thought of Chang Tsai*. Cambridge: Cambridge University Press.

Keith, Ronald C. (1991). Chinese Politics and the New Theory of "Rule of Law". *The China Quarterly, 125*, 109–18.

——, & Lin, Zhiqiu (2003). The "Falun Gong Problem": Politics and the Struggle for the Rule of Law in China. *The China Quarterly, 175*, 623–42.

Kim, Singmoon (2009). Self-Transformation and Civil Society: Lockean vs. Confucian. *Dao: A Journal of Comparative Philosophy, VIII(4)*, 383–401.

——(2011). The Virtue of Incivility: Confucian Communitarianism Beyond Docility. *Philosophy and Social Criticism, 37(1)*, 25–48.

Ko, Dorothy (1994). *Teachers of the Inner Chambers: Women and Culture in Seventeenth-Century China*. Stanford, CA: Stanford University Press.

Kupperman, Joel J. (1991). *Character*. New York: Oxford Univesity Press.

Lauren, Paul Gordon (1998). *The Evolution of International Human Rights: Visions Seen*. Philadelphia: University of Pennsylvania Press.

Lee, Ming-huei (2008). Wang Yangming's Philosophy and Modern Theories of Democracy: A Reconstructive Interpretation. *Dao: A Journal of Comparative Philosophy, 7:3*, 283–94.

Lee, Ming-huei 李明輝 (1991a). 儒學如何開出民主與科學? [How Can Confucianism Generate Democracy and Science?]. In 《儒家與現代意識》 [*Confucianism and Modern Consciousness*]. Taibei: Wenlu chubanshe, 1–17.

——(2001). 牟宗三思想中的儒学与康德 [Confucianism and Kant in Mou Zongsan's Thought]. In 《当代儒学的自我转化》 [*The Self-Transformation of Contemporary Confucianism*]. Beijing: Zhongguo Shehui Kexue Chubanshe, 48–80.

——(2005a). 性善说与民主政治 [Theories of Good Nature and Democratic Politics]. In 《儒家视野下的政治思想》 [*Political Thought in Confucian Perspective*]. Beijing: Beijing daxue chubanshe, 22–46.

——(2005b). 存心伦理学、责任伦理学与儒家思想 [Ethics of Conviction, Ethics of Responsibility, and Confucian Thought]. In 《儒家视野下的政治思想》 [*Political Thought in Confucian Perspective*]. Beijing: Beijing daxue chubanshe, 66–87.

——(2005c). 儒家政治哲学与责任伦理学 [Confucian Political Philosophy and

Ethics of Responsibility]. In 《儒家视野下的政治思想》 [*Political Thought in Confucian Perspective*]. Beijing: Beijing daxue chubanshe, 109–19.

——Lee, Ming-huei (2008). Wang Yangming's Philosophy and Modern Theories of Democracy: A Reconstructive Interpretation. *Dao: A Journal of Comparative Philosophy, 7:3,* 283–94.

Lee, Pauline (2000). Li Zhi and John Stuart Mill: A Confucian Feminist Critique of Liberal Feminism. In Li, Chenyang (ed.), *The Sage and the Second Sex: Confucianism, Ethics, and Gender.* Chicago: Open Court, 113–32.

——(2011). *Li Zhi* 李贽 *(1527–1602), Confucianism and The Virtue of Desire.* Albany, NY: SUNY Press.

Legge, James (1967). *Li Chi: Book of Rites.* New York: University Books.

——(1985). *The Ch'un Ts'ew with The Tso Chuen.* Taipei: Southern Materials Center.

Levey, M. (1991) *Chu Hsi as a "Neo-Confucian": Chu Hsi's Critique of Heterodoxy, Heresy, and the "Confucian" Tradition.* Unpublished University of Chicago: Chicago, IL.

Li, Buyun (2001). On The Three Existential Types of Human Rights. In Angle, Stephen C., & Svensson, Marina (eds), *Chinese Human Rights Reader.* Armonk, New York: M. E.Sharpe, 333–43.

Li, Chenyang (2012). Equality and Inequality in Confucianism. *Dao: A Journal of Comparative Philosophy 12: 3.*

Li, Lanfen 李兰芬 (2008). 《当代中国德治研究》 [*Research in Contemporary Chinese Virtue Politics*]. Beijing: Renmin chubanshe.

Li, Yushi 栗玉仕 (1996). 伦理本位与以德治国——梁漱溟社会伦理思想研究 [Ethical Basis and Using Virtue for Governance: Research on Liang Shuming's Social Ethical Thought]. 《齐鲁学刊》 [*Qilu Journal*], 6, 12–18.

Liang, Qichao (2001). On Rights Consciousness. In Angle, Stephen C., & Svensson, Marina (eds.), *Chinese Human Rights Reader.* Armonk, New York: M. E.Sharpe, 5–15.

Lin, Anwu 林安梧 (1998). 《儒學革命論：後新儒學哲學的問題向度》 [*A Confucian Revolution: Problematic Aspects of Post-New-Confucian Philosophy*]. Taibei: Xuesheng Shuju.

——(2004). 从"外王"到"内圣"：以"社会公义"论为核心的儒学——后新儒学的崭新思考 [From 'Outer Kingship' to 'Inner Sagehood': Taking 'Social Justice' as the Core of Confucianism—Brand New Reflections on Post-New-Confucianism]. *Zhejiang shehui kexue, 1,*

——(2008). 后新儒学及"公民儒学"相关问题之探讨 [Investigating Issues Concerning Post-New-Confucianism and 'Civic Confucianism']. *Qiushi xuekan, 1,* 13–20.

Liu, Lydia H. (1995). *Transligual Practice: Literature, National Culture, and Translated Modernity in China, 1900–1937.* Stanford: Stanford University Press.

Liu, Shao-chi (1964). *How to Be a Good Communist.* Beijing: Foreign Language Press.

Lo, Chung-shu (1949). *Human Rights in the Chinese Tradition*. New York: Columbia University Press.

Luo, Guojie 罗国杰, & Xia, Weidong 夏伟东 (2001). 论 "以德治国" 的历史、理论与实践 [On the History, Theory, and Practice of 'Use Virtue to Govern the State'. «高校理论战线» [*The Theoretical Line in Higher Education*], 6, 6–14.

Luo, Qinshun (1987). (Bloom, Irene, trans.) *Knowledge Painfully Acquired*. New York: Columbia University Press.

Luo, Zhitian 罗志田 (2007). 天下与世界：清末士人 关于人类社会认知的转变——侧重梁启超的观念 [All-under-Heaven and World: The Transformation of Late-Qing Intellectuals' Understanding of Human Society]. «中国社会科学» [*Chinese Social Sciences*], 5, 191–204.

Lynn, Richard John (1994). *The Classic of Changes: A New Translation of the I Ching, as Interpreted by Wang Bi*. New York: Columbia University Press.

Macauley, Melissa (1998). *Social Power and Legal Culture: Litigation Masters in Late Imperial China*. Stanford, CA: Stanford University Press.

McDowell, John (1979). Virtue and Reason. *The Monist*, 62, 331–50.

McNamee, Stephen J., & Miller, Robert K., Jr. (2009). *The Meritocrcy Myth*. Lanham: Rowman & Littlefield.

Makeham, John (2003). The Retrospective Creation of New Confucianism. In Makeham, John (ed.), *New Confucianism: A Critical Examination*. New York: Palgrave, 25–53.

———(2008). *Lost Soul: "Confucianism" in Contemporary Chinese Academic Discourse*. Cambridge: Harvard University Asia Center.

Mann, Susan, & Cheng, Yu-yin (2001). *Under Confucian Eyes: Writings on Gender in Chinese History*. Berkeley: University of California Press.

Maritain, Jacques (1949). Introduction. In UNESCO (Ed.), *Human Rights: Comments and Interpretations*. New York: Columbia University Press, 9–17.

Makeham, John (ed.) (2012). *Learning to Emulate the Wise: The Genesis of Chinese Philosophy as an Adcademic Discipline in Twentieth-Century China*. Hong Kong: Chinese University of Hong Kong Press.

Mencius (1970). (Lau, D. C., trans.) *Mencius*. London: Penguin.

Mengzi (2008). (Van Norden, Bryan, trans.) *Mengzi: With Selections from Traditional Commentaries*. Indianapolis: Hackett.

Metz, Thaddeus. (2001). Respect for Persons and Perfectionist Politics. *Philosophy and Public Affairs*, 30(4), 417–42.

Metzger, Thomas A. (2005). *A Cloud Across the Pacific: Essays on the Clash Between Chinese and Western Political Theories Today*. Hong Kong: Chinese University of Hong Kong Press.

———(unpublished). The Problem of Factual and Normative Continuity with the Tradition in Modern Chinese Thought.

Meyers, Diana (1997). Emotion and Heterodox Moral Perception. In Meyers, Diana (ed.), *Feminists Rethink the Self*. Boulder, Colorado: Westview, 197–218.

Mou, Zongsan, Zhang, Junmai, Xu, Fuguan, & Tang, Junyi (1989). 为中国文化

敬告世界人士宣言 [A Manifesto to the World's People On Behalf of Chinese Culture]. In Feng, Zusheng 封祖盛 (ed.), 《当代新儒家》 [*Contemporary Confucianism*]. Beijing: Sanlian Shudian, 1–52.

Mou, Zongsan 牟宗三 (1954). 《王陽明致良知教》 [*Wang Yangming's Teaching of Extending Good Knowing*]. Taibei: Zhongguo wenhus shuju.

——(1975). 《現象與物自身》 [*Phenomena and Things-in-Themselves*]. Taibei: Xuesheng Shuju.

——(1983). 《中國哲學十九講》 [*Nineteen Lectures on Chinese Philosophy*]. Taibei: Xuesheng Shuju.

——(1989). 《五十自述》 [*Autobiography at Fifty*]. Taibei: Ehu chubanshe.

——(1991). 政道與治道 [*Authority and Governance*]. Taipei: Xuesheng Shuju.

——(1992). 《道德的理想主義》 [*Moral Idealism*]. Taibei: Xuesheng Shuju.

——(2005). 论黑格尔的辩证法 [On Hegel's Dialectical Method]. In 《生命的学问》 [*Life Learning*]. Guilin: Guangxi Shifan Daxue chubanshe, 176–86.

Munro, Donald (1969). *The Concept of Man in Ancient China*. Stanford: Stanford University Press.

——(1977). *The Concept of Man in Contemporary China*. Ann Arbor: University of Michigan Press.

Neville, Robert Cummings (2000). *Boston Confucianism: Portable Tradition in the Late-Modern World*. Albany: SUNY Press.

——(2008). *Ritual and Deference: Extending Chinese Philosophy in a Comparative Context*. Albany: SUNY Press.

Nylan, Michael (2008). Boundaries of the Body and Body Politic in Early Confucian Thoguht. In Bell, Daniel A (ed.), *Territorial Boundaries and Confucianism*. Princeton: Princeton University Press, 85–110.

Ocko, Jonathan K., & Gilmartin, David (2009). State, Sovereignty, and the People: A Comparison of the 'Rule of Law' in China and India. *Journal of Asian Studies*, 68:1, 55–100.

Olberding, Amy (2009). 'Ascending the Hall': Style and Moral Improvement in the *Analects*. *Philosophy East & West*, 59:4, 503–22.

Ownby, David (2009). Kang Xiaoguang: Social Science, Civil Society, and Confucian Religion. *China Perspectives*, 4.

Parekh, Bhikhu (1999). Non-Ethnocentric Universalism. In Dunne, Tim, & Wheeler, Nicholas J. (eds), *Human Rights in Global Politics*. Cambridge: Cambridge University Press, 128–59.

Peerenboom, Randall P. (1998). Confucian Harmony and Freedom of Thought: The Right to Think Versus Right Thinking. In DeBary, Wm. Theodore, & Wei-ming, Tu (eds.), *Confucianism and Human Rights*. New York: Columbia University Press, 235–60.

——(2002). *China's Long March toward Rule of Law*. Cambridge: Cambridge University Press.

Peng, Guoxiang 彭国翔 (2010). 道德与知识：从宋明理学到现代新儒学 — 对现代新儒学的一个发生学解说 [Morality and Knowledge: From Song-Ming

Neo-Confucianism to Contemporary New Confucianism—A Geneological Narrative of Contemporary New Confucianism]. In «儒家传统与中国哲学：新世纪的回顾与前瞻» [*The Confucian Tradition and Chinese Philosophy: Review and Prospect of a New Century*]. Shijiazhuang: Hebei renmin chubanshe, 169–96.

Philpott, Dan (2010). Sovereignty. *The Stanford Encyclopedia of Philosophy, Summer 2010 Edition.*

Pines, Yuri (2009). *Envisioning Eternal Empire: Chinese Political Thought in the Warring States Era.* Honolulu: University of Hawaii Press.

Punzo, Vincent A. (1996). After Kohlberg: Virtue Ethics and the Recovery of the Moral Self. *Philosophical Psychology, 9(1),* 7–23.

Rawls, John (1999). *The Law of Peoples.* Cambridge, MA: Harvard University Press.

Roberts, Robert C. (1991). Virtues and Rules. *Philosophy and Phenomenological Research, LI (2),* 325–43.

Rosemont Jr., Henry (1988). Why Take Rights Seriously? A Confucian Critique. In Rouner, Leroy S. (ed.), *Human Rights and the World's Religions.* Notre Dame: University of Notre Dame Press, 167–82.

———(1998). Human Rights: A Bill of Worries. In deBary, William Theodore, & Tu, Wei-ming (eds), *Confucianism and Human Rights.* New York: Columbia University Press, 54–66.

Rosenlee, Lisa Li-Hsiang (2006). *Confucianism and Women: A Philosophical Interpretation.* Albany: SUNY Press.

Sarkissian, Hagop (2010). Minor tweaks, major payoffs: The problems and promise of situationism in moral philosophy. *Philosopher's Imprint, 10(9).*

Schnall, S., Haidt, J., Clore, G. L., & Jordan, A. H. (2008). Disgust as embodied moral judgment. *Pers Soc Psychol Bull, 34(8),* 1096–109.

Schwitzgebel, Eric (2009). Do Ethicists Steal More Books? *Philosophical Psychology, 22,* 711–25.

Seligman, Adam B., Weller, Robert P., Puett, Michael J., & Simon, Bennett (2008). *Ritual and its Consequences: An Essay in the Limits of Sincerity.* New York: Oxford University Press.

Sen, Amartya (2000). Merit and Justice. In Arrow, Kenneth, Bowles, Samuel, & Durlauf, Steven N. (eds), *Meritocracy and Economic Inequality.* Princeton: Princeton University Press.

Shan, Yuhua 单玉华 (1998). 治法与德治辨析 [Distinguishing Rule by Law and Rule by Virtue]. «法学家» [*The Jurist*], 6, 20–8.

Sher, George (1997). *Beyond Neutrality: Perfectionism and Politics.* Cambridge: Cambridge University Press.

Shusterman, Richard (1997). *Practicing Philosophy: Pragmatism and the Philosophical Life.* New York: Routledge.

Slingerland, Edward (2011). The Situationist Critique and Early Confucian Virtue Ethics. *Ethics, 121(2),* 390–419.

Slote, Michael (2001). *Morals from Motives*. Oxford: Oxford University Press.

Snow, Nancy E. (2010). *Virtue as Social Intelligence: An Empirically Grounded Theory*. New York: Routledge.

Song, Ruozhao (1999). Analects for Women. In deBary, William Theodore, & Bloom, Irene (eds), *Sources of Chinese Tradition*, vol. 1. New York: Columbia University Press, 827–31.

Swanton, Christine (2003). *Virtue Ethics: A Pluralistic View*. Oxford: Oxford University Press.

Tan, Soor-hoon (2004). *Confucian Democracy: A Deweyan Reconstruction*. Albany: SUNY Press.

———(2010). Authoritative Master Kong (Confucius) in an Authoritarian Age. *Dao: A Journal of Comparative Philosophy, 9(2)*, 137–49.

———(unpublished). Why Confucian Democracy?

Tang, Zhonggang 汤忠钢 (2008). 《德性与政治：牟宗三新儒家政治哲学研究》 [*Virtue and Politics: Research on Mou Zongsan's New Confucian Political Philosophy*]. Beijing: Zhongguo Yanshi chubanshe.

Tessman, Lisa (2005). *Burdened Virtues: Virtue Ethics for Liberatory Struggles*. Oxford: Oxford University Press.

Tiwald, Justin (2008). A Right of Rebellion in the *Mengzi*? *Dao: A Journal of Comparative Philosophy, 7:3*, 269–82.

Tiwald, Justin (2011a). Confucianism and Human Rights. In Cushman, Thomas (ed.), *The Routledge Handbook of Human Rig hts*. New York: Routledge.

———(2011b). Review of Stephen C. Angle, *Sagehood: The Contemporary Significance of Neo-Confucian Philosophy*. *Dao: A Journal of Comparative Philosophy, 10(2)*, 231–34.

———(2011c). Reply to Stephen Angle. *Dao: A Journal of Comparative Philosophy, 10(2)*, 241–3.

Tu, Wei-ming (1991). Cultural China: The Periphery as the Center. *Daedulus, 120:2*, 1–32.

———(1996). *A Confucian Perspective on Human Rights: The Inaugural Wu Teh Yao Memorial Lecture*. Singapore.

Van Norden, Bryan W. (2007). *Virtue Ethics and Consequentialism in Early Chinese Philosophy*. New York: Cambridge University Press.

Wakeman, Frederic, Jr. (1973). *History and Will: Philosophical Perspectives of Mao Tse-tung's Thought*. Berkeley: University of California Press.

Walsh, Sean Patrick (unpublished). Varieties of Moral Luck in Ethical and Political Philosophy for Confucius and Aristotle.

Wang, Dade 王大德 (1996). 牟宗三先生良知坎陷說之詮釋 [An Interpretation of Mr. Mou Zongsan's Theory of Restriction of Good Knowing]. In Lee, Ming-huei 李明輝 (ed.), 《牟宗三先生與中國哲學之重建》 [*Mr. Mou Zongsan and the Reconstruction of Chinese Philosophy*]. Taibei: Wenlu Press, 399–412.

Wang, Keping (2003). Some Possible Effects of 'Rule by Virtue' in Chinese

Society Today. from http://bic.cass.cn/English/InfoShow/Article_ Show_Conference_Show_1.asp?ID=346&Title=The%20Roles%20of%20 Values%20and%20Ethics%20in%20Contemporary%20China&strNavigati on=Home-%3EForum&BigClassID=4&SmallClassID=9

Wang, Mengou 王夢鷗 (1980). 《禮記今註今譯》 [*Book of Rites*]. Taipei: Shangwu Press.

Wang, Robin R. (ed.). (2003). *Images of Women in Chinese Thought and Culture: Writings from the Pre-Qin Period through the Song Dynasty*. Indianapolis: Hackett.

Wang, Yangming (1963). (Chan, Wing-tsit, trans.) *Instructions for Practical Living*. New York: Columbia University Press.

Wang, Yangming 王陽明 (1983). 《傳習錄詳註集評》 [*Record of Practice with Detailed Annotations and Collected Commentary*]. Taipei: Xuesheng Shuju.

Wawrytko, Sandra A. (2000). Prudery and Prurience: Historical Roots of the Confucian Conundrum Concerning Women, Sexuality, and Power. In Li, Chenyang (ed.), *The Sage and the Second Sex: Confucianism, Ethics, and Gender*. Chicago: Open Court, 163–97.

Wilson, Thomas A. (1996). The Ritual Formation of Confucian Orthodoxy and the Descendants of the Sage. *Journal of Asian Studies*, *55(3)*, 559–84.

Winston, Kenneth (2005). The Internal Morality of Chinese Legalism. *Singapore Journal of Legal Studies*, 313–47.

Wood, Alan T. (1995). *Limits to Autocracy: From Sung Neo-Confucianism to a Doctrine of Political Rights*. Honolulu: University of Hawaii Press.

Woodruff, Paul (2001). *Reverence: Renewing a Forgotten Virtue*. Oxford: Oxford University Press.

Xu, Empress (1999). Instructions for the Inner Quarters. In deBary, William Theodore, & Bloom, Irene (eds), *Sources of Chinese Tradition*, vol. 1. New York: Columbia University Press, 831–36.

Xu, Fuguan 徐復觀 (1980). 《學術與政治之間》 [*Between Scholarship and Politics*]. Taipei: Xuesheng shuju.

Xunzi (1998–94). *Xunzi: A Translation and Study of the Complete Works*. Stanford: Stanford University Press.

Xunzi, 荀子 (1979). (Li Tisheng 李滌生, ed., trans.) 《荀子集釋》 [*Xunzi, with Collected Interpretations*]. Taipei: Xuesheng Shuju.

Yang, Bojun (1984). *Mengzi Yizhu*. Hong Kong: China Press, Hong Kong Branch.

Yearley, Lee H. (1990). *Mencius and Aquinas: Theories of Virtue and Conceptions of Courage*. Albany: SUNY Press.

Young, Iris Marion (1990). Five Faces of Oppression. In *Justice and the Politics of Difference*. Princeton: Princeton University Press, 39–65.

Yu, Dan 于丹 (2006). 《于丹《论语》心得》 [*Yu Dan's Insights Into the Analects*]. Beijing: Zhonghua Shuju.

Yu, Ying-Shih 余英時 (2004). 现代儒学的回顾与展望 [Review of and Prospects for Contemporary Confucianism]. In «现代儒学的回顾与展望» [*Review of and Prospects for Contemporary Confucianism*]. Beijing: Sanlian Shudian, 132–86.

Zhang, Feng (2010). The Tianxia System: World Order in a Chinese Utopia. *China Heritage Quarterly*, 21, 1–4.

Zhang, Shizhao 章士钊 (2000). «章士钊全集» [*Complete Works of Zhang Shizhao*]. Shanghai: Wenhui Chubanshe.

Zhao, Tingyang 赵汀阳 (2005). «天下体系：世界制度哲学导论» [*The All-Under-Heaven System: An Introduction to the Philosophy of a World Institution*]. Nanjing: Jiangsu jiaoyu chubanshe.

——(2006a). "预付人权"：一种非西方的普遍人权理论 ["Credit Human Rights": A Non-Western Universal Theory of Human Rights]. *Zhongguo Shehui Kexue*, 4, 17–30.

——(2006b). Rethinking Empire from a Chinese Concept 'All-under-Heaven' (Tian-xia 天下). *Social Identities*, 12(1), 29–41.

——(2008). The Self and the Other: An Unanswered Question in Confucian Theory. *Frontiers of Philosophy in China*, 3:2, 163–76.

——(2009a). «坏世界研究:作为第一哲学的政治哲学» [*Investigations of the Bad World: Political Philosophy as the First Philosophy*]. Beijing: Renmin daxue chubanshe.

——(2009b). A Political World Philosophy in terms of All-under-heaven (Tian-xia). *Diogenes*, 221, 5–18.

——(Forthcoming). All-Under-Heaven and Methodological Relationism: An Old Story and New World Peace. In Fred Dallmayr and Zhao Tingyang (eds), Chinese *Political Thought Today: Debates and Perspectives* (Lexington: University of Kentucky Press).

Zheng, Jiadong 郑家栋 (2000). «牟宗三» [*Mou Zongsan*]. Taibei: Dongda Tushu gongsi.

Zhu, Xi (1991a). (Ebrey, Patricia Buckley, trans.) *Chu Hsi's Family Rituals: A Twelfth-Century Chinese Manual for the Performance of Cappings, Weddings, Funerals, and Ancestral Rites*. Princeton: Princeton University Press.

——(1991b). (Wittenborn, Allan, trans.) *Further Reflections on Things at Hand*. Lanham: University Press of America.

—— & Lu, Zuqian (1967). (Chan, Wing-tsit, trans.) *Reflections on Things at Hand*. New York: Columbia University Press.

Index and Glossary of Chinese Terms